The Air Pilot's **Manual**

Volume 6

Human Factors and Pilot Performance

Safety, First Aid and Survival

Trevor Thom

Revised & edited by
Peter D. Godwin

Airlife England

Coventry University

Nothing in this manual supersedes any legislation, rules, regulations or procedures contained in any operational document issued by The Stationery Office, the Civil Aviation Authority, the manufacturers of aircraft, engines and systems, or by the operators of aircraft throughout the world. Note that as maps and charts are changed regularly, those extracts reproduced in this book must not be used for flight planning or flight operations.

Copyright © 1997 Aviation Theory Centre

ISBN 1 85310 930 4

First edition published 1994
Reprinted 1995
Reprinted 1997
Second edition 1997
Reprinted 1998, 1999
Reprinted with revisions 2001

Origination by Bookworks Ltd, Ireland.

Printed in England by Livesey Ltd, Shrewsbury, England.

A Technical Aviation Publications Ltd title published
under licence by

Airlife Publishing Ltd
101 Longden Road, Shrewsbury SY3 9EB, Shropshire, England
Website: www.airlifebooks.com E-mail: airlife@airlifebooks.com

The Air Pilot's **Manual**

Volume 6

Contents

Editorial Team

Trevor Thom
A former Boeing 757 and 767 Captain with a European airline, Trevor has also flown the Airbus A320, Boeing 727, McDonnell Douglas DC-9 and Fokker F-27. He has been active in the International Federation of Airline Pilots' Associations (IFALPA), based in London, and was a member of the IFALPA Aeroplane Design and Operations Group. He also served as IFALPA representative to the Society of Automotive Engineers (SAE) S7 Flight-Deck Design Committee, a body which makes recommendations to the aviation industry, especially the manufacturers. Prior to his airline career Trevor was a Lecturer in Mathematics and Physics, and an Aviation Ground Instructor and Flying Instructor. He is a double degree graduate from the University of Melbourne and also holds a Diploma of Education.

Peter Godwin
Head of Training at Bonus Aviation, Cranfield (formerly Leavesden Flight Centre), Peter has amassed over 14,000 instructional flying hours as a fixed-wing and helicopter instructor. He has edited this series since 1995 and recently updated it to cover the JAR-FCL. As a member of the CAA Panel of Examiners, he is a CAA Flight Examiner for the Private Pilot's Licence (FEPPL[A]), Commercial Pilot's Licence (FECPL[A]), Flight Instructor Examiner (FIE[A]), as well as an Instrument Rating and Class Rating Examiner. A Fellow of the Royal Institute of Navigation (FRIN), Peter is currently training flying instructors and applicants for the Commercial Pilot's Licence and Instrument Rating. He has been Vice Chairman and subsequently Chairman of the Flight Training Committee on behalf of the General Aviation Manufacturers' and Traders' Association (GAMTA) since 1992 and is a regular lecturer at AOPA Flight Instructor seminars. In 1999 Peter was awarded the Pike Trophy by The Guild of Air Pilots and Air Navigators for his contribution to the maintenance of high standards of flying instruction and flight safety. Previously he was Chief Pilot for an air charter company and Chief Instructor for the Cabair group of companies based at Denham and Elstree.

Robert Johnson
An experienced aviator, Bob edited the first edition of this manual and produced many of the illustrations. His aviation experience includes flying a Cessna Citation II-SP executive jet, a DC-3 (Dakota) and light aircraft as Chief Pilot for an international university based in Switzerland, and seven years on Fokker F27, Lockheed Electra and McDonnell Douglas DC-9 airliners. Prior to this he was an Air Taxi Pilot and also gained technical experience as a Draughtsman on airborne mineral survey work in Australia.

Bill Constable
An accomplished Aviation Ground Instructor, Charter Pilot, Senior Flying Instructor and Chief Pilot, Bill has over thirty years' experience in aviation. He is a qualified Meteorological Observer and served with the Royal Navy prior to his aviation career.

Ian Suren
Ian is a former Chief, Personnel Licensing and Training with ICAO in Montreal, a position which he held for 10 years. Prior to this he was Senior Examiner in charge of Flight Crew Licence Examinations with the Australian Department of Civil Aviation. He also held Flight Navigator and Commercial Pilot Licences.

Warren Yeates
Warren has been involved with editing, indexing, desktop publishing and printing Trevor Thom manuals since 1988 for UK, US and Australian markets. He currently runs a publishing services company in Ireland.

Acknowledgements
The Civil Aviation Authority, British Aerospace, Boeing and McDonnell Douglas; Graeme Dennerstein, Daryl Guest, Frank Horwill, Michael Leahy and Peter Loughnan for medical comments; Captain R. W. K. Snell (CAA Flight Examiner [ret.]); Airtour International.

Introduction

Human Factors and Pilot Performance

The **human factor** is the most important factor in aviation. Human skills have led to the design of very fine aircraft, and human factors (i.e. the performance of the ground engineer, the air traffic controller, and the pilot) play a major role in safe operation of these aircraft during every flight.

The human factor is vital.

Human factors not only play a major role in the *safe* operation of aircraft – they also play a major role in *unsafe* operation, leading to incidents and accidents. On a less dramatic note, less-than-optimal operation of an aircraft is inefficient – costing time, money and stress – and is best avoided. Always aim for optimum performance, and learn from each flight so that the next one can be even better.

What is the Human Factor?
The human factor is the performance and behaviour of the individual, and of the group. It involves internal psychological and physical aspects of the individual, as well as interaction with other people, with the machine and the equipment in use, and with the operating environment.

There are other terms in common usage with a similar meaning to *human factors,* such as *human aspects* and *human elements,* as well as *ergonomics,* which is the study of the efficiency of people in their operating environment.

Optimising Human Performance
Aviation is a complex working environment, and optimising the role of people in it involves consideration of many aspects of human performance and behaviour, including:
- personal fitness and well-being;
- operating (flying) skills;
- thinking ability (*cognitive* process, i.e. information processing);
- judgement and decision-making abilities (airmanship);
- communication skills;
- leadership qualities and crew coordination (in a professional environment);
- design and layout of displays and controls on the flight deck; and
- design of operating procedures, and their presentation in operating manuals, checklists and charts.

Minimising Human Error

Human error is a fact of life – *"We are only human"* – but it is a reasonable aim to set out to minimise the occurrence of errors and their effects. This can be done by:

- good selection of people (in a professional environment);
- good training;
- good design – matching the machine, controls, displays and operating procedures to human characteristics (physical and psychological);
- providing a good working environment (low noise level, comfortable temperature, no vibration); and
- good operating procedures – such as good cockpit checklists, and cross-checking and crew cooperation in two-pilot cockpits.

The Aim of this Book

This book concentrates on the performance and the behaviour of the individual pilot (and of the crew as a unit, in larger aircraft), with the aim being to optimise the results in terms of:

- safety and efficiency of the operation; and
- well-being of the individual.

It will also enable the reader to pass the relevant CAA *Human Performance and Limitations* examinations.

Safety, First Aid and Survival

The second section in the book supplies a good working knowledge of this important area of flight operations.

Also, those planning a trip over water or through remote areas of the world, particularly in a light aircraft, need to prepare for survival in a hostile environment. This section will help give an understanding of the factors involved, and enable an evaluation of the appropriate safety equipment that should be carried.

Section **One**

Human Factors and **Pilot Performance**

Human Physiology and High Altitudes

To be proficient pilots, we need a basic understanding of how the human body operates. This will help us to appreciate the demands and influences that flying places on us, and be aware of the operational controls we sometimes need to exert over ourselves in maintaining safe flight operations.

The Nervous System

The body contains a vast network of cells which carry information in the form of nerve impulses to and from all of its parts. These impulses are the means by which all bodily activity occurs.

The brain – the master controller – and the spinal chord together form the **central nervous system,** which is responsible for the integration of virtually all nervous activity in the body.

The remaining nervous tissue – the *peripheral nervous system* – includes the *autonomic nervous system,* which controls various bodily functions that are not consciously directed, including:

☐ **the regular beating of the heart;**
☐ **intestinal movements;**
☐ **sweating; and**
☐ **salivation.**

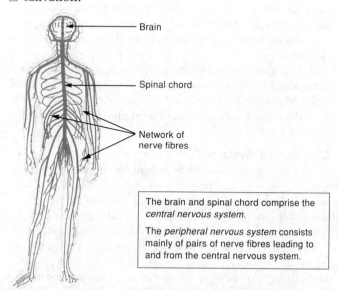

Brain

Spinal chord

Network of
nerve fibres

The brain and spinal chord comprise the
central nervous system.

The *peripheral nervous system* consists
mainly of pairs of nerve fibres leading to
and from the central nervous system.

■ Figure 1-1 **The nervous system facilitates all bodily activity**

Other functions, such as the need to move an arm, hand and fingers to turn the pages of this book, require our conscious intervention. An activity such as flying an aeroplane certainly requires conscious intervention! Although training and experience can reduce the amount of effort we need to make in conducting a flight, it can never become an entirely automatic activity like the heart beat.

The Brain

The brain exerts control by sending electrical signals down channels of nerve cells to the various parts of the body. These channels are referred to simply as *nerves,* and each muscle, organ or sense in the body has one or more nerves connecting it to the brain.

> The brain controls the body.

As well as sending out signals to the various parts of the body, the brain also receives signals from them, which it then processes, perhaps sending out another signal in response. For instance, a finger may send a message that it is in contact with a hot metal plate, to which the brain responds by sending messages to various muscles telling them to contract, thereby withdrawing the finger from the plate.

A sudden and unexpected noise may cause fright, to which the brain responds by quickly preparing the body for action – electrical signals are transmitted to appropriate muscles, and certain chemicals are released (adrenalin, for instance) to speed up the rate of metabolism and prepare the body to 'fight or flee'. The constant interplay of transmitted signals and reception of feedback signals is a never-ending activity of the brain right throughout life, even when we are asleep.

The brain is also involved in the many automatic bodily functions carried out in the autonomic nervous system (such as control of the senses, body temperature, breathing rate and depth, pulse rate, the digestive process, and blood pressure). More about the brain in Chapters 6 and 7.

The Circulatory System

The circulatory, or *cardiovascular,* system moves **blood** around the body, carrying oxygen and nutrients to the body tissues, and taking waste products, such as carbon dioxide, away from them.

> The circulatory system moves blood around the body.

Blood is composed of red and white blood cells, or *corpuscles.* The red blood cells contain the iron-rich pigment *haemoglobin,* whose principal function is the transport of oxygen around the body. The white blood cells, of which there are various types, protect the body against foreign substances and are involved in the production of antibodies, a special kind of blood protein that circulates in the blood plasma (straw-coloured fluid in which the blood cells are suspended). The antibodies attack any substance that the body regards as foreign or dangerous.

The Blood Vessels

The blood vessels form a system of arteries, capillaries and veins known as the *vascular system*.

> The heart pumps blood into the arteries.

Arteries carry blood into the body, away from the heart, and *veins* carry blood back to the heart. The walls of the veins are thinner and less elastic than the walls of the arteries, and the veins contain valves to prevent the reverse flow of blood. The smallest blood vessels are the *capillaries*, which form a network in most tissues, and enable an exchange of oxygen and other matter with individual cells in the body tissues.

The circulation of blood through the blood vessels and the tissues is known as the *systemic circulation*. A second system – the *pulmonary circulation* – diverts the blood which reaches the heart into capillaries situated in the walls of the two air reservoirs – the lungs.

> The lungs deliver oxygen to the blood, and remove waste carbon dioxide from it.

The bloodstream passes through the lungs, which remove the carbon dioxide from the blood and add oxygen to it. The oxygenated blood then returns to the heart, where it is pumped into the *aorta* – the main artery – and then carried around the body through the systemic circulation.

> The blood carries oxygen to the body tissues, and carries waste away.

The bloodstream also collects nutrients from the gastro-intestinal system for distribution to the body tissues, and carries waste matter back to where it is removed by the gastro-intestinal system (as faeces) and the kidneys (as urine).

On reaching the heart, the deoxygenated blood is again pumped through the lungs to remove the carbon dioxide which it has accumulated in its journey through the body (including the brain), and to obtain a fresh charge of oxygen.

It is necessary for the blood to be continuously replenished with oxygen which it has given out to the tissues, and at the same time rid itself of the carbon dioxide which it has acquired there.

Summary

The circulatory system consists of:

☐ **a central pump** – the heart – which is a hollow muscular organ capable of contracting as part of its pumping action;

☐ **a series of connecting blood vessels** which consist of the arteries – conveying the blood from the heart to the tissues – and the veins – returning the blood from the tissues to the heart;

☐ **a number of very fine vessels,** known as capillaries – found in the body tissues, and forming the connection between the arteries and the veins.

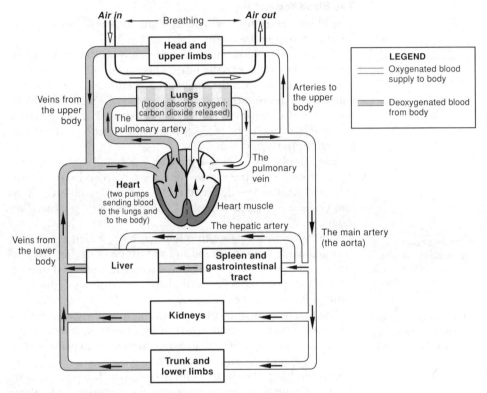

■ *Figure 1-2* **Schematic of the circulatory (or cardiovascular) system**

The Heart

The heart is a strong muscle, about the size of a closed fist, which is divided into two sides, each with two chambers. The muscle fibres of the heart all contract at the same time, forcing blood through the one-way heart valves and moving it on through the network of arteries. This causes a pressure pulse which can be felt at various parts of the body where the arteries are near the surface (such as on the wrist and the side of the neck).

The heart is a muscle which pumps blood.

The chambers in the heart separate the blood as it is received from the veins in its deoxygenated state and sent to the lungs through the pulmonary artery, and then received from the lungs after oxygenation (and removal of the carbon dioxide) through the pulmonary vein and pumped into the arteries again.

The amount of blood pumped by the heart depends upon the size of the heart, the heart rate (or *pulse* rate), and the strength of the heart contraction. This is controlled principally by the autonomic nervous system, and so requires no conscious thought on our part.

Blood Pressure

Blood pressure is a measure of the pressure of the blood against the walls of the main arteries. It is highest during the period when the lower heart chambers are contracting, known as *systolic* pressure, and is lowest when the chambers are relaxing and refilling with blood, known as *diastolic* pressure. The normal range varies with age, but a healthy young adult will typically have a systolic pressure of about 120 millimetres (mm) of mercury, and a diastolic pressure of 80 mm – written as 120/80.

Respiration

The respiratory process supplies energy-giving oxygen to the body, and removes carbon dioxide.

The process of respiration brings oxygen into the body and removes carbon dioxide. It happens in two stages: the first stage occurs in the lungs – *external* respiration – and the second stage takes place in the body tissues – *internal* respiration.

The body needs a continuous supply of oxygen.

The body has a permanent need for oxygen; it is used in the energy-producing 'burning' process that goes on in every cell of the body tissues. The body is unable to store oxygen permanently – hence the need for continuous breathing. Any interruption to breathing lasting more than a few minutes may lead to permanent physical damage, especially of the brain, and to possible death.

Breathing Rate

The autonomic nervous system detects both the need for more blood to certain parts of the body, and the amount of carbon dioxide (CO_2) in the blood. The carbon dioxide in the blood returning to the heart, and then to the lungs, is a waste product from the consumption of oxygen (O_2) in the tissues to produce energy.

A higher than normal amount of carbon dioxide means that a lot of oxygen has been burned, and therefore there is a need for more replacement oxygen around the body. As a result of a high carbon dioxide content in the blood, the breathing rate is automatically increased to bring more oxygen into the lungs for the bloodstream to absorb.

External Respiration

Two processes occur in the lungs:

☐ **Energy-giving oxygen,** breathed in from outside the body, diffuses through the thin walls of the lungs and into the blood, whose red blood cells carry it to the body tissues.

☐ **Waste carbon dioxide,** returned to the lungs in the bloodstream, diffuses through the walls into the air, which is then breathed out.

Internal Respiration

Two processes occur in the body tissues, the reverse of those occurring in the lungs:

- **Oxygen,** brought to the body tissue by the red blood cells, diffuses through the very thin capillary and body-cell walls into the body tissue, where it is burned up to produce energy.

- **Carbon dioxide,** a waste product in the body tissues from the burning of oxygen, diffuses back into the capillaries and is carried away in the bloodstream.

> *The body tissues burn oxygen to give energy, and the blood removes waste carbon dioxide.*

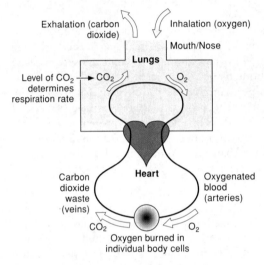

■ *Figure 1-3* **The two-stage respiration process**

The Lungs

The two lungs are the organs in which the waste carbon dioxide in the blood, which is returned from around the body, is exchanged with oxygen brought in by freshly breathed air.

> *The lungs absorb oxygen, and expel waste carbon dioxide.*

The lungs are housed within the chest cavity, protected by the rib cage, and have a muscular, curved diaphragm beneath them. The diaphragm can be flattened by contraction of the muscles, which expands the chest cavity, and draws fresh air in through the mouth and/or nose. This function is normally controlled by the autonomic nervous system without our conscious intervention, although we can consciously increase the rate and depth of our breathing if we want to.

The lowered pressure in the chest cavity draws the air down through the bronchial passage, which divides into two tubes, one going to each lung. The two tubes divide into smaller and smaller tubes, ending in millions of small sacs with very thin walls known as *alveoli,* which are surrounded by blood capillaries.

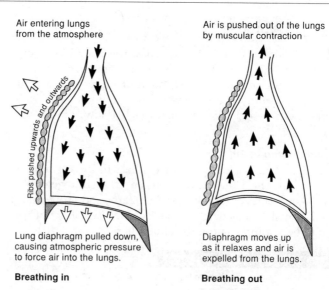

Air entering lungs from the atmosphere

Air is pushed out of the lungs by muscular contraction

Ribs pushed upwards and outwards

Lung diaphragm pulled down, causing atmospheric pressure to force air into the lungs.

Diaphragm moves up as it relaxes and air is expelled from the lungs.

Breathing in   **Breathing out**

■ *Figure 1-4* **Expanding the chest cavity draws air into the lungs**

Haemoglobin in the red blood cells accepts oxygen from the lungs and transports it to the body tissues.

Oxygen molecules that diffuse through the walls of the alveoli sacs and into the bloodstream attach themselves to the *haemoglobin* in the red blood cells, which have an affinity for oxygen, and are transported to the body tissues requiring oxygen. The oxygen attached to the haemoglobin causes the blood to look very red, whereas the oxygen–deficient blood returning through the veins looks somewhat bluer.

A high level of waste carbon dioxide in the lungs causes an increased breathing rate.

Chemical sensors in the lungs detect the level of waste carbon dioxide and, to a lesser extent the level of oxygen, and send messages to the brain. A high level of carbon dioxide (or a low level of oxygen) returning to the lungs in the blood is interpreted automatically by the brain as a need for more oxygen. A lot of carbon dioxide means that a lot of oxygen has been burned in the body tissues. The brain then responds automatically by speeding up the respiration rate to increase the supply of oxygen.

Each breath when we are resting is about one-half litre – only one-tenth of the lung capacity of five litres. This means that a lot of used air remains in the lungs. With the constant transfer of oxygen into the bloodstream and the addition of carbon dioxide out of the bloodstream, the air in the lungs will have a much higher concentration of carbon dioxide than the surrounding atmospheric air, and a lower concentration of oxygen. This is increasingly the case as altitude is gained. The air in the lungs is also saturated with water vapour (as witnessed by the fog it forms when we breathe out on a cold day).

Flying at Altitude

The human body is designed to function normally in the lower levels of the atmosphere, where the air is fairly dense. Aircraft, however, operate above sea level, often at quite high altitudes where the air density is very low, exposing the pilot to possible oxygen deficiency and other problems such as low ambient temperatures.

The Composition of Air

Air is a mixture of various gases that is held to the earth by the force of gravity. The main gases are oxygen (21%), nitrogen (78%), with small quantities of carbon dioxide (0.03%) and ozone, and an extremely variable percentage of water vapour (which is not considered to be a component of the atmosphere).

COMPOSITION OF AIR	
Gas	Volume (%)
Nitrogen	78%
Oxygen	21%
Other gases (argon, carbon dioxide, neon, helium, etc.)	1%
Total	100%

THE ATMOSPHERE is held to the earth by the force of gravity and, because air is compressible, it packs in around the earth's surface. As altitude is gained, the air thins out, with fewer and fewer molecules in the same volume, but the percentage composition of the air does not change. Total air pressure falls with altitude, as does the partial pressure of each of the gases in the air. (Total air pressure is a sum of all of the partial pressures.)

The natural oxygen supply decreases with altitude.

OXYGEN (O_2). The main source of oxygen in the atmosphere is the process of photosynthesis in plants. This uses carbon dioxide and water for the purposes of the plant – one of the resulting products being oxygen, which is needed by animals for their purposes. In this way, the plant world supports the animal world, providing it with oxygen, as well as being a source of food.

Oxygen is essential for animals because it is a necessary component of the 'burning' process that produces energy in the body tissues. An oxygen deficiency can have a devastating effect on a person, therefore the supply of oxygen to a pilot, in the form of fresh air of a suitable density, or supplemented by an additional supply of oxygen, is of critical importance.

The body and brain need oxygen.

NITROGEN (N$_2$) is the most plentiful gas in air, but it is not directly used by the body in the respiration process. It is used in the building of cells in both plants and animals, and saturates the body cells and tissues. Excess nitrogen in the tissues can cause problems, however, as any diver who has suffered *the bends* can tell you.

CARBON DIOXIDE (CO$_2$) is produced in the burning process, when oxygen combines with carbon, and forms about 0.03% of the atmosphere. Since the Industrial Revolution the wide-spread combustion of fossil fuels (oil, diesel and petrol) has led to a significant increase in the amount of carbon dioxide present in the atmosphere. This is a major contributor to global warming.

Carbon dioxide is also produced when oxygen is burned in the body tissues, and is carried to the lungs in the bloodstream through the veins and expelled in the breath. The human body is much more sensitive to changes in carbon dioxide levels than to changes in oxygen levels.

WATER VAPOUR, whilst not considered to be a component of the atmosphere, is carried in the air and plays a very important role in the weather. When the saturation point for water is reached, the water vapour condenses out as liquid water droplets and forms cloud, fog, rain, or dew.

The percentage of water vapour in the air varies from almost none over dry, desert areas to about 5% in warm, humid air. At high altitudes, above the level where clouds form, there is little water vapour.

OZONE is a molecule containing three oxygen atoms (O$_3$), whereas normal oxygen contains two (O$_2$). It is formed when air or oxygen is subjected to electrical discharges, and is poisonous if breathed in large amounts. It is found in the stratosphere, and prevents a lot of the sun's damaging ultraviolet radiation from reaching the earth's surface (hence the concern about holes in the ozone layer). The presence of ozone in the earth's atmosphere is a consideration when flying at extremely high altitudes for long periods.

Hypoxia

A lack of sufficient oxygen to the body (and brain) is called **hypoxia**.

Air pressure and density decrease with altitude. As an aeroplane climbs, the density of the air in which it is flying gradually reduces. The less dense the air, the lower the mass of oxygen taken into the lungs in each breath. Also, because of the lower partial pressure of oxygen at altitude (i.e. fewer molecules), less oxygen will diffuse across the alveoli membranes into the bloodstream.

A high cabin altitude, therefore, means that less oxygen will be transported around the body, and less energy will be generated (including in the brain). In this oxygen-deficient condition, a pilot is less able to think clearly and less able to perform physically.

Above about 8,000 feet cabin altitude, the effects of oxygen deprivation may start to become apparent in some pilots, especially if the pilot is active or under stress. At 10,000 feet, most people can still cope with the diminished oxygen supply, but above 10,000 feet supplementary oxygen is required (i.e. oxygen supplied through a mask), if a marked deterioration in performance is not to occur. The effects of oxygen deprivation are very personal in that they may differ from person to person, and become apparent at different cabin altitudes. In some people, night vision, for instance, might start to deteriorate at 4,000 feet cabin altitude – in others it might start to deteriorate at a higher cabin altitude. The effects of oxygen deprivation will eventually be the same, but some people are more resilient than others. In general terms, 10,000 feet cabin altitude is considered to be the critical cabin altitude above which flight crew should wear an oxygen mask.

At 14,000 feet without supplementary oxygen, performance will be very poor, and at 18,000 feet the pilot may become unconscious; this will occur at lower altitudes if the pilot is a smoker, or is unfit or fatigued. Rapid rates of ascent can allow higher altitudes to be reached before severe symptoms occur. In these circumstances, unconsciousness may occur before any or many of the symptoms of hypoxia appear. At 18,000 feet the partial pressure of oxygen in the air is about *half* that at sea level.

A lack of oxygen (hypoxia) leads to poor performance, even unconsciousness.

The initial symptoms of hypoxia may hardly be noticeable to the sufferer, and in fact they often include feelings of *euphoria*. The brain is affected quite early, so a false sense of security and well-being may be present. Physical movements will become clumsy, but the pilot may not notice this.

Difficulty in concentrating, faulty judgement, moodiness, drowsiness, indecision, giddiness, physical clumsiness, a headache, deterioration of vision, a high pulse rate, blue lips and blue fingernails (cyanosis), and tingling of the skin may all follow, ending in loss of consciousness. Throughout all of this pilots will probably feel euphoric and as if doing a great job. Hypoxia is subtle and it sneaks up on you!

A pilot may not notice hypoxia (a lack of oxygen).

Susceptibility to hypoxia is increased by anything which reduces the oxygen available to the brain, such as a high cabin altitude (of course), high or low temperatures, illness, stress, fatigue, physical activity, or smoke in the cockpit.

Very high positive g-loadings, say when pulling a high-speed acrobatic aircraft quickly out of a steep dive and experiencing 5g, will force the blood into the legs and lower regions of the body, and temporarily starve the brain of oxygen. This could lead to a *greyout* (when vision is affected) or a *blackout* (unconsciousness). Such g-loadings, however, are not achievable in typical light aircraft. (See *Sensing Acceleration* on page 47.)

Pressurised Cabins

Pressurised cabins can lead to hypoxia if they depressurise.

> Pressurised cabins improve the oxygen supply at altitude.

Advanced aeroplanes have pressurised cabins which allow the cabin to hold air at a higher pressure than in the outside atmosphere. For instance, an aeroplane flying at 35,000 feet may have a cabin that is pressurised *(pumped up)* to the same pressure level found at 5,000 feet in the outside atmosphere, eliminating the need for the pilot and passengers to be wearing oxygen masks – a significant improvement in comfort and convenience.

> If a cabin depressurises, supplemental oxygen may be required.

The situation, of course, changes if the aeroplane depressurises at high altitudes for some reason and the cabin air escapes, reducing the partial pressure of oxygen in the air available to the pilot. The suddenly lower pressure surrounding the body in a rapid depressurisation causes a sudden exhalation of breath (as the air pressure in the lungs tries to equalise with the external air pressure). The same volume in the lungs will now contain fewer oxygen molecules. Supplementary oxygen then becomes vital, and it is usually obtained through a mask until the pilot descends to a lower altitude (below 10,000 feet), where there is sufficient oxygen available and the mask can be removed.

Time of Useful Consciousness

If a person is suddenly deprived of an adequate supply of oxygen, unconsciousness will follow. This is a very important consideration for a high-flying pressurised aircraft that suffers depressurisation.

The cells of the brain are particularly sensitive to a lack of oxygen. Total cessation of the oxygen supply to the brain results in unconsciousness in 6 to 8 seconds and irreversible damage ensues if the oxygen supply is not restored within 4 minutes.

The time available for pilots to perform useful tasks *without* a supplementary oxygen supply, and before severe hypoxia sets in, is known as the **time of useful consciousness (TUC),** which gets shorter and shorter the higher the altitude. The pilots *must* get the masks on and receive oxygen well within this period, if flight safety is to be preserved.

TIME OF USEFUL CONSCIOUSNESS		
Altitude above sea level	**Sudden failure of oxygen supply**	
	Moderate activity	**Minimal activity**
22,000 feet	5 minutes	10 minutes
25,000 feet	2 minutes	3 minutes
28,000 feet	1 minute	$1^1/_2$ minutes
30,000 feet	45 seconds	$1^1/_4$ minutes
35,000 feet	30 seconds	45 seconds
40,000 feet	12 seconds	15 seconds

Remaining conscious is paramount for the pilot, even if the passengers become unconscious for a short period. You must think of yourself first, since the safety of all on board depends upon your well-being.

How To Avoid Hypoxia

To avoid hypoxia it is best to be reasonably fit, to have no cigarette smoke in the cockpit, and to ensure that oxygen is used at the higher cabin altitudes, and definitely above 10,000 feet. Remember that lack of oxygen can lead to a feeling of euphoria and a lack of judgement (a similar effect perhaps to alcohol). Self-discipline must be imposed and the oxygen mask donned when the altitude approaches 10,000 feet.

Types of Hypoxia

Hypoxia caused by a lack of oxygen in the air is called *hypoxic hypoxia.*

Hypoxia caused by an inability of the blood to carry oxygen is called *anaemic hypoxia,* and may be due to a medical condition (anaemia) or to carbon monoxide poisoning in the blood (from a faulty engine exhaust system or from smoking).

The reduction of the oxygen-carrying capacity of the blood by smoking has the same effect as increasing the cabin altitude by 4,000 to 5,000 feet; the effect on you will worsen as the aeroplane climbs to higher altitudes. Hypoxia can also result following a loss of blood – for instance, after a person has made a blood donation.

Barotrauma

Another effect of increasing cabin altitude is that gases trapped in parts of your body – such as the stomach, intestines, sinuses, middle ear, or in a decaying tooth – will want to expand as external pressure decreases. Either they will be able to escape to the atmosphere, or they may be trapped and possibly cause pain, known as *barotrauma.*

As cabin altitude increases, gases in the body expand.

Hyperventilation

Hyperventilation can occur when the body 'over-breathes' due to some psychological distress such as fear or anxiety. It is a self-per-petuating cycle, in which a feeling of breathlessness develops – one is unable to 'catch one's breath' – and continues even if the triggering influence is removed. Even though the person is now over-breathing, he or she still feels breathless, which tends to add to the anxiety and so promote the over-breathing.

Hyperventilation flushes the carbon dioxide out of the blood and disturbs its chemical balance; this produces symptoms of numbness and tingling in the lips, fingertips and toes. The further effects may include palpitations, an increased pulse rate, sweating, chest pain, blurred vision, dizziness, fainting and ringing in the ears, muscle spasms, drowsiness, and unconsciousness.

Donning an oxygen mask will not help treat hyperventilation.

Dealing with Hyperventilation

In working out how to treat a person experiencing breathing dif-ficulties, it is necessary to first establish whether the problem is hyperventilation (over-breathing) or hypoxia (too little oxygen). **Hypoxia is the more urgent situation to treat.**

The best procedure to deal with hyperventilation is to try and calm the person, both by being calm yourself and by talking nor-mally to them. Allocating simple distracting tasks in the cockpit may also help the person to take it easy.

☐ **Hyperventilation can be remedied** by consciously slowing down the breathing rate (talking is a good way of doing this).

☐ **A suggested direct remedy** for hyperventilation is to breathe into and out of a bag to increase the carbon dioxide level in the blood.

☐ **If recovery is not evident,** then assume that hypoxia rather than hyperventilation is the problem.

NOTE If you have a passenger who is breathing abnormally and experiencing symptoms that could be caused by either hypoxia or hyperventilation, but you have a low cabin altitude (say below 10,000 feet) where hypoxia is not a consideration, assume that hyperventilation is the cause and apply the appropriate remedy.

Decompression Sickness

Decompression sickness can follow scuba diving. Scuba diving and flying do not mix.

When the body is deep under water it is subjected to strong pressures, and certain gases, such as nitrogen, are absorbed into the blood. The deeper and longer the dive, the more this absorption occurs. If the pressure on the body is then reduced – for example, by returning to the surface from a great depth or, even worse, by flying in an aeroplane at high cabin altitudes – the gases (especially nitrogen) may form bubbles in the bloodstream. (You can see the same effect caused by a suddenly reduced pressure when the top is removed from gaseous drinks and bubbles of gas come out of solution.)

Gas bubbles in the blood will cause great pain and some immobilisation in the shoulders, arms and joints. This serious complaint is called **decompression sickness** or *the bends*. The remedy is to return the body to a region of high pressure for a lengthy period of time (say in a decompression chamber), and then gradually return it to normal lower pressures over a period of hours or days.

In an aircraft, the best you can do if *the bends* is suspected is to descend to a low altitude, where air pressure is greater. Even landing may not provide a sufficient pressure increase to remedy the problem, in which case seek medical assistance without delay.

■ *Figure 1-5* **Scuba diving just prior to flying can have serious consequences**

As a guide, do not fly within 12 hours of any scuba diving where compressed air was used to breathe, even if only to shallow depths. Scuba diving at depths below approximately 30 feet for long periods should *not* be considered in the 24 hours prior to flying! Snorkelling will not cause decompression sickness, only the underwater breathing associated with scuba or deep-sea diving.

The risk of suffering decompression sickness increases with the depth to which you dive, the rate at which you resurface, how soon and how high you fly, how quickly the cabin altitude increases, age, obesity, fatigue, and re-exposure to decompression within 24 hours.

Carbon Monoxide Poisoning

Carbon monoxide is produced during the combustion of fuel in the engine. It is present in engine exhaust gases and in cigarette smoke, both of which can sometimes be found in the cockpit.

Carbon monoxide is poison.

Susceptibility to carbon monoxide poisoning increases as the cabin altitude increases.

Haemoglobin in the blood prefers carbon monoxide to oxygen.

Carbon monoxide is a colourless, odourless and tasteless gas for which haemoglobin in the blood has an enormous affinity. The prime function of haemoglobin is to transport oxygen from the lungs throughout the body to act as 'fuel'.

If carbon monoxide molecules are present in the air inhaled into the lungs, then the haemoglobin will transport them in preference to oxygen, causing the body and the brain to suffer oxygen starvation, even though oxygen is present in the air. Haemoglobin shows a far greater affinity for carbon monoxide (poisonous, and just what we do not need) than for oxygen (what we do need).

Do not breathe carbon monoxide.

The performance of a pilot in an environment contaminated by carbon monoxide will be seriously impaired. Recovery, even on pure oxygen, may take several days. Carbon monoxide poisoning is serious and can be fatal!

Many cabin heating systems use warm air from around the engine and exhaust manifold as their source of heat. Any leaks in the engine exhaust system can allow carbon monoxide to enter the cabin in the heating air and possibly through open windows and cracks. To minimise the effect of any carbon monoxide that enters the cockpit in this way, fresh air should always be used in conjunction with cabin heat.

Regular checks and maintenance of the aircraft are essential. Even though carbon monoxide is odourless, it may be associated with other exhaust gases that do have an odour. Engine smells in the cabin are a warning that carbon monoxide may be present.

Symptoms of Carbon Monoxide Poisoning:
☐ headache, dizziness and nausea;
☐ deterioration in vision;
☐ impaired judgement;
☐ personality change;
☐ impaired memory;
☐ slower breathing rate;
☐ loss of muscular power;
☐ convulsions;
☐ coma, and eventually death.

If Carbon Monoxide Is Suspected in the Cabin:
☐ shut off the cabin heat;
☐ stop all smoking;
☐ increase the supply of fresh air through vents and windows; and
☐ land as soon as possible.

Many operators place carbon monoxide detectors in the cockpit. The most common type contains crystals that change colour when carbon monoxide is present. These detectors only cost a few pounds and are a wise investment, but they do have a limited life, so check the expiry date. If the detector is date-expired it may not indicate the presence of carbon monoxide, and so may lull you into a false sense of security.

Upper Respiratory Tract Problems

The common cold, hay fever, sinusitis, tonsillitis or any similar condition can lead to blocked ears. This can mean trouble for a pilot because the equalisation of pressure on either side of the eardrum is not possible when the *Eustachian tubes,* which connect the ears and the nasal passages, are blocked by a cold or similar infection. In the training environment, problems are more likely to occur on descent than when climbing, as even low-powered aircraft can change altitude rapidly on descent, giving rise to rapid pressure changes.

Blocked ears can sometimes be cleared by holding your nose and blowing hard (a technique known as the *Valsalva* movement), by chewing, swallowing or yawning. The best advice is, however, if you have a cold, do not fly.

Problems can also arise in the sinuses, which are cavities in the head connected by narrow tubes to the nasal/throat passages. Such blockages can cause great pain, especially during descent, so do not fly with sinus problems. This applies to flight in any aircraft; even though pressure changes in a pressurised cabin will be less as the aircraft changes altitude (compared with an unpressurised cabin), there is always the risk of a sudden depressurisation, in which case the pressure changes can be dramatic.

> Do not fly with a cold or sinus problem.

The possible serious effects of upper respiratory tract infections on aviators are covered in more detail in Chapter 3, *Hearing and Balance* and Chapter 4, *Am I Fit to Fly?*

Now complete: **Exercises 1 – Human Physiology and High Altitudes** *(Exercises and Answers at back of book.)*

Coventry University

Lanchester Library

Tel 02476 887575

Borrowed Items 04/10/2016 17:10
XXXXX9995

em Title	Due Date
38001005639244	25/10/2016
The air pilot's manual .	
38001003659210	11/10/2016
* The air pilot's manual.	

* Indicates items borrowed today
Thankyou for using this unit

www.coventry.ac.uk

Eyesight and Visual Illusions

The eyes provide us with a **visual** image of the environment. They are the most important sensory organs for flying, although their messages to the brain are often backed up by messages from other sensory organs, including the balance mechanisms in the inner ear *(vestibular* inputs), as well as skin and muscular feeling from all over the body ('seat-of-the-pants' inputs, known more technically as *somatosensory* inputs).

Each eye acts as a natural and very sophisticated camera. Its basic function is in collecting light rays coming from an object, using the lens to focus these rays into an image on a screen (the *retina),* and then converting this image into electrical signals which are then sent via the optic nerve to the brain. In this way we 'see'.

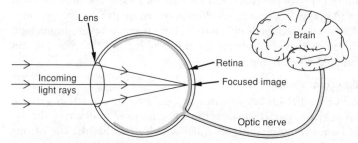

■ *Figure 2-1* **The basic components of vision**

The connection of the optic nerve to the brain is so close and integral, and the importance of the messages sent via it to the brain so immense, that the two eyes can almost be considered an extension of the brain.

The Eyes Move in their Sockets

The eye is roughly the shape of a ball, hence it is often referred to as an eyeball. Each eye has a series of muscles that can be used to rotate it in its socket, thereby allowing it to follow a moving object without you having to move your whole head. Conversely, it means you can also keep focused on a stationary object even though your head might be moving, for instance in a turn.

To keep tracking a moving object with your two eyes, they need to act in harmony with one another, and this means coordinated control of the two sets of muscles, one set for each eye, by the brain. In a fatigued person, this coordination sometimes fails, and the result is quite different images from each eye, resulting in *double vision.*

When focusing on very near objects, the visual axis of each eye will be turned-in slightly; when focusing on distant objects, say more than six metres away, the visual axes of your two eyes will be roughly parallel.

■ *Figure 2-2* **Focusing on a near object, and on a far object**

The natural tendency, when you are *not* trying to focus on any particular object and you are – for instance, just gazing out the window into an empty blue sky, is for the eyes to focus somewhere in the range of one to two metres. This is referred to as *empty field myopia* (empty field short-sightedness).

A pilot flying visually must continually scan the sky for other aircraft and for obstacles, and then focus on any that are observed. In an empty sky, it requires effort to focus on distant objects, since the eyes tend to focus on a much closer point. It is very important, therefore, that the eyes are fit and healthy, and that you are not fatigued when flying.

> *It requires effort to focus on distant and very close objects.*

Binocular Vision

A normal person has two functioning eyes that together provide binocular vision. *Binocular* is the adjective used to describe the use of both eyes, as against *monocular* which describes the use of one eye only. Two eyes are better than one for a number of reasons.

One reason is protection against the **blind spot** in each eye. The blind spot is the small area on the retina of the eye where the *nerve fibres* from the light-sensitive cells *(rods* and *cones)* on the retina lead into the optic nerve. There is therefore no space at this spot on the retina for light-sensitive cells, and hence any light falling here will not register, i.e. it is a blind spot.

> *Each eye has a blind spot.*

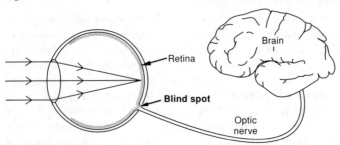

■ *Figure 2-3* **The blind spot**

It is not possible for an image of an object to fall on the blind spot of *both* eyes simultaneously. Even when an image falls on the blind spot of one eye, and is therefore not registered, the brain will receive a message from the other, and so the object will be seen. People with only one functioning eye, of course, do not have this protection, and run a greater risk of not seeing other aircraft in flight. (More about this later.)

Another advantage of two eyes is **binocular vision,** which is the ability to focus both eyes on one object at the same time. Light from a particular object, especially a near one, will enter each eye at a slightly different angle, causing the images formed by each eye to be different. The brain uses these two different images as one means of estimating the distance of nearby objects – the difference in the two images being greater for near objects than for far objects.

You can observe this effect by holding a pencil or a finger up against a distant background, closing one eye at a time and viewing it through the other. Each eye will provide a different image – the pencil or finger will be seen from different angles, and its relationship to the background will be different.

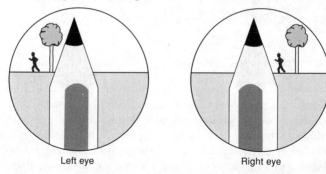

Left eye   Right eye

■ *Figure 2-4* **Binocular vision – different view from left and right eyes**

With normal two-dimensional photographs or films projected onto a screen, each eye receives an identical image, so the impression of depth and reality is lost to some extent. Attempts have been made to artificially replicate binocular vision and its three-dimensional (3-D) effect by using 3-D films and 3-D photographs. This is done, not by presenting a real three-dimensional situation, but by presenting a slightly different two-dimensional picture to each eye, with objects seen from slightly different angles and in slightly different positions relative to the background. The brain then forms a more realistic three-dimensional picture than is possible when each eye receives an identical picture.

The Structure of the Eye

The main components of the eye are the cornea and lens, the retina, and the optic nerve.

Light passes into the eye through the cornea and the lens, which focus the light rays onto a screen, the retina, at the back of the eye. The retina converts the image made by the received light into electrical signals which are then sent via the optic nerve to the brain – and so we 'see'.

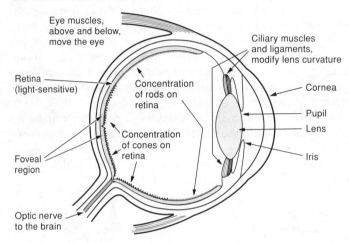

Eye muscles, above and below, move the eye

Ciliary muscles and ligaments, modify lens curvature

Retina (light-sensitive)

Concentration of rods on retina

Cornea

Pupil

Lens

Concentration of cones on retina

Iris

Foveal region

Optic nerve to the brain

■ *Figure 2-5* **The structure of the eye**

The Cornea

The cornea is a transparent cap over the lens, through which the light rays first pass. Its surfaces are curved and some refraction of the light occurs as it passes through the cornea. Unlike the lens, whose edge is surrounded by the 'ciliary' muscles, there are no muscles attached to the cornea, and so we cannot alter its shape and refractive abilities. The eye has eyelids which can close over the cornea for protection and to assist in spreading lubrication. Most of the movement comes from a large upper eyelid, and less movement from the smaller and weaker lower eyelid.

The Iris

Between the cornea and the lens is a coloured membrane known as the *iris*. The colour of the iris determines the colour of the eye. At the centre of the iris is a small round aperture known as the *pupil*. The pupil changes its size to restrict the amount of light entering the lens. In very bright light, the pupil becomes quite small; in very dim conditions, the pupil widens to allow more light to enter.

The Lens

Muscles alter the curvature of the lens to alter focusing.

The lens, like the cornea, is transparent to light, but we change its shape with the ciliary muscles surrounding it, allowing us to focus the light rays. When the muscles are relaxed, the lens tends to flatten, and the reduced curvature of its surfaces means less refraction of the light rays, i.e. less focusing. The muscles can be used to squeeze the lens, which increases the curvature of the lens surfaces, thereby increasing the amount of refraction and the amount of focusing – the greater the curvature, the greater the focusing. This occurs when you focus on a very near object.

The ability of an eye to change its focus, e.g. from a far object to a near object, is known as *accommodation*.

The power of the eyes to accommodate varies, especially with tiredness and with age. When a person is fatigued, accommodation diminishes, the result being blurred images. Also, with increasing age the lens becomes less flexible, and less able to modify its curvature. This reduced focusing capability that is noticed by middle-aged people means that starting to use glasses is usually necessary sometime in the forties.

The ability to focus deteriorates with tiredness, and with age.

The Retina

The retina is the 'screen' which collects images.

The *retina* is a light-sensitive layer located at the back of the eye. It is the screen onto which the lens focuses images, which are converted to electrical signals that pass along the optic nerve to the brain.

The retina contains two types of light-sensitive (or photo-sensitive) cells: cones and rods.

Cones in the central area are sensitive to colours and detail by day.

CONES are concentrated around the central section of the retina, especially the *foveal* region directly opposite the lens. Cones are sensitive to colour, small details, and distant objects, and are most effective in daylight, and less effective in darkness. They provide the best visual acuity (the ability to resolve fine detail). The foveal region is where we focus most objects and it is this area of the retina which provides our central vision in good light conditions. Objects focused on the foveal region in very dim light (as at night) will not stimulate the cones to transmit a message along the optic nerve, so the image will therefore not be 'seen' by us.

Rods in the peripheral area are sensitive to greys and movement.

RODS are concentrated in a band outside the central foveal area. They are sensitive to movement, but not to detail or colour, and so 'see' only in shades of black, white, and grey, rather than the colours seen by the cones. Rods are effective in both daylight and darkness, and are responsible for our *peripheral* vision (i.e. off-centre vision), which helps our orientation and night vision. Objects in dim light, such as at night, are therefore most easily noticed when their image falls somewhere on the peripheral area of the retina where the rods are concentrated. You can achieve this by looking slightly to the side of an object at night, rather than directly at it as you would during daylight.

Sight Is Very Sensitive

Rods and cones are really the nerve endings of the vital optic nerve. As an extension of the brain, they will be affected by anything that affects the brain. With a shortage of oxygen (hypoxia), or an excess of alcohol, medication, or other drugs, your sight will be one of the first things to suffer. High positive g-loadings, such as in very strenuous acrobatic manoeuvres, will force the blood into the lower regions of the body and temporarily starve the brain of blood, leading to a *greyout* (only black-and-white vision) or even unconsciousness *(blackout)*.

The Optic Nerve and the Blind Spot

There is no place for cones or rods on the area of the retina where the nerves bundle together to form the big optic nerve. Any image that falls on this area will therefore not be 'seen' – in other words, there is a *blind spot* on the retina of each eye.

You can observe the existence of the blind spot in each eye by viewing Figure 2-6. Hold the page at arm's length, cover your right eye, and then with your left eye focus on the aeroplane on the right. It will be clearly recognisable as a biplane because it will be focused on your fovea (cone vision). If it were coloured, you would also be able to detect this. The helicopter on the left will be visible in your peripheral vision (rod vision), but it may not be defined clearly enough for you to recognise it as a helicopter, nor will you see its colour. You will, however, be aware that there are two potential collision risks: the aeroplane in focus through the right windscreen, and some other aircraft not clearly defined (because you are not looking directly at it and focusing on it) in the left windscreen.

Now move the page closer to your open left eye, continuing to focus on the aeroplane (right windscreen). At some point, the helicopter will disappear from your peripheral vision, and then come back into view as you bring the page even closer. The time when the image is not seen is when it falls on the optic nerve blind spot on your retina. The lack of rods or cones here means that the image is not detected. The left windscreen at this time appears empty – a dangerous situation which significantly increases the collision risk. Repeat the experiment by concentrating your right eye on the helicopter, in which case the biplane will disappear from view when its image falls on the blind spot of your right eye.

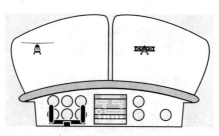

■ Figure 2-6 **Your blind spot**

Binocular vision protects you from blind spots.

Now repeat the experiment with both eyes open. Both aircraft should remain in view at all times, because the eyes are designed so that the image from a particular object cannot fall on the blind spots of both eyes simultaneously. This is another advantage of binocular vision.

Be careful when you are scanning the sky that another aircraft is not blocked from view by the magnetic compass or some part of the windscreen structure. If it is blocked from the view of both eyes, you will not see it at all; if it is blocked from the view of only one eye, you will lose the blind spot protection provided by binocular vision.

Normal Functions of the Eye

Visual Acuity – The Clarity of What We See

Visual acuity (seeing clearly and sharply) is vital to a pilot.

Visual acuity is the ability of the eye to see clearly and sharply. Perfect visual acuity means that the eye sees the object exactly as it is, clearly and without distortion, no matter how distant the object is. The degree of visual acuity varies between different people and also between the two eyes of any one person, as well as for the single eye at different times. This depends upon whether the person is fatigued, suffering hypoxia (lack of oxygen), or under the influence of alcohol or some other drug.

To describe differences in visual acuity, the standard is considered to be what a 'normal' eye is capable of seeing clearly at a particular distance. The eye test chart usually has lines of letters readable for a normal eye from 36, 24, 18, 12, 9, 6 and 5 metres respectively. (The large letter at the top of eye charts is sized that a person with normal sight can read it from a distance of 60 metres.)

The standard testing distance between the eye and the eye chart is 6 metres; the normal eye is capable of seeing clearly letters of a certain size at this distance. If another eye at 6 metres cannot read the 6-metre line clearly, and can only identify letters on the chart that a normal eye can see clearly at 9 metres, then the 'abnormal' eye is said to have '6/9' vision. This is compared with the '6/6' vision of the so-called normal eye.

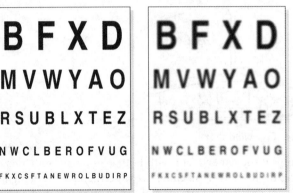

■ *Figure 2-7* **An eye chart seen with 6/6 vision and 6/9 vision**

The best visual acuity within the individual eye occurs when the image is focused sharply by a high-quality cornea and lens onto the central foveal region of a healthy retina, where the cone receptors predominate. The cone receptors are very sensitive to small details and send very sharp, colourful images to the brain.

Light rays that are focused on the retina away from the central foveal region in areas where there are not so many cone receptors, but more rod receptors, will not be seen as clearly, nor will they be in colour. Visual acuity will therefore be less for these images.

To illustrate the difference between central and peripheral vision, look at the words on this page. You must move your eyes so that the image of the word that you want to read falls on the central foveal region. Whilst you can clearly read the word you are looking at right now, you will not be able to read words some distance away from it – up, down, or sideways from it – unless you move your eyeball so that the image of that word falls on the central high-visual-acuity area of the retina.

Glare

When flying at high altitudes, especially above cloud layers or flying into a rising or setting sun, the pilot is exposed to light of very high intensity, possibly coming from all angles.

Whereas the eyes are protected from light coming from above by the forehead, eyebrows, eyelashes, and strong upper eyelid, they are not so well protected from light coming from below. Bright sunlight reflected from cloud tops, for instance, can be particularly bothersome because of this lack of natural protection.

In conditions of glare, it is advisable to protect your eyes by using high-quality sunglasses that reduce glare but not your visual acuity.

Avoid glare from strong sunlight by wearing sunglasses.

The contrast between the glare of a very bright outside environment and the darker cockpit interior may also make it difficult for the eyes to adjust quickly enough to read instruments and charts inside the cockpit.

Effect of Flickering Lights

Helicopter pilots should be aware that bright flickering lights can bring on epileptic-type fits in some people. On the ground this effect can be seen when driving along a sunlit avenue of trees, where areas of light and shade are constantly changing. Common airborne causes are the shadows of rotating helicopter blades or windmilling propellers in bright sunshine. These problems usually occur at 'flash' frequencies of between 5 Hz and 20 Hz. For instance, a 2-bladed helicopter rotor at 240 rpm would give 8 flashes per second.

Common symptoms of this effect are feelings of unease or discomfort. Susceptible passengers should wear sunglasses, cover the window, or close and cover their eyes. People so affected by flickering lights should not operate as helicopter pilots. See AIC 125/1996 (Pink 130).

Depth Perception

Binocular vision aids depth perception.

The eyes and your brain use many clues and memories of past experience to help you in judging distance. Some items are mathematical, such as the relative size of objects – a bigger object appearing to be nearer than a smaller object. Also, binocular vision (the slightly different images of a nearby object relative to its background seen by each eye) assists in depth perception when the object is near.

Texture aids depth perception.

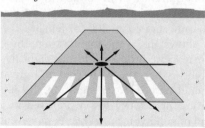

■ Figure 2-8 **Texture moves outward from the aiming point as you approach it**

Texture also assists in depth perception: the more visible the texture, the closer the object appears to be. On final approach as you near the runway, its texture will appear to flow outwards in all directions from the point on which you are focused. This is one means by which you can visually maintain a constant approach slope to the aiming point – adjusting descent angle and track so that the point from which the texture appears to be moving outwards remains at the desired aiming point.

Texture is also used for the estimation of height – for instance, as you approach flare height for a landing, the actual texture of the runway or the grass passing by the cockpit becomes increasingly noticeable.

Relative motion also aids in depth perception. Near objects generally appear to pass by the windscreen faster than more distant objects. This helps a visual pilot estimate height above the runway before and during the flare – the closer the aeroplane is to the runway, the faster the runway surface and the surrounding environment appears to pass by.

> *Relative motion aids depth perception.*

Depth perception can also be difficult in hazy or misty conditions, where edges are blurred, colours are muted, and light rays may be refracted unusually. This gives the impression of greater distance, an impression reinforced by the fact that we often have to look at distant objects through a smoggy or hazy atmosphere.

> *In haze or mist, objects may be closer than what they appear to be.*

In hazy conditions, the object might be closer than what it seems; in very clear conditions, the object might be further away than it seems. On hazy days you might touch down earlier than expected; on very clear nights, you might flare a little too soon.

Colour Vision

Colours are detected in the central foveal region of the retina by the cone receptors, which are only active in fairly bright light. By differentiating between the various wavelengths of light in the visible spectrum (red light with its longer wavelength, through to violet light with its shorter wavelength), the average eye can distinguish over one hundred hues (single wavelength colours) and one thousand shades.

There are some eyes that cannot distinguish any colours at all, even in bright light, but this total colour-blindness is very rare. Males are susceptible to colour blindness, with about 1 in 12 caucasian males having some colour blindness (better called *defective colour vision*), compared with only about 1 in 200 for females.

Defective colour vision shows up as trouble distinguishing between red and green. It may cause problems during night flying, as well as in poor visibility, when the white, red and green navigation lights of other aircraft are used for recognition, and also when visual light signals from the control tower are used in a radio–failure situation instead of radio voice messages (a rare event nowadays).

Adaptation of the Eyes to Darkness

At night, there are some special considerations regarding vision. Since your attention during night flying will be both inside and outside the cockpit, care should be taken to ensure that your eyes can continuously function at near maximum efficiency. It takes the eyes some minutes to adapt to a dark environment, as most of us have experienced when walking into a darkened cinema and stumble across other patrons in an attempt to find an empty seat.

The rate at which *dark adaptation* of the eyes occurs depends to a large extent on the contrast between the brightness of light previously experienced and the degree of darkness of the new environment.

Whereas the cones, concentrated in the central region of the retina, adjust quickly to variations in light intensity, the rods (which are most important for night vision) take some 30 minutes to adapt fully to darkness. In dim light the cones become less effective, or even totally ineffective, and there is a chemical change in the rods to increase their sensitivity.

Protecting Your Night Vision

To assist in night adaptation, it is good airmanship to **avoid bright white lights** (landing lights, strobes, flashlights, etc.) in the 30 minutes prior to night flight, and also while in flight. Exposure to bright light, even for just a second or two, can cause a loss of night adaptation which will then require many minutes to return.

Since bright lights will impair your outside vision at night, it is good airmanship to keep the cockpit lighting at a reasonably low level, but not so low that you cannot see your charts, or find the fuel selector.

A good oxygen supply is also essential for good night vision, which can begin to deteriorate at cabin altitudes as low as 4,000 feet. At cabin altitudes above 10,000 feet, make sure that you don an oxygen mask and use supplementary oxygen.

Scanning for Other Aircraft by Day

The central (foveal) region of the retina provides the best vision, but only during daylight, and not in darkness. Aeroplanes and other objects are best seen by day if you can focus their image on the foveal region, and you do this by looking directly at them.

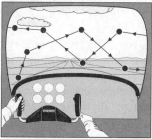

■ *Figure 2-9* **Scanning by day**

The most effective method of scanning for other aircraft for collision avoidance during daylight hours is to use a series of short, regularly spaced eye movements to search each 10° sector of the sky. Systematically focusing on different segments of the sky for short intervals is a better technique than continuously sweeping the sky.

You may be on a collision course with another aircraft if there is no apparent relative motion between you and the other aircraft, especially if the other aircraft appears to be getting bigger and bigger in the windscreen. Because of the lack of movement across your windscreen, an aircraft on a collision course with you will be more difficult to spot than one that is not on a collision course. Any relative movement of an object against its background usually makes it easier to notice in your peripheral vision.

The image of the other aircraft may not increase in size much at first, but, shortly before impact, it would rapidly increase in size.

The time available for you to avoid a collision may be quite brief, depending upon when you see the other aircraft and the rate of closure. If you are flying at 100 knots and it is flying at 500 knots in the opposite direction, the rate of closure is 600 knots, i.e. 10 nautical miles per minute.

If you spot the other aircraft at a distance of 1 nm, you only have ⅒ of a minute, i.e. 6 seconds, to potential impact. If you are a vigilant pilot, and spot it at 3 nautical miles (nm), you have 18 seconds in which to act. In hazy or low-visibility conditions, your ability to see other aircraft and objects whose edges might be blurred will be diminished and, if you can see them, they may *appear* to be further away than their actual distance, i.e. you might be closer than you think.

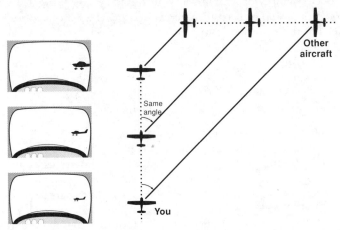

■ *Figure 2-10* **A potential collision**

When trying to search for other aircraft in an empty sky, we often have trouble because of *empty field myopia*, the natural tendency of a resting eye to focus at 1 to 2 metres, and not at infinity as we might think. Consequently, distant aircraft may not be noticed; or sometimes a dust particle, a scratch, or an insect on the windscreen might be mistaken for a distant aeroplane. To avoid this empty-field myopia, you should focus on any available distant object, such as a cloud or a landmark, to lengthen your focus. If the sky is empty of clouds or other objects, then focus briefly on a relatively distant part of the aeroplane like a wingtip as a means of lengthening your focus.

Having spotted an aeroplane in an otherwise empty sky, be aware that it could be closer to you than it appears to be, because you have no other object with which to compare its size.

Scanning for Other Aircraft by Night

Peripheral vision is more effective than central vision at night.

Because the central foveal region of the retina containing mainly cones is *not* effective by night, causing a night blind spot in your central vision, you need to rely to a greater extent on your peripheral vision which is provided by the rods in the outer band of the retina. **An object at night** will be more readily visible when you are looking to the side of it by 10 or 20°, rather than directly at it. Colour will not be perceived by the rods, and so your night vision will be in black, white, and shades of grey, and objects will not be as sharply defined as in daytime central vision.

The most effective way to use your eyes during night flight is to scan small sectors of sky more *slowly* than in daylight, to permit 'off-centre' viewing of objects in your *peripheral vision*. Because you may not be able to see the aircraft shape at night, you will have to determine its direction of travel making use of its visible lighting:

☐ the flashing red beacon;
☐ the red navigation light on the left wingtip;
☐ the green navigation light on the right wingtip; and
☐ a steady white light on the tail.

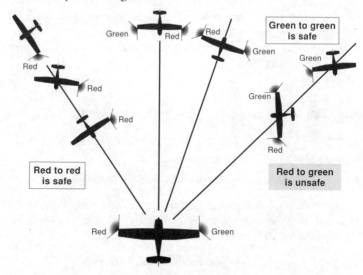

■ *Figure 2-11* **Using navigation lights to evaluate and avoid collisions at night**

Visual Illusions

Sometimes what we 'see' in our brain is not the precise reality because images sent from the eyes can sometimes be misinterpreted by the brain.

Autokinesis

The visual illusion of *autokinesis* (self-motion) can occur at night if you stare continuously at a single light against a generally dark background. It will appear to move, perhaps in an oscillating fashion, after only a few seconds of staring at it, even though in fact it is stationary. You could lose spatial orientation if you use it as your single point of reference. The more you try to concentrate on it, the more it may appear to oscillate.

You can guard against autokinesis at night by maintaining movement of your eyes in normal scanning, and by monitoring the flight instruments frequently to ensure correct attitude.

Keep your eyes moving and check the flight instruments.

Unless you have a distant object in view at night, your eyes will tend to focus at a point about one to two metres ahead of you, especially if you are an older person with 'tired eyes', and you may miss sighting distant objects. This *empty field myopia* or *night myopia* (short-sightedness) can be combated by searching for *distant* lights and focusing briefly on them.

Beware also of false horizons at night (see later in this chapter).

False Expectations

We expect that a pencil will be smaller than a tree, so when we see the image of a pencil beside the image of a tree that is occupying the same angular area on the retina, we assume that the tree is further away. This is usually the case, but need not be, e.g. if the tree is a miniature one.

What we see

What we expect

The reality

■ Figure 2-12 **What we 'see' is sometimes not how it really is**

Similarly, a small, dark image formed on the retina could be a distant, but rapidly approaching aircraft, or it could be a speck of dirt or dust, or an insect spot, on the windscreen.

■ Figure 2-13 **Is it a distant aircraft, or a speck on the windscreen?**

If we spend most of our time landing on the one runway, we get very used to its width and length, and how it should look on approach. Landing on a different runway, which has a different width and/or length, may present us with quite a different view on approach, even though we are on the correct slope; its appearance at the correct flare height might also be different.

It is quite common for a pilot familiar with a small country airfield to flare too high on the first landing at a large international airport where the runways are usually long and wide.

Interpreting Patterns

The brain often has to make sense of a pattern of lines, and the interpretation may not always be correct, as can be seen from some of the figures which follow.

■ Figure 2-14 **Is this a two-bladed propeller on a radial engine, or a Mexican riding a bicycle?**

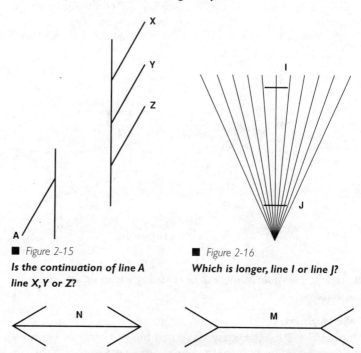

■ Figure 2-15
Is the continuation of line A line X, Y or Z?

■ Figure 2-16
Which is longer, line I or line J?

■ Figure 2-17 **Is line N longer or shorter than line M, or are they the same length?**

Does a stick bend upwards as I put it into a bucket of water? No, it does not, but it certainly looks as though it does because our brain and eyes assume light travels in straight lines, which is not always the case, as we know from an understanding of refraction.

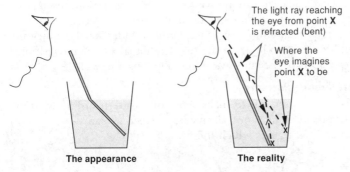

The light ray reaching the eye from point **X** is refracted (bent)

Where the eye imagines point **X** to be

The appearance   The reality

■ *Figure 2-18* **Does a stick bend upwards as I put it into a bucket of water?**

An aeroplane on approach through heavy rain can sometimes experience quite a build-up of water on the windscreen, which refracts the light rays on their way to the pilot's eyes, perhaps causing an illusion like the 'bent stick'. Knowledge of this effect can be some protection for the pilot.

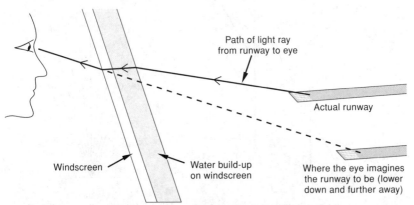

Path of light ray from runway to eye

Actual runway

Windscreen

Water build-up on windscreen

Where the eye imagines the runway to be (lower down and further away)

■ *Figure 2-19* **A visual illusion can be caused by a layer of water on the windscreen**

False Horizons
Sloping cloud layers by day, or angled lines or areas of lights by night, can sometimes present a pilot with a false horizon that can be very misleading. Make use of your flight instruments to confirm your flight attitude.

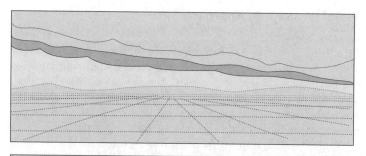

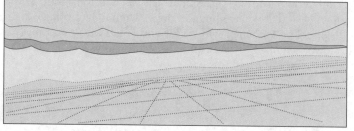

■ Figure 2-20 **A sloping cloud layer that is more prominent than the horizon can cause a strong visual illusion of a false horizon – check your attitude indicator and balance ball regularly**

■ Figure 2-21 **A visual illusion of same level due to a sloping cloud layer (do not change level prematurely)**

■ Figure 2-22 **What the pilot sees through the windscreen; and what might be seen if the pilot had x-ray vision (sloping cloud layer)**

Visual Illusions on Approach

Runway Slope

Most runways are of standard width and on flat ground. On every approach, you should try to achieve the same flightpath angle to the horizontal, and your eyes will become accustomed to this, allowing you to make consistently good approaches along an acceptable approach slope merely by keeping your view of the runway through the windscreen in a standard perspective.

Approaching a **sloping runway**, however, the perspective will be different. A runway that slopes *upwards* will look longer, and you will feel that you are high on slope, when in fact you are right on slope. The tendency will be for you to go lower and make a shallower approach. If you know that the runway does have an upslope, you can avoid this tendency.

> *Allow for a different perspective when approaching a sloping runway.*

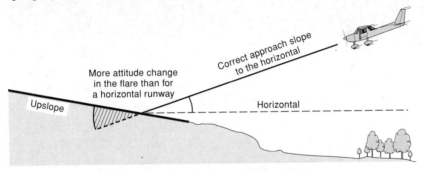

■ *Figure 2-23* **An upward sloping runway creates a 'too-high' illusion**

A runway that slopes *downwards* will look shorter, and you will feel that you are low on slope, when in fact you are on slope. The tendency will be for you to go higher and make a steeper approach. If you know that the runway does have a downslope, you can avoid this tendency.

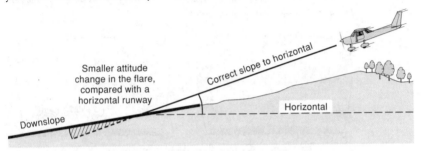

■ *Figure 2-24* **A downward sloping runway creates a 'too-low' illusion**

If you know the runway slope, you can allow for it in your visual estimation of whether you are high or low on slope (Figure 2-25).

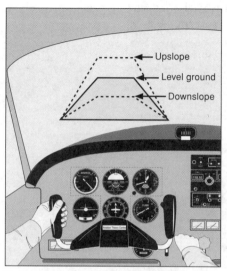

■ Figure 2-25 **How runways of different slopes should appear at the same point on final approach to land**

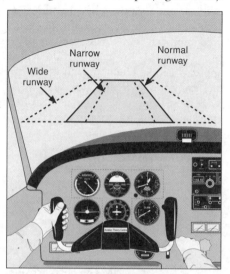

■ Figure 2-26 **How runways of different widths should appear at the same point on final**

Runway Size

A runway that is *larger* than usual will appear to be closer than it really is. Conversely, a runway that is *smaller* than usual will appear to be further away than it really is.

A *wide* runway, because of the angle at which you view it peripherally in the final stages of the approach and landing, will cause an illusion of being too low, and you may flare and hold-off too high as a result. This may lead to 'dropping–in' for a heavy landing. Conversely, a *narrow* runway will cause an illusion of being too high, and you may delay the flare and make contact with the runway earlier (and harder) than expected.

If you know that the runway is wider or narrower than what you are familiar with, then you can allow for this in your visual judgement of flare height and hold–off prior to touchdown (Figure 2–26).

Haze

In hazy conditions, you may be *closer* to the runway than you appear to be, an illusion that may lead to an unnecessarily hard landing if you are not prepared for the effect of haze on your vision.

The Night Approach

It is preferable to **make a powered approach at night,** rather than a glide approach, providing a normal well-controlled approach at normal speeds. In modern training aircraft, the powered approach is generally used by day also. Power gives the pilot more control, a lower rate of descent and, therefore, a less-steep approach slope. The approach to the aiming point should be stable, using any available aids, such as the runway lighting and a VASI (visual approach slope indicator system) if available. The *red-on-white* VASI is commonly used throughout the world, but there are other types in use also.

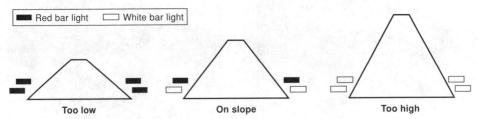

■ *Figure 2-27* **Perspectives on approach using a VASI**

Using the runway edge lighting only, correct tracking and slope is achieved when the runway perspective is the same as in daylight. For correct tracking, the runway should appear symmetrical in the windscreen. Guidance on achieving the correct approach slope is obtained from the apparent spacing between the runway edge lights.

If the aeroplane is below slope, the runway lights will appear to be closer together. If the aeroplane is flying above slope, then the runway lights will appear to be further apart. Attention should also be paid to the airspeed indicator throughout the approach, to ensure that the correct airspeed is being maintained.

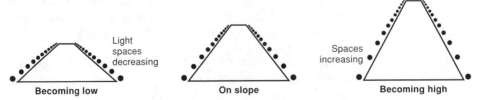

■ *Figure 2-28* **Perspectives on approach using runway edge lighting**

A VASI will provide correct slope guidance by day or night, but the perspective provided by runway edge lighting may be slightly misleading if you do not allow for any runway slope.

The 'Black-Hole' Approach

Flying an approach to a runway without other visible references can often be difficult. This can occur when approaching a runway on a dark night where the only lights visible are the runway edge lights, with no town lights or street lights to be seen, and no indication of the nature of the surrounding terrain. This is what is known as 'a black-hole approach'.

Black-hole approach   **Approach with good ground reference**

■ *Figure 2-29* **Visual information is considerably less in a 'black-hole' situation**

The tendency is to think that you are higher than in fact you are, resulting in an urge to fly down, and fly a lower and flatter approach. Approach aids such as an electronic glideslope (instrument landing system – ILS) or a VASI can help you to resist this unwanted tendency. If these aids are not available, you can resist the temptation to fly too low an approach by monitoring the vertical speed indicator (VSI) to ensure that the rate of descent is reasonable for the approach slope that you wish to maintain.

Black-hole approaches are common at night on tropical atolls, at desert airfields, or on approaches to land on runways that are surrounded by water.

Similar situations to a black-hole approach arise in **white-out** conditions where the ground is covered with snow, making it fairly featureless. The lack of features around the runway make depth and slope perception much more difficult. See Figure 2-30.

White-out approach   Good perspective (normal)

■ Figure 2-30 *Snow considerably restricts the visual perspective information*

Glasses and Contact Lenses

Faulty focusing by the eye can result naturally from a lens that has become less flexible with age and cannot be made curved enough to focus nearby objects, or it can result from a lens that is not shaped correctly. In almost all cases, artificial lenses in the form of glasses or contact lenses can be made to correct the specific deficiency and restore clear vision.

Artificial lenses can compensate for most deficiencies in an eye lens.

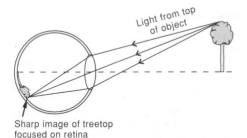

■ Figure 2-31 *Normal vision, without the need for correction*

Short-Sightedness (Myopia)

Short-sightedness (myopia) is a common problem. It occurs when the eye is relaxed and the cornea and lens focus the rays from a distant object not on the retina, but in front of it. By the time the light rays reach the retina they have moved apart and are no longer concentrated at a point. The resultant image formed on the retina is therefore out of focus.

A short-sighted person might see near objects clearly, but distant objects (which require less focusing) might be blurred.

Poor distant vision caused by short–sightedness can be corrected by using an artificial concave lens to reduce the overall refraction of the light rays. The light rays will then focus at a greater distance behind the lens, which ideally will be on the retina.

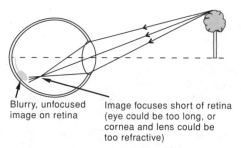

Blurry, unfocused image on retina

Image focuses short of retina (eye could be too long, or cornea and lens could be too refractive)

■ Figure 2-32 **Short-sightedness (myopia) – image focuses short of the retina**

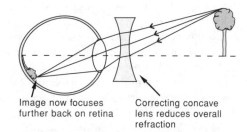

Image now focuses further back on retina

Correcting concave lens reduces overall refraction

■ Figure 2-33 **Short-sightedness corrected using a concave lens**

Long-Sightedness (Hyperopia or Hypermetropia)

Long-sightedness (hyperopia) occurs when the eye is relaxed and the cornea and lens do not focus the rays from an object before they reach the retina. The resulting image formed on the retina will therefore not be in focus. The point of focus for the rays is beyond the retina. A long-sighted person might see distant objects clearly, but near objects that need more focusing might be blurred.

Long-sightedness (hyperopia) can be corrected by a conscious effort to focus the image, or by using an artificial convex lens to increase the overall refraction of the light rays so that they focus earlier, ideally on the retina.

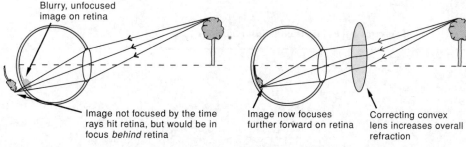

Blurry, unfocused image on retina

Image not focused by the time rays hit retina, but would be in focus *behind* retina

■ Figure 2-34 **Long-sightedness (hyperopia) – image not focused by the time the light rays reach the retina**

Image now focuses further forward on retina

Correcting convex lens increases overall refraction

■ Figure 2-35 **Long-sightedness corrected using a convex lens**

A form of long-sightedness that occurs quite naturally in people in their forties or older is *presbyopia*. It is caused by the lens material losing some of its flexibility and so the muscles are less able to increase its curvature. Rays, especially from near objects, will not be focused by the time they reach the retina, i.e. the eyes have lost some of their ability to accommodate for near vision. This is when people say that their arms are not long enough, i.e. not long enough to hold a book or newspaper at a distance where their eyes are capable of focusing the words.

Near vision (for reading) visually deteriorates with age (presbyopia).

Presbyopic people, with diminished near-vision, may have distant vision that requires no correction. The solution for them, to improve reading vision without affecting distant vision, is to use half-glasses with a half-moon convex lens in the lower half to increase the refraction, and nothing in the upper half.

Astigmatism

Astigmatism occurs when the curvature of the cornea, and less commonly the curvature of the lens, is not perfectly round, i.e. may be ellipsoid rather than spheroid. This causes uneven refraction of the various light rays passing through the lens, and the formation of distorted images. It can be corrected by a lens which has varying curvature over its surface.

■ *Figure 2-36*

Half-glasses improve near-vision without affecting distant-vision

Glasses for Flying

If you are required to wear glasses when flying, you should carry a second pair to guard against loss or damage to the first pair.

Conclusion

A pilot should always handle any vision deficiency and/or correction under the supervision of an expert. For information about vision correction requirements for pilots see AIC 135/1997 (Pink 155).

Now complete **Exercises 2 – Eyesight and Visual Illusions.**

Hearing and Balance

The Ears

The ear is a very important organ for two senses – for hearing, and for balance. *Hearing* allows us to perceive sounds and to interpret them; the sense of *balance* lets us know which way is up and whether we are accelerating or not. Balance is the next most important sense for a pilot after vision.

Sound is defined as energy that we can hear with our ears. It is often very useful and pleasant, as with voice messages and music, but excessive sound may be annoying and fatiguing, and can even lead to damage within the ear. Irregular, unwanted, and unpleasant sound is called *noise*, and is best filtered out if we can find a means to do it.

Sound signals are caused by pressure variations travelling through the air as pressure waves, and these cause sensitive membranes like the eardrum to vibrate. The inner ear translates these pressure vibrations into electrical signals which are sent via the auditory nerve to the brain, where they are interpreted.

Similarly, **balance and acceleration signals** from the balance mechanism in the inner ear pass to the brain as electrical signals for interpretation. The interpretation is sometimes tricky in the case of an airborne pilot, since the brain is used to the person generally being upright on the earth's surface.

The ears are used for hearing and for balance.

The Structure of the Ear

The ear is divided into three areas: the outer, middle, and inner ear.

THE OUTER EAR includes:
- **the external ear** (known medically as the *pinna* or *auricle*), which is used as a megaphone to gather the sound signals;
- **the outer canal** through which the pressure waves pass; and
- **the eardrum,** which is caused to vibrate in harmony with the pressure waves.

Any obstruction to the outer canal, such as earplugs or an excess of wax, can reduce the sound pressure waves reaching the eardrum. Similarly a padded cover over the external ear will reduce the sound waves entering the ear, unless the cover is a headset that blocks external noise, but has a small speaker for radio and interphone messages.

THE MIDDLE EAR is an air-filled cavity containing three small bones, known as *ossicles,* which are forced to move by the vibrating eardrum, converting the pressure wave energy into mechanical energy of motion. The ossicles are arranged like a series of levers to increase the effect of the initial movement. This energy then passes on to the cochlea in the inner ear.

The air in the middle ear is maintained at ambient pressure via the *Eustachian tube,* which connects the interior of the middle ear to the nasal passages. There is (or should be) no leakage of air across the eardrum, and there should be easy passage of air through the Eustachian tube, when needed, to equalise pressures – for instance, when climbing or descending. This is sometimes hindered by swelling and inflammation when a person has a cold, and can lead to serious consequences (explained later) if a person flies with a cold or similar infection.

> *The Eustachian tubes equalise pressure either side of the eardrums.*

Interference to the movement of the three small ossicles or their joints will reduce or distort the sound signal. This can be caused by ear infections, damage to the bones or joints, or a blocked ear with air trapped inside the middle ear *(barotitis).*

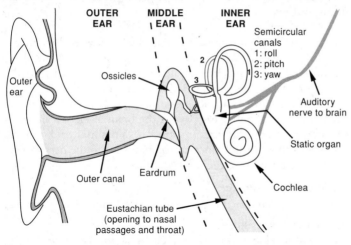

■ *Figure 3-1* **The structure of the ear**

THE INNER EAR contains two very important pieces of apparatus:

- ☐ The *cochlea* for hearing; it converts the mechanical energy from the ossicles into electrical signals which then travel via the auditory nerve to the brain for interpretation.
- ☐ The *vestibular apparatus,* consisting of the *static organ* and the *semi-circular canals;* these contain fluid and small hairs that convert gravity and acceleration forces into electrical signals which are sent to the brain for interpretation.

Fluid in the cochlea is moved by the mechanical energy from the ossicles, and this causes a wavy movement of small hairs protruding into the fluid. The movement is converted to electrical signals at the bottom of each hair, and these signals are sent along the *auditory nerve* to the brain.

Excessive noise can lead to damage of the hairs in the cochlea, and infection or injury can damage the auditory nerve, possibly causing ringing in the ears (tinnitus).

The ear is never switched off, and loud noises can stir us from even the deepest sleep. For this reason, a quiet room is best if you want to sleep soundly. It is interesting to note how you can extract messages important for you out of a noisy background – for instance, a radio message directed at you, the sound of your own child on a crowded beach, or your own name mentioned in a distant conversation – known as 'the cocktail party effect'.

The comments that follow apply to the *hearing* aspects of the ear. The *balance* aspects, i.e. the gravity and acceleration signals from the semi-circular canals of the middle ear, will be discussed shortly.

Hearing

What is Sound?

Sound is what we hear, and each sound can be defined by:

☐ **Frequency or pitch:** the number of pressure waves per second (or hertz, Hz) that the sound source produces. Perfect human hearing is in the range of 20 Hz to 20,000 Hz, and voices use the frequency range 500 Hz to 3,000 Hz.

☐ **Loudness or intensity:** the strength or amplitude of the pressure waves, measured in decibels (dB), a logarithmic scale where an increase of 20 dB signifies an increase in intensity of 10 times (20 dB is 10 times as loud as 0 dB, the threshold of hearing; 40 dB is 10 times louder again, i.e. 100 times as loud as 0 dB; 60 dB is 1,000 times as loud as 0 dB and 100 times as loud as 20 dB; an increase from 80 dB to 100 dB is an increase in loudness by a factor of 10).

☐ **Duration:** how long the sound lasts (the longer you are exposed to loud noise, the more damage it can do to your hearing).

Fatigue and Damage From Noise

Loud noise can damage hearing.

Unwanted sound, especially if it is loud and disagreeable, is *noise*. It can be mentally fatiguing through its effect on our ears, but it also affects the rest of our body, especially if it is associated with vibration as is often the case. Noise can interfere with communications, and with our concentration.

Extreme noise levels can also do permanent damage to our ears, with duration of exposure as important as loudness.

NOISE LEVELS OF TYPICAL SOUNDS	
130 dB	Standing near a jet aircraft (noise becoming painful)
120 dB	Standing near a piston-engined aircraft (noise becoming uncomfortable). Several hours per day for 3 months could lead to deafness.
110 dB	Maximum recommended for up to 30 minutes' exposure
100 dB	Maximum recommended for 2 hours' exposure
90 dB	Maximum recommended for 8 hours' exposure (a working day)
80 dB	Standing near heavy machinery. Above 80 dB for long periods can lead to temporary or permanent hearing loss.
60 dB	Loud street noise, trucks, etc.
50 dB	Conversation in a noisy factory
40 dB	Office noise
30 dB	Quiet conversation
20 dB	Whispering
0 dB	The threshold of hearing

Loss of Hearing

A person can experience a temporary hearing loss after exposure to noise. The noise of an engine, for instance, may no longer be heard after a while even though the engine noise is still there. Some factory workers lose the ability to hear frequencies that they are subjected to all day long. A temporary hearing loss may disappear after a few hours or after a few days.

Exposure to high noise levels for long periods can also lead to a *permanent* hearing loss, especially in the high-frequency range. This is a risk area for pilots who are exposed to a noisy work environment for long periods. Put it together with visits to the car races, noisy discotheques, plus a top set of loudspeakers at home, and you are in a high risk environment from the point of view of your hearing. Very, very gradually, and imperceptibly, a person can lose the ability to hear certain sounds clearly, speech becomes more difficult to comprehend, and radio communications become more difficult.

Sudden, unexpected loud noises greater than about 130 dB, such as an explosion or the sound of an impact, can cause damage to hearing, possibly even physical damage to the eardrum or to the small and delicate ossicle bones behind the eardrum.

Hearing loss can also result from:

☐ **Problems in the conduction** of the sound, through a blocked outer canal (ear wax), fluid or pressure problems in the middle ear (barotrauma caused by a cold, for instance), or faulty ossicle bones and joints – this is known as *conductive* hearing loss.

◻ **Loss of sensitivity** of the hair cells in the cochlea, through exposure to noise, infection, or age – this is known as a *sensory* or *noise-induced* hearing loss.

◻ *Presbycusis,* a natural loss of hearing ability with increasing age, especially in the higher frequencies, (down about 5% by age 60 and 10% by age 70).

◻ **Alcoholism,** or excessive use of medications.

Preventing or Minimising Hearing Loss

A noise-induced hearing loss may develop gradually over a period of years without the person noticing – something which cannot be reversed, hence the need for prevention rather than cure. As pilots, we are lucky in that we have regular audiometry tests which can be monitored over the years to look for any gradual loss of hearing, especially in the higher frequencies.

Wear hearing protection in noisy environments.

Try to wear hearing protection when in noisy areas. A good noise-cancelling **headset** is highly recommended for the cockpit, and earplugs or earmuffs for when you are moving around outside the aircraft. **Earplugs** can reduce noise by about 20 dB, and good earmuffs by about 40 dB.

Headsets protect your hearing and aid radio communications.

The radio headset, especially if it is well sealed, will block out background noise but not affect radio communications. You should use the *squelch* control on the radio, if available, to reduce unwanted background hash, and you should keep the volume turned down as much as possible without disturbing your comprehension of voice messages.

Unprotected exposure to jet-engine noise close up can be hazardous to the sensitive balance mechanism in the ears also – another reason to wear hearing protection outside the aircraft.

Balance

Sensing Acceleration

The human body does not sense motion in a straight line at a steady speed, except by visual means, since muscular sensations and the balance organs of the inner ear do not sense *unaccelerated* motion.

The body can sense accelerations (changes in speed), but not speed itself.

Sometimes, when you are a passenger on one of two trains travelling on parallel tracks, it is difficult to know whether your train is moving, the other train is moving, or both trains are moving – even with your eyes open. A steady speed in a straight line is unaccelerated 1g motion, as is being stationary, and so the muscles and balance organs will not sense motion in this situation at a steady speed.

The human body, with its muscular sensations ('seat-of-the-pants' or 'proprioceptive' sensing) and balance organ of the inner ear, however, *does* react to *acceleration,* i.e. changes in either speed or direction. For instance, as an elevator accelerates upwards, you experience more than 1g and feel heavier than normal, reverting to your normal 'weight' once the elevator has reached a steady speed. As it slows down, you tend to keep on going, experiencing less than 1g and feeling lighter than usual. You revert to normal 1g feeling once the elevator has stopped. Your body also reacts to changes in *angular* speed, i.e. to angular acceleration – for instance, when you roll into a banked turn, or when you spin.

The g-force changes in an elevator are only fractional compared with those experienced by a pilot, especially in aerobatic manoeuvres such as loops and in steep turns. In a 60° banked turn, for instance, you will experience 2g and feel double your weight.

In normal flying, the g-force changes are also only fractional and have no significant effect on the body. In strenuous aerobatics, however, forces of +4g or more for a sustained period, say when pulling out of a steep dive, will have a significant effect. The blood will be forced towards the lower extremities and away from the brain, causing a loss of vision due to the lack of oxygen, leading to *greyout* and, eventually, *blackout.*

If *negative* g-forces are experienced – for instance, if the control column is suddenly pushed forward and held there – the blood rushes to the head. In an extreme case of negative g, the lower eyelids will move up and cover the eyes, giving an impression of *red-out.*

How the Balance Mechanism Works

Sensing Angular Accelerations

The inner ear contains a balance organ consisting of three **semi-circular canals** connected at a sac. They contain fluid which can flow in the canal, and move gelatinous material into which hairs from the base of the canal protrude. Any movement of the fluid will move the gelatinous material and the hairs. Small nerve cells at the base of each hair convert this movement into an electrical signal which is sent to the brain for interpretation.

The three semicircular canals are at right angles to each other, like the pitch–roll–yaw planes of an aeroplane, and can detect angular accelerations (in pitch, roll and yaw).

During angular acceleration, the relevant semicircular canal accelerates away from the fluid, which is 'left behind'. This causes the fluid to flow in the semicircular canal in a direction opposite to the angular acceleration, and bend the sensory hairs, which send an angular acceleration message to the brain.

Three semicircular canals in the inner ear sense angular accelerations in the three planes.

■ *Figure 3-2* **The semicircular canals for roll, pitch and yaw**

Once the angular acceleration has ceased, and a steady angular speed is maintained, the fluid ends up moving with the canal, i.e. there is no longer any relative motion between the fluid and the canal, and so the sensory hairs on the canal wall no longer bend. The semicircular canals no longer sense any turning motion because there is no angular acceleration, even though a steady turn is continuing.

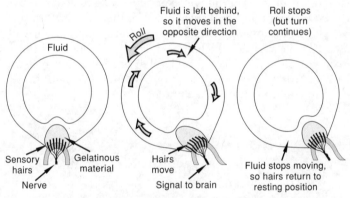

■ *Figure 3-3* **Angular acceleration**

Sensing Gravity and Linear Accelerations

Gravity and linear accelerations or decelerations are detected in a similar fashion by sensory hairs in the sac, which is sometimes known as the **static organ**. The hairs protrude into a gelatinous material called the *cupula* containing small crystals called *otoliths*.

The cupula has a resting position when the head is upright, and the brain interprets the message sent from the small hairs at this time as 'up', i.e. the cupula is supported by a 1g force directly upwards. If the head is tilted to one side, or forward or back, then the cupula moves under the force of gravity and takes up a new position, bending the hairs, which then send a different signal to the brain.

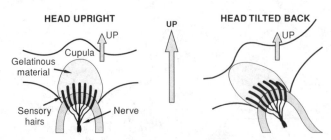

■ *Figure 3-4* **The cupula sends a message as to which way is 'up'**

The cupula detects the direction of g-forces, but cannot distinguish their origin – the force of gravity, or a centripetal force, which will not be vertical, pulling you into a coordinated turn. We must remember that the body was designed for fairly slow motion on the face of the earth, with a basic 1g force of gravity exerted on it, and not really for the three-dimensional forces we experience in flight.

For instance, sitting firmly in your seat in a perfectly coordinated 60° banked turn, you will experience a 2g force exerted by the seat on your body at an angle of 60° to the vertical. With your eyes closed, you might feel that you are still sitting upright with respect to the vertical which, in fact, is not the case. It is sometimes difficult to know if you are level or in a banked turn, hence the need to use your eyes to look outside or at the flight instruments to confirm your actual attitude.

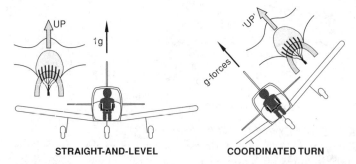

■ *Figure 3-5* **'Up' is the direction of the g-forces exerted on your body, according to your static organ**

The cupula in the static organ also detects linear accelerations. During a linear acceleration, the body accelerates away from it and the cupula is temporarily 'left behind', causing the hairs to bend and send a new signal to the brain. They will return to their normal position once the body is no longer accelerating and is moving at a steady speed (which may be zero).

The static organ in the inner ear senses gravity (weight) and linear accelerations.

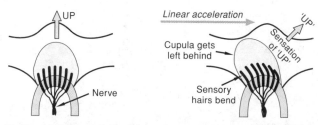

■ Figure 3-6 **The cupula detects linear accelerations**

NOTE If you compare Figure 3-6 with the one regarding 'which way is up' (Figure 3-4), you will see that the relative position of the cupula during a linear acceleration is similar to that when the head is tilted back; this can lead to an illusion of tumbling backwards, when in fact you are accelerating.

Orientation

Orientation – the ability to determine your position in space – is usually achieved by some combination of three senses:

☐ **vision** – the most powerful sense of all;
☐ **balance** – the vestibular sense (gravity, acceleration, and angular acceleration); and
☐ **'seat-of-the-pants'** (bodily feel or the *proprioceptive* sense).

In most situations, each of the three senses reinforces the others, but this is not always the case in flight. Each of these senses can sometimes have its messages misinterpreted by the brain, and you must guard against this. Not knowing your attitude in space (i.e. which way is up) is called *spatial disorientation*. Usually, the most reliable sense is vision! Hence the need to rely on your flight instruments.

Vision is your most powerful sense.

Vestibular Illusions Involving Rolling

The Illusion of Level Flight While In a Steady Turn

The semicircular canals can send good signals to the brain whilst the aircraft is rolling at a reasonable rate into or out of a turn, i.e. during any angular acceleration, but once in a steady turn the fluid motion stops and the signals cease. The sensation of rolling ceases. The static organ senses the direction of the g-forces, not only gravity, and the brain interprets this direction as 'up', which it may not be. Therefore, in a steady turn, your vestibular apparatus might indicate a false 'up'. You are now in a steady turn, but receiving no vestibular signals that a turn is occurring.

To avoid this illusion, **use your eyes,** either to refer to the natural horizon, or to the flight instruments (which may be difficult to interpret for an untrained instrument pilot).

Sight is more reliable than balance.

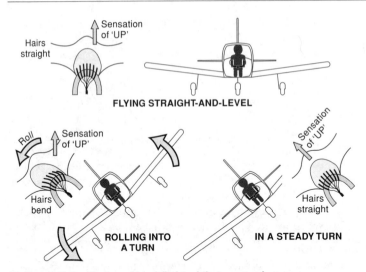

■ *Figure 3-7* **An illusion of level flight while in a steady turn**

The Illusion of being in Level Flight While Slowly Banking into a Shallow Turn

Another illusion of level flight can occur when the aeroplane banks over very slowly, perhaps while the pilot is distracted reading the navigation chart. The rate of roll is insufficient to cause any movement of fluid in the semicircular canals, hence there is no impression of angular acceleration and no impression of either entering or being in a turn. Once again, the solution is to use your eyes and the natural or artificial horizon to return to wings level.

> *Your balance mechanism may not sense slow banking.*

The 'Leans'

The 'leans' is the illusion of the aeroplane being banked when in fact the wings are level. The leans will be accentuated if the pilot has no visual references, and, once again, can occur in the following manner.

An aeroplane has been in a steady turn for 15 seconds, time enough for the initial movement of fluid in the semicircular canals to have ceased and the vestibular apparatus to have forgotten that it is in a turn, or maybe the aeroplane has banked gently unbeknown to the pilot. Anyway, the situation is that the aeroplane is in a turn, but the vestibular apparatus is not sending any signals to the brain to indicate this – the vestibular apparatus senses wings-level even though the aeroplane is banked, say to the left.

> *In a lengthy, steady banked turn, your balance mechanism senses 'wings-level.'*

The pilot now rolls right to level the wings. The vestibular apparatus registers this roll to the right, but it does so from what it sensed as a wings-level situation rather than the left turn that in reality it was. It now senses the situation as a right banked turn, even though the wings in reality are level – this is an illusion.

The tendency is for the pilot to feel as if he is leaning into an unwanted turn to the right, and to roll back in the other direction to what felt like wings-level, i.e. into the original left turn. If things get out of hand, a 'graveyard spiral' in the original direction of turn could be the undesired result. Once again, your eyes should come to your rescue! Check the natural horizon or the artificial horizon on the attitude indicator.

STEADY TURN

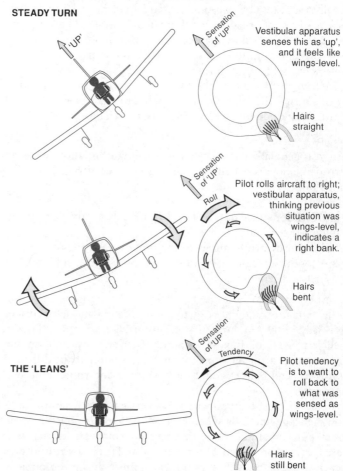

Vestibular apparatus senses this as 'up', and it feels like wings-level.

Hairs straight

Pilot rolls aircraft to right; vestibular apparatus, thinking previous situation was wings-level, indicates a right bank.

Hairs bent

THE 'LEANS'

Pilot tendency is to want to roll back to what was sensed as wings-level.

Hairs still bent

■ *Figure 3-8* **The 'leans' after rolling wings-level from a steady turn**

You can expect two illusions in every normal steady turn:
☐ **first of all,** the illusion, once you have settled into the turn for 10 or 15 seconds, that the wings are level when they are not; and then

☐ **a second illusion,** after you have rolled out of the turn to wings-level, of turning in the opposite direction, with a tendency to want to roll back out of the imagined turn.

Figure 3-8 illustrates the situation. You can overcome this illusion by using your eyes to look at the real or artificial horizon.

Keep Your Head Upright

The illusions caused by shifting the semicircular canals out of their normal plane of rotation are known as *Coriolis* illusions. The means of avoiding any Coriolis illusion is to hold your head in a steady upright position relative to your body and minimise its movement, and keep all turns coordinated (ball in the centre).

We have discussed here the situation regarding rolling into and out of a turn – the same situation applies to changes in pitch and in yaw using the semicircular canals relative to those axes.

Vertigo

Vertigo is generally experienced as a feeling of rotation, when in fact no rotation is actually occurring (or vice versa). It can be caused by:
☐ **disease;**
☐ **accelerations** that disturb the delicate balance mechanisms in the inner ear; and
☐ **sudden pressure changes** in the inner ear; strong blowing of the nose or sneezing can do this quite violently, and bring on a spell of dizziness.

Vertigo can also be brought on by a flashing light, such as a strobe light or sunlight reflecting off rotating propeller blades (especially in the case of helicopter rotor blades) – this is known as **flicker vertigo.** If you wish to experience vertigo on the ground, you can bring it on by spinning around about 20 times with your head held low, and then stand up and try to walk in a straight line.

Avoid flashing lights.

Similar forces on your body occur when an aeroplane is manoeuvring, especially when high g-loadings are pulled in steep turns, spins, spiral dives, etc., and vertigo can occur, especially if there is no visual reference to the horizon. This is the reason why non-instrument-rated (i.e. VFR) pilots are asking for trouble if they enter cloud and lose the advantage of visual reference to the horizon!

Check your flight instruments.

A form of vertigo known as **pressure vertigo** can result from the effect on the balance apparatus following inwards failure of the eardrums due to blocked Eustachian tubes. This could occur, in an extreme case, if flying with a cold or other similar infection, when pressure changes outside the ear while descending at a high rate or from a great height cannot be equalised inside the ear.

Do not fly with a cold.

Vestibular and 'Seat-of-the-Pants' Illusions Caused by Accelerations and g-forces

The Illusion of Climbing When In a Turn

In a turn, the body experiences a force on the seat-of-the-pants greater than 1g normally exerted on it by the seat in straight-and-level flight, the same feeling as if the aeroplane was being pulled up from straight-and-level into a climb.

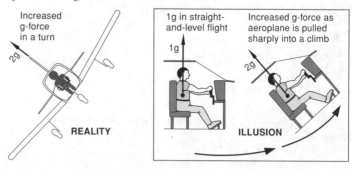

Increased g-force in a turn

2g

REALITY

1g in straight-and-level flight

1g

Increased g-force as aeroplane is pulled sharply into a climb

2g

ILLUSION

■ *Figure 3-9* **The illusion of climbing when in a turn**

Turns can feel like climbs.

The pilot must avoid the tendency to push the control column forward to stop the imagined climb – it will only send the aeroplane into a descending turn. (The semicircular canal fluid may have settled down and stopped indicating a roll, so you will not be getting any sense of a turn from the vestibular apparatus.)

The Illusion of Descending after being in a Turn

Rolling out of a lengthy turn can feel like a descent.

After being in a steady turn for some time, the body gradually gets used to the increased g-forces. Immediately after rolling back to wings-level, and reducing the g-forces to just 1g, the body feels this reduced g-force as less than 1g, the same effect as pushing the nose over into a descent. Use your eyes to check the horizon or the flight instruments to avoid making incorrect inputs on the controls.

The Tumbling-Backwards Illusion Caused by Strong Linear Acceleration

In a state of rest or steady velocity (i.e. no acceleration), the body experiences an upward force from the seat. If you now accelerate strongly, there is a further force from the back of the seat accelerating you forwards, and your vestibular apparatus, as well as the seat-of-your-pants, interprets this as a g-force angled forwards.

Accelerating forward may feel like tumbling backwards.

Since you are used to g-forces always being 'up', you interpret the tilted direction of the new g-force as being 'up'; in other words, you must have tumbled backwards. This is known as the *oculogravic* illusion or the *somatogravic* illusion. The tendency is, as a result of this illusion of tumbling backwards during strong accelerations, to want to push the nose of the aeroplane down – a tendency which you can avoid if you use your eyes.

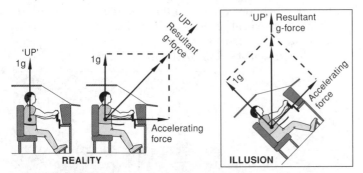

■ *Figure 3-10* **Rapid acceleration creates the illusion of tumbling backwards**

Similarly, pushing the nose forward strongly, to level off from a climb or enter a descent from straight-and-level, will also exert a force on your back, which may create the illusion of tumbling backwards.

The Illusion of Pitching Forwards Caused by Strong Linear Deceleration

The converse happens when you are travelling fast, and then decelerate rapidly. The seat-belt now exerts a force on you, and the resultant g-force from this and the force of gravity is now angled backwards. You sense this direction as 'up', so you imagine that you must have pitched forward. The tendency is to pull the control column back, which you can resist if you use your eyes.

Slowing down may feel like tumbling forwards.

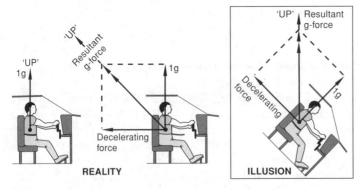

■ *Figure 3-11* **Rapid deceleration creates the illusion of pitching forwards**

Motion Sickness

Motion sickness, also called airsickness, is often caused by the balance mechanisms of the inner ear continually being over-stimulated by accelerations. This can be caused by turbulence, or manoeuvres such as steep turns or spins, in which forces other than the normal 1g that the body is used to will be experienced. A hot, smelly cockpit does not help!

Psychological aspects can also play a role in the onset of motion sickness – for instance, a fear of flying or apprehension at seeing the horizon at different angles.

Motion sickness can also be caused by a mis-matching of balance signals from the ears and visual signals from the eyes. For example, an experienced pilot practising instrument flying in a fixed-base (non-moving) simulator may experience motion sickness because the visual sense (what is seen on the flight instruments, which may be a steep bank) is different to the vestibular signals being received from the ears (1g straight-and-level).

Many pilots have experienced airsickness, especially early in their training when stress levels are higher than normal, and slightly unusual attitudes and g-forces are encountered perhaps for the first time, so do not be discouraged if you experience it occasionally.

To avoid airsickness:
- ☐ **fly the aeroplane smoothly** and coordinated;
- ☐ **avoid manoeuvres** involving unusual g-forces;
- ☐ **avoid areas of turbulence;**
- ☐ **ventilate** the cabin with a good supply of fresh air;
- ☐ **involve a potentially airsick passenger** in the operation of the flight, especially if this involves looking outside the aeroplane and into the distance (e.g. to help identify ground references);
- ☐ **as a last resort,** recline the airsick passenger's seat to reduce the effect of the vertical accelerations and keep an airsickness bag handy; and
- ☐ **land** as soon as is reasonably possible (if necessary).

Now complete **Exercises 3 – Hearing and Balance.**

Am I Fit to Fly?

Before each flight you must ask yourself, "Am I fit to fly? Do I feel well? Am I able to perform the physical and mental tasks that may be required of me as pilot-in-command?"

During the course of your training, you should read this chapter through several times but, right at this early stage, it will suffice if you just note the paragraph headings, and then read those paragraphs relevant to you.

Physical Fitness

As a pilot, you should maintain a reasonable degree of physical fitness. It allows better physical and mental performance during flight and in the long term, and quite apart from flying, improves your chances of a long and healthy life.

Keep physically fit.

Keeping fit takes some effort, and this effort must be continuous for fitness to be retained; but it can also be good fun and very recreational. Walking, jogging, digging in the garden, cycling, swimming – in fact anything that steadily raises your pulse rate will improve your fitness.

If you are grossly unfit or obese, then allow yourself several diet-conscious months with moderate exercise that is gradually increased, and consider medical supervision. It might seem like a long haul, but the quality of life and your self-perception will improve along with your fitness. Physical activity also promotes a hunger for healthy foods as well as encouraging good sleeping patterns.

Physical fitness helps pilots cope better with stress, tiredness, fatigue and the reduced availability of oxygen at higher levels in the atmosphere.

Mental Fitness

Flying an aeroplane involves physical activity but the main work-load on a pilot is intellectual. Mental fitness is vital to safe flying, but it can be degraded by:

Keep mentally fit.

- ☐ medication;
- ☐ drugs, including alcohol and cigarettes;
- ☐ stress;
- ☐ personal or family problems;
- ☐ lack of sleep or poor eating habits; and
- ☐ fatigue or allowing oneself to become over-tired.

Illness and Drugs (including alcohol and smoking)

A reasonably innocuous complaint on the ground (such as the common cold) may have serious effects under the stress of flying and high altitudes.

Medical drugs taken to combat an illness may impair flying abilities and physical comfort in flight. 'Recreational drugs' such as alcohol, marijuana, LSD, etc. must **never** be mixed with flying and a person dependent upon these may not be fit to hold a pilot's licence. See AIC 58/00 (Pink 4) for more information.

Be careful with medicines and drugs.

Smoking also significantly decreases a pilot's capacity to per-form by reducing the amount of oxygen carried in the blood, replacing it with the useless and potentially poisonous by-prod-ucts of cigarette smoke. A pilot does not have to be the active smoker to suffer the effects; smoke from any person in the cockpit (or anywhere in the aircraft, if it is small) will affect everyone.

Medical Checks

Regular checks by an Aviation Medical Examiner are required to monitor your general health, both physical and mental. Major items in the medical test include checks of the central nervous sys-tem (including eyesight), the cardiovascular system (including heart and blood pressure), the kidneys (using a urine test), hearing ability, and the respiratory system (ears, nose, throat and lungs), especially the Eustachian tubes for their ability to allow pressure to equalise either side of the eardrums.

Regular medical checks verify your general health and fitness, but occasional bouts of sickness or injury may make you tempo-rarily unfit to fly, particularly if medication is involved. If in doubt consult an Aviation Medical Examiner.

If you are travelling to tropical countries, seek medical advice about taking precautions against malaria. Not many people are aware that over 2,000 cases are reported in the UK annually, and in 1991, twelve of these patients died. AIC 97/00 (Pink 10) dated 12 January contains details on malaria prevention.

Do not assume that because you have a disability you may not be able to hold a pilot's licence. There are many people with disabilities who are permitted to fly. Check with an Aviation Medical Examiner.

■ *Figure 4-1* **A partial disablement may not disqualify you from holding a pilot's licence**

Pilots carry a heavy responsibility to themselves and to the general community, and so medical fitness in general, and on the day of flight in particular, is most important.

Medication

Until cleared by a doctor, it is safest to assume that *any* drug or medication will temporarily ground you.

A list of common medications considered incompatible with flying includes:

- ☐ **antibiotics** (e.g. penicillin) used to combat infection;
- ☐ **tranquillisers,** antidepressants and sedatives;
- ☐ **stimulants** (caffeine, amphetamines) used to maintain wakefulness or suppress appetite;
- ☐ **antihistamines,** often used to combat colds and hay fever;
- ☐ **drugs for the relief** of high blood pressure;
- ☐ **analgesics** to relieve pain;
- ☐ **anaesthetics** (used for local, general or dental purposes) usually require about 24 hours before returning to flight.

BLOOD AND BONE MARROW DONATION. Blood donation is a safe procedure for aircrew, provided a suitable time is allowed after the donation before flight. In some cases there is a slight risk of fainting after donation. If you do donate blood, do not fly for at least 24 hours afterwards. In the case of bone marrow donation you should not fly for at least 48 hours afterwards, because a general anaesthetic is involved. See AIC 14/1998 (Pink 166).

Alcohol

A pilot who has 'had a drink' is obliged not to fly if under the influence of alcohol or any drug which will impair the ability to perform pilot duties. **Alcohol and flying should never be mixed!**

■ *Figure 4-2* **Alcohol is dangerous when associated with flying**

Even *small* quantities of alcohol in the blood can impair one's performance, with the added danger of relieving anxiety so that the person thinks he is performing marvellously. Alcohol severely affects a person's judgment and abilities. High altitudes, where there is less oxygen, worsens the effect.

> Alcohol impairs performance.

It takes time for the body to remove alcohol and, as a general rule, a pilot should not fly for at least 8 hours after drinking small quantities of alcohol and increase this time if greater quantities are consumed. After heavy drinking, alcohol may still be in the blood 30 hours later. Sleep will *not* speed up the removal process; in fact it slows the body processes down and the elimination of alcohol may take even longer.

> Alcohol disturbs sleep.

NOTE The average time required to eliminate one unit of alcohol from the blood is one hour.

People who are dependent upon alcohol (alcoholics) should not hold a pilot's licence.

A drunk person should not be permitted on board an aeroplane as a passenger.

Upper Respiratory Tract Problems

Each eardrum has ambient pressure from the outer ear on one side and air pressure in the middle ear on the other side – the middle ear being an air-filled cavity connected indirectly to ambient air via the Eustachian tube, nose and throat. The function of each Eustachian tube is to allow the air pressure in the middle ear to equalise with ambient pressure.

During a climb, atmospheric pressure on the outer parts of the body decreases. The differential pressure across the eardrum forces out the eardrum and also causes air to flow from the inner ear through the Eustachian tube in each ear into the throat to equalise the pressures.

Most training aeroplanes have a low rate of climb (500 ft/min or less), allowing adequate time for pressure equalisation to occur through the Eustachian tubes, which means that ear problems during the climb are generally not serious. **During descent,** however, difficulties with the ears may be more serious due to high rates of descent and problems with pressure equalisation.

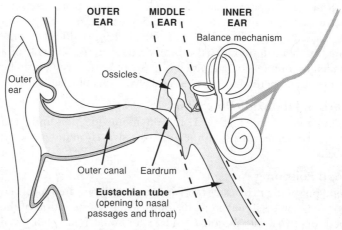

OUTER EAR   MIDDLE EAR   INNER EAR

Balance mechanism

Ossicles

Outer ear

Outer canal   Eardrum

Eustachian tube
(opening to nasal
passages and throat)

■ Figure 4-3 **The Eustachian tube equalises pressure either side of the eardrum**

Flying with a cold can cause problems, especially on descent.

As atmospheric pressure on the outer parts of the body increases during a descent, it pushes the eardrums in. Ideally, some air will flow from the throat and nasal passages via each Eustachian tube into the inner ear and equalise the pressure. However, the nature of the Eustachian tubes is such that air will not move into them from the nasal passages as readily as it moves out, and so any swelling or blocking can lead to problems. High rates of descent worsen the situation.

Flying with a common cold or other upper respiratory tract infection is asking for trouble. The **blocked Eustachian tubes** which usually accompany such a complaint will lead to problems with pressure equalisation, especially on descent (when ambient pressure changes can be high even in low-performance aircraft).

- **Pain in the ears** could be severe, which is very distracting.
- **There is a danger of the eardrums collapsing** inwards as the external pressure builds up, giving rise to a loss of hearing which may or may not be permanent.
- **The balance mechanisms** could be affected in extreme cases, a situation known as pressure vertigo.

Blocked ears can sometimes be cleared by holding the nose and blowing hard (a technique known as the *Valsalva* movement), by chewing, swallowing or yawning. The best advice is, however, **if you have a cold, do not fly.**

Problems can also arise in the sinuses, which are cavities in the head connected by narrow tubes to the nasal/throat passages. Blockages can cause great pain, especially during descent. For this reason, do not fly with sinus problems, or any problems to do with your upper respiratory tract. This applies to flight in any aircraft – pressurised or unpressurised. Even though pressure changes in a pressurised cabin will be less as an aircraft changes altitude (compared with an unpressurised cabin), there is always the risk of a sudden decompression, in which case the pressure changes can be dramatic, and perhaps cause serious damage to a blocked ear.

Carbon Monoxide Poisoning

As mentioned in Chapter 1, carbon monoxide poisoning can occur if engine exhaust fumes or excessive cigarette smoke is inhaled.

> Exhaust fumes are poison.

Food Poisoning

Food poisoning may result from an improperly prepared meal and its onset may be almost immediate following consumption of the food, or it may not become evident for some hours, but, even then, its onset may be very sudden. The stomach pains, nausea, diarrhoea, vomiting, etc., that accompany food poisoning can make it physically impossible to perform pilot duties.

> Food poisoning can kill.

It is a good practice, for the half day prior to flight, to avoid foods that are often associated with food poisoning, including shellfish, fish, mayonnaise, creams, over-ripe and thin-skinned fruits, uncooked foods such as salads and raw foods, and old food (e.g. food that has been cooked and stored for some time). If you suspect that some effects of food poisoning are imminent from something bad that you have eaten, **do not fly!**

Glasses and Contact Lenses

If you are required by the Aviation Medical Examiner to wear glasses to correct your sight, then you must wear them as required. It is also compulsory to carry a spare pair of glasses whenever you are flying.

> If you wear glasses or contact lenses, you must carry a spare pair of glasses when flying.

If you wear contact lenses, note the relevant requirements in AIC 135/1997 (Pink 155). Before your Medical Certificate can be endorsed to approve the wearing of contact lenses you must provide a report from an ophthalmologist including details of your field of vision, unaided and corrected visual acuity, corrective lenses prescription, and confirmation that the contact lenses have been worn constantly and successfully for over 8 hours a day for at least one month.

If your Certificate is endorsed to permit the use of contact lenses for flying you must carry a pair of ordinary spectacles at all times while exercising the privileges of the licence.

Bifocal contact lenses for the correction of presbyopia are unsuitable for use in flying. Any near-vision correction must be provided by 'look over' spectacles. In such cases, therefore, suitable bifocal spectacles should be carried for emergency use.

Pilots considering refractive surgery for vision correction should refer to the CAA Medical Division before undertaking the procedure.

For more information about vision correction requirements for pilots see AIC 135/1997 (Pink 155).

If flying in bright sunlight, especially above clouds, it is good practice to wear a high-quality set of sunglasses.

Smoking

Smoking is detrimental to good health, both in the short term and in the long term.

In the short term – carbon monoxide, which is present in cigarette smoke, is absorbed into the blood in preference to oxygen. This reduces the body's ability to produce energy (including in the brain). The diminished supply of oxygen to the body and brain becomes very noticeable at higher altitudes where cigarette smoke in the cabin can significantly decrease the pilot's performance (even if not actually smoking the cigarette!).

In the long term – it is now generally accepted that cigarette smoking plays a significant role in cardiovascular (heart) and other diseases. If you want to live a long and healthy life, then you should not smoke.

Smoking is bad.

Incidentally, smoking in the cockpit is banned by many airline captains, and, in some countries, smoking by everyone, including passengers, is banned in aircraft and airports.

Fatigue and Sleep Deprivation

Do not fly when fatigued.

Fatigue, tiredness and sleep deprivation can lower a pilot's mental and physical capacity quite dramatically. The nature of flying is such that moderate levels of these complaints are involved. As a pilot, you must train yourself to cope with them, and to recognise when your **personal limits** are being approached. However, a deeply tired or fatigued pilot should not be flying!

Fatigue can become deep-seated and chronic if personal psychological or emotional problems are not solved, preventing deep rest and good sleep over a prolonged period. Chronic fatigue will be cured when the problems are solved, or at least being coped with, and the person can relax and unstress. As a pilot, you should prohibit yourself from flying until this is the case.

Short-term fatigue can be caused by overwork, mental stress, an uncomfortable body position, a recent lack of sleep, *living it up* a bit too much, lack of oxygen or lack of food. Sleep and rest are essential!

To guard against fatigue that is detrimental to flight safety, you should:

- [ ] **have your psychological** and emotional life under control;
- [ ] **be reasonably fit;**
- [ ] **eat regularly;**
- [ ] **ensure you are not deprived** of having adequate and effective sleep;
- [ ] **ensure that cockpit comfort** is optimised and that energy foods and drink are available on long flights; and
- [ ] **exercise your limbs** occasionally and, if practicable, land to stretch your legs at least every four hours.

Now complete **Exercises 4 – Am I Fit to Fly?**

Stress Management, Fatigue and Sleep

Stress Management

Stress

In the course of normal activity we respond to stimuli, or demands, placed on us in response to our actions and by our environment. These demands can be mental or physical, and if they create a pressure overload, we are *adversely affected* and stress results. The cause of the stress is called a **stressor**.

Exposure to constant stress can bring about changes in the balance of hormones in the body, which threatens the health. Also, the existence of one form of stress tends to diminish the resistance to other forms.

Stressors cause stress.

A potential stressor can be *acute* in the sense that it is immediate and disappears after a short time; another can be *chronic*, long lasting, and fatiguing. It is important for general health, and for longevity, that all pressures and demands are managed so as not to be stressful for us as much as possible.

Stress management is a vital skill for the modern pilot to develop. It requires learning how to deal with pressure and disallow it from:

☐ **overwhelming** the ability to respond properly; and/or
☐ **disrupting** the ability to operate smoothly, correctly and efficiently in the cockpit and on the ground in the course of conducting a flight.

Stress accumulates.

Any individual demand on ourselves is a potential stressor if not managed properly. Also, combinations of demands which are individually small can be potentially overloading. For example, radio calls coming in to a pilot who is making a difficult crosswind approach, say in turbulent conditions in poor visibility or at night. A system malfunction at this time would further increase the load.

Some stress is good.

A small amount of pressure can raise our arousal level into the optimum area and can actually improve our performance by making us more alert. An overload of pressure, however, can move us beyond this, maybe into the 'panic' area, and affect us adversely, causing poor performance.

The aim when flying is for the load to be kept at a manageable level, well below the overload level (but not so low that we are not stimulated or alert).

Responding to Demands and Stimuli

Every person functions under some form of pressure, which serves as a stimulus to act. The person responds to 'demands'. For a pilot, these demands are many and varied and will include feedback on how well the desired flightpath and airspeed are being maintained, cockpit procedures, navigation requirements, radio procedures, and so on, often happening almost simultaneously.

How well a person handles these demands varies with the person's ability or capacity to respond, and this may depend on:

☐ **general health;**
☐ **personality,** and how at ease the person feels;
☐ **having a happy** and organised personal life;
☐ **sufficient rest** having been taken;
☐ **the degree of preparation** for the task; and
☐ **the person's intelligence** and aptitude for the activity.

A particular situation can cause differing degrees of difficulty for different people, and in the same person under different circumstances. The situation can be a stressor for one person and 'normal life' for another. For instance, a strong crosswind on final approach will be more demanding for a beginning pilot than for an experienced one. However, if the experienced pilot was tired or fatigued, concerned about family life, and trying to cope with an emergency, then the stress level might also be high during the crosswind approach.

Overload

If the demands become too much, the person becomes overloaded, and performance usually drops. This can have serious consequences in aviation.

Different people can cope with different levels of pressure. Each one of us, though, has probably been overloaded at one time or another. It is important then that we develop a strategy to prevent overloads, or to cope with them if they occur.

Family and social life should be under control. If not, this can cause a high level of stress. Generally good health and fitness is also important.

Always be well rested and well prepared, so that you can approach the task in a responsible, but natural and easy manner. Knowledge, experience and flight proficiency will allow you to keep stress levels manageable, and make correct decisions quickly and efficiently. This requires effort during your training and prior to every flight.

Being fit, rested, and experienced reduces stress.

Perceived Pressures

Stress is the adverse effect on the mind and body of an overload of pressure. When we react to perceived pressures, a response is usually demanded from the brain. These perceived pressures may not, in fact, be real pressures – something which is very important for us to appreciate when we find ourselves having to deal with a potential overload.

The first question to ask, once you decide that you want to reduce the level of stress, is: "Does the stressor – the item causing the stress – really exist?" For instance, a slamming door may cause your body to react in the same way as an explosion since, in each case, the body receives a shock, even though in the case of the slamming door there is no danger. The same applies to perceived emotional stresses, many of which turn out to be imaginary. Once you realise that the danger does not exist in reality, the stress gradually dissipates.

Tolerance to pressure demands varies a lot between individuals, with some people being able to tolerate a much higher level than others. The tolerance to new stress also varies within the one individual, depending upon the current level of stress, and the time of day (according to the personal body clock). Increasing age may also lead to a decrease in tolerance to stress, something older pilots and their younger colleagues need to be aware of.

Physical Stress – Fight or Flight?

A sudden fright, like the perception of physical danger, causes your brain to rapidly prepare for action. The adrenal gland sends out the hormone *adrenalin* which stimulates your body physically to meet the threat – to fight or to flee. You have no doubt experienced the sudden rush of adrenalin on occasions. The heart rate increases quickly, certain blood vessels constrict to divert blood to where it is most needed for physical action, and many other changes occur in the body.

Your performance will, most probably, be enhanced, within the limits of your experience and training. Your responses may be quick and exact – the well-practised ones may even be automatic – and you will be very sensitive to your surroundings. In cases like this the stimuli can enhance the level at which you function.

Whether you 'fight or flee' depends on many things, including personality and aptitude (or suitability) for the job, and the level of perceived danger.

Non-Physical Stress

Emotional overload will cause stress.

Some stressful situations arise, not from a perceived physical threat, but from intellectual, psychological and emotional causes. These could be the pressure of time (too much to do in too little time), difficult decisions to be made (to continue into deteriorating weather ahead or to divert to an alternate aerodrome), a lack of self-confidence, a strained personal relationship, or an emotional overload.

Some psychological or emotional demands, such as a failing personal relationship, can be debilitating on a long-term or chronic basis, whereas some intellectual pressure can prepare you for quick mental activity. Some stimuli can be performance-enhancing; other types can inhibit your performance.

Arousal

How well you can handle a task depends to a large extent on your state of arousal. Many types of stimuli increase your arousal level – for instance, a fright – whereas other types decrease your arousal level, such as fatigue.

A *low* level of arousal is associated with deep sleep, fatigue, sleep deprivation, a lack of motivation, and low body temperature, which will occur naturally when internal body temperature is at a low point in its daily circadian rhythm.

A *high* level of arousal is associated with fear, panic, and under-confidence.

Being under-aroused – for instance, overly casual or apathetic – may lead to poor performance of a task; being over-aroused – for instance, highly keyed up and tense – may also lead to poor performance.

Between these two extremes, however, there is a region of *optimum* arousal leading to optimum performance of the task. The measure of your performance may be the speed with which you respond to the situation, the intensity and accuracy of your response, how well you are coordinated in your response, and how quickly you react in modifying your response as the situation changes. Your response to the situation will be best in the region of optimum arousal, between low and high arousal.

> Optimum arousal facilitates optimum performance.

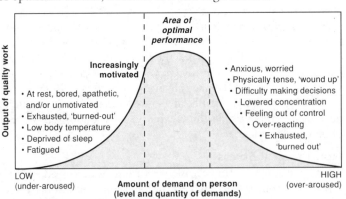

■ Figure 5-1 **Optimum arousal facilitates optimum performance**

Poor performance will be the result at both extremes of the arousal scale; good performance will be the result in the central region where arousal is optimum. This connection between state of arousal and level of performance can be shown graphically (Figure 5-1).

For peak performance during take-off, landing and emergencies, you should be in the intermediate area of arousal – aroused, but not over-aroused.

For satisfactory performance in the relatively low workload period of a long-haul cruise, a moderate level of arousal is adequate (but not under-arousal where you might miss important things such as a reporting point and heading change, or a developing emergency).

Stressors

An experience causing stress is known as a **stressor**. Stressors can be divided into two classes:

☐ **environmental or physical stressors** – these include such items as noise and physical contact; and

☐ **intellectual, psychological, and emotional stressors** – these are often related to problems at home and at work.

Environmental or Physical Stressors

Keep the working environment comfortable.

If you are working in an environment that differs from the ideal environment for man – for instance in an environment which is excessively hot, cold, noisy, damp, dry, turbulent, vibrating, dark, light, smelly, or lacking in oxygen – you can become tired and stressed more quickly than otherwise.

STRESS CAUSED BY HEAT (HYPERTHERMIA). In very high environmental temperatures, say 35°C and above, the body struggles to keep its internal temperature at just under 37°C and prevent itself from overheating (known as *hyperthermia*). The perspiration rate, heart rate and blood pressure all increase. In a humid atmosphere, as opposed to a dry atmosphere, your perspiration will tend *not* to evaporate, hence no latent heat is absorbed into the air from your skin and the underlying blood, so there is a greater tendency for your body to overheat.

To minimise heat stress you should try to control the environmental temperature if at all possible (but, unfortunately, not every aircraft has an air-conditioning system), and, most importantly, **drink enough fluids**. Water is ideal. Try to take a drink *before* you actually become thirsty, since thirst is a sign that you are already on the way to becoming dehydrated.

Remember that tasks outside the cockpit prior to flight, such as loading the aircraft or flight planning, or even just standing or sitting in high temperatures, may cause your body to overheat and/or dehydrate. Take appropriate measures by drinking fluids, staying under shade, and not rushing.

STRESS CAUSED BY COLD (HYPOTHERMIA). In a cold environment, the body automatically sends more blood to the body core, rather than to the extremities. This is an attempt to keep the internal temperature at about 37°C by minimising heat loss from the skin. Heat loss can occur by:

- **radiation** from exposed areas of skin, especially from your head which has many blood vessels near the surface of your scalp;
- **conduction** as wind flows across your skin and carries heat away, which is known as the *wind chill factor*; and
- **evaporation** of perspiration or other moisture from your skin, which causes cooling by absorbing heat from the skin and underlying blood vessels, and using it to change the state of the moisture from liquid to vapour (latent heat).

In low temperatures, your toes and fingers may feel cold, your muscles might feel stiff and weak, you may feel tired and drowsy, and you might start to shiver – this is an attempt by your body to generate warmth by muscle activity. It is said that "if your hands and feet feel comfortable, then all is well".

STRESS CAUSED BY VIBRATION. Vibrations transmitted to the body from the aircraft via the seat, seat-belts and the floor can make you feel uncomfortable, distract you from your main tasks, and lead to fatigue.

A vibrating instrument panel may make the instruments difficult to read. Severe vibration may even cause your eyeballs to vibrate, making it almost impossible to read your flight instruments or your navigation charts, or to scan for other aircraft. Even though it might be impossible to reduce the vibration from the aircraft itself, the vibration reaching your body can be reduced by well-mounted and well-cushioned seats.

STRESS CAUSED BY TURBULENCE. Turbulence will cause irregular movements of the aircraft, varying from fairly small movements when flying through slight turbulence to unbelievably strong movements associated with severe turbulence that may even damage the aircraft. Turbulence can cause discomfort to the pilot and passengers by shaking them around, exerting unusual g-forces on them, and perhaps causing motion sickness. It may cause the instrument panel to vibrate or the eyeballs to judder, making it difficult to read the instruments, and it may make the aircraft very difficult to control.

STRESS CAUSED BY NOISE. Excessive noise in the cockpit, especially if it is high-pitched and loud, can cause stress and fatigue. An industry limit for continuous noise is 85 dB (decibels), with ear protection required above this level. Noise levels in a typical cockpit are in the range 75–80 dB, but this is only background noise, with noise from radio messages superimposed on it. Noise above about 90 dB will cause stress that raises your arousal into the poor performance area, making you irritable, and leading to fatigue. Above about 80 dB, you should wear protection to avoid stress damage to your ears.

Stress can also be caused by having to strain to understand radio messages against a high background noise level. With your ears protected from background engine and air noise by a high-quality headset, you should be able to hear radio messages even when the volume is quite low.

STRESS CAUSED BY BEING UNCOMFORTABLE. The nature of our job as pilots is that we are confined to sitting in small cockpits for long periods of time. The stress of sitting in a noisy, vibrating aircraft for long periods, and having to cope with the usual problems of flight, such as turbulence, navigation, radio calls, and so on, can lead to an accumulation of stress and fatigue.

The best means of combating this form of stress is to keep yourself fit, be well rested prior to flight, maintain a good posture with your tail tucked well back into the seat and your lower back well supported, and exercise periodically by wriggling your toes and feet and stretching your arms.

It is also important to be appropriately dressed for the job. Wearing too much or too little clothing will make you uncomfortable and is thus distracting. You should also make sure that your clothes fit well. There are few things worse than a tight shirt collar, tight trousers, or tight shoes.

STRESS CAUSED BY FEELING UNWELL. If feeling unwell, you may be easily overloaded and prone to becoming fatigued. Your body will be using up a lot of your energy to combat the illness, and so you will have less energy available for other tasks. Your general performance will be much lower than normal.

If you have a headache, an upper respiratory tract infection (such as a cold), a sporting and other injury, a stomach upset, or a sneezing attack, you should consider whether it is a responsible decision to commence your flight. If you feel unwell in flight, then you should consider landing and resting.

Motion sickness (feeling airsick) can make a person feel very low and uninterested in events. It is not confined to new student pilots and passengers — on rare occasions even experienced pilots feel airsick. Their knowledge that it might cause them to feel apathetic, however, is protection to some extent against lowered performance.

A pilot will also be subject to stress unnecessarily if not eating regularly or eating well, the result possibly being *hypoglycemia*, a low blood sugar level. Its symptoms are headache, stomach pain,

Use a high-quality headset.

Keep fit and well.

lack of energy, nervousness and shaking, and can be relieved in the short term by eating a snack.

STRESS CAUSED BY EYE STRAIN. Eye strain due to impaired vision or poor lighting can cause stress. Impaired vision can be remedied with glasses or contact lenses. The solution to bad lighting is obvious – turn the lights up! This need not mean that the whole cockpit be brightly lit when all you need to see are the instruments and your charts – simply turn the instrument lights up and use a small spotlight, if available, for your charts. If the main cabin lights are turned up too bright at night, you may have to strain your eyes to scan outside for other aircraft and weather.

STRESS CAUSED BY FLASHING LIGHTS. A flashing light is designed to attract attention, usually to other vehicles or aircraft. Seeing a flashing light will raise your level of alertness. If, however, the warning does not apply to you, the flashing light may be very distracting and even fatiguing. For instance, a flashing amber light from a fuel truck parked right in front of your cockpit at night can be very distracting if you are trying to complete your flight preparation tasks – ask the driver to move a little! Reflected light from your own strobe lights when flying in cloud at night can be highly distracting, so turn the strobes off temporarily – other aircraft will not be able to see them while you are in cloud anyway.

Avoid flashing lights.

STRESS CAUSED BY CONCENTRATION. Skill stress which leads to fatigue can result if you have to maintain a high level of performance for an extended period – for instance, hand-flying on instruments in turbulent IFR conditions, or even just straight-and-level visual flying for a student pilot.

STRESS CAUSED BY LACK OF SLEEP. A lack of restful sleep leaves a pilot fatigued, and needing to struggle to stay awake to handle the demands of flying. The pilot has to fight off sleep, and really force concentration, leading to a high stress level and even deeper fatigue. It is a vicious circle. The solution to this is, of course, not to fly unless well rested.

Rest properly.

Psychological and Emotional Stressors

Psychological or emotional stress can arise from a number of sources. It could be work-related (a difficult flight about to begin, or a strained relationship with management or colleagues), or it could have a domestic cause (marital or financial problems).

The result of psychological stress is that a pilot may be over-aroused and move into the area of poor performance:

- **concentrating on a single problem** and not maintaining a good overview of the flight;
- **exhibiting poor judgement;**

- ☐ **becoming disoriented** quite easily;
- ☐ **being distracted** from prime tasks;
- ☐ **taking a resigned attitude** to problems that arise ("why does this always happen to me?"); and
- ☐ **becoming fatigued** at an early stage.

WORK-RELATED PSYCHOLOGICAL STRESS. Most pilots experience a certain amount of apprehension regarding a forthcoming flight, but this is quite normal and can raise the level of arousal into the optimum area for good performance. A pilot who is stressed and over-anxious, however, may be too highly aroused to perform well – a common situation with inexperienced student pilots, and in many experienced pilots who are facing a demanding flight.

PSYCHOLOGICAL & EMOTIONAL STRESS. Psychological and emotional stress can be caused by problems at home. Domestic-related stress can be very damaging to a pilot. If distracted by emotional problems during highly charged periods such as following the death of a spouse or child, a divorce, or when experiencing severe financial difficulties, a responsible pilot should consider grounding himself. Domestic-related problems can lead to lack of sleep, chronic fatigue, emotional instability, and a dangerous flight operation.

Anxiety

Anxiety is the extreme worry that results when a person is overloaded, particularly for prolonged periods. It is a state of being uneasy, apprehensive or worried about what may happen, and experiencing a generalised pervasive fear.

An anxious person will probably perform poorly – the condition is often apparent to a sensitive observer (such as a flying instructor or cockpit colleague) by signs of:

- ☐ **physical discomfort,** such as perspiring, nervous twitching, a dry mouth, breathing difficulties, panting, increased heart rate;
- ☐ **inappropriate behaviour,** such as laughing or singing at inappropriate times, painstaking self-control, extreme over-cooperation, rapid changes in emotion, impulsiveness or extreme passivity;
- ☐ **mood changes,** perhaps from extreme light-heartedness to depression;
- ☐ **unreasonable behaviour** towards other people, unnecessary anger, impatient and rude behaviour, etc.;
- ☐ **fatigue** – the extreme and deep tiredness that can result from being under pressure for too long;

☐ **incorrect thought processes,** poor concentration, or concentrating on one point to the exclusion of others, an inability to set reasonable priorities, forgetting important items such as the use of flaps for take-off or on final approach, or failing to read a checklist.

A person suffering from a *chronic stress overload* may show a personality change, behave poorly and erratically towards others, perform at a low level, become ill with stomach pains or headaches, drink, smoke or eat excessively, and may well become accident-prone.

Anxiety is a dangerous condition for a pilot to be suffering from, and top priority should be given to reducing the anxiety level before making a flight. It may be advisable to seek medical attention, but certainly the best antidote is to remove the cause (if it can be identified) as much as possible and give yourself plenty of deep rest.

Over-anxiousness causes poor performance.

Handling Pressure

Some pressure or stimulus is needed to alert you and to enhance your performance. The risk is, not the activity itself, but an *overload* of it, and an inability to cope with the demands.

The best way to handle pressure is to be physically and psychologically well prepared. This means being fit, well rested, on top of your job, on top of your life, and ready to face challenges. It is also sensible to reduce the level of unwanted stress if you can, giving you a greater capacity to handle any new situations that might arise. This can be achieved by resolving emotional problems at least to a point where they do not interfere with your work.

Reduce unnecessary risks.

Knowledge is also important, such as knowing the emergency procedures for your aeroplane so that you can cope with basic emergencies. You must also learn to manage your time efficiently so that you are never rushed. Stress can also be reduced if you control your environment as much as possible, keeping unwanted noise and vibration to a minimum, for instance, and maintaining a comfortable ambient temperature.

Manage your time.

Prepare Yourself Physically
☐ **Keep fit** and well-exercised.
☐ **Eat well** and eat regularly.
☐ **Sleep well** and go flying with plenty of sleep-hours in credit.
☐ **Take time out** to relax.
☐ **Manage your time** so that you do not have to rush.
☐ **Control your physical environment** (noise, temperature, humidity).

Prepare Yourself Psychologically

☐ **Be well prepared** regarding knowledge, skills, and standard operating procedures.

☐ **Have well-placed confidence** in your ability.

☐ **Leave your domestic and financial worries at home** – preferably arrange your life so that you have these matters well under control – have a well-rounded social and/or family life.

☐ **Do not procrastinate** – tackle your problems and solve them, or at least have a timetable for attempting to solve them.

☐ **Do not be afraid to discuss** your doubts and worries with appropriate people, with an aim to removing or minimising any unnecessary stress or anxiety.

☐ **Do not allow yourself to become over-excited** about non-events, or to become resigned and pessimistic unnecessarily – control your psychological environment.

Techniques of Stress Management

You will have prepared yourself in general terms to manage the normal demands of life, as suggested above, by the way you think and behave (cognitive/behavioural techniques), relaxation, and by managing your time. But sometimes you find yourself in one of those situations that arise where, even though you are generally in control of your life, the current situation seems about to get out of hand. You need to recognise this, and take appropriate action.

Recognise a Potential Overload

The first step in coping with a potential overload is to recognise its presence. As we have seen, a certain amount of pressure is essential if we are to live a normal life and handle everyday problems, both at home and in our workplace, but an overload can drastically reduce our performance and our happiness.

Avoid stress overloads.

Remember that we respond to perceived pressures (rather than actual pressures), and to our perceived ability to handle these pressures (rather than our actual ability). After consideration, you might find that the excessive pressures are not there to begin with or, if they are, your ability is such that you can confidently handle them.

Take Action

Coping satisfactorily with stress usually involves taking action to:

☐ remove the cause; or

☐ remove yourself.

For instance, you can minimise the cause of noise stress by wearing a good headset. You can minimise the cause of domestic unhappiness by discussing matters openly with your partner. These actions will remove or reduce the cause of the stress.

On the other hand, you can remove the stress caused from learning to fly aerobatics, by giving up aerobatics and taking up something less demanding – in other words by removing yourself from the scene.

You can remove the stress of flying in severe turbulence near a thunderstorm by turning back or landing – you will not remove the turbulence, but you will take yourself away from its stressful effect. You can remove (or reduce) the stress caused by an unhappy relationship by moving out, physically and psychologically.

> Remove the cause of unwanted stress.

Acute stress is usually easily relieved. For instance, if you are under pressure of time to solve an undercarriage problem during an approach to land, make a missed approach and join a holding pattern. You can now take longer to resolve the problem, and the pressure of time is relieved.

Chronic long-term stress is another matter, and resolving it may mean a change in lifestyle or activity. Consult your spouse, your doctor, your adviser, your minister or priest, a friend, a counsellor, or some other appropriate person. Prolonged exposure to stress will accelerate the ageing process, unbalance the body chemistry, and lead to mental and physical illness – certainly no way to have a happy life.

Unacceptable Means of Coping with Stress

There are some means of trying to cope with stress that are not really acceptable if you want to be a pilot, such as:

☐ **closing your eyes** to the problem and pretending it does not exist; or

☐ **taking medication, drugs or alcohol** to relieve the symptoms of the stress, but not its cause.

The body and mind have certain **defence mechanisms** that sometimes operate subconsciously to remove painful matters from our consciousness. Defence mechanisms remove the symptoms but not the cause, and this can be dangerous for a pilot. Common defence mechanisms include:

☐ **lack of awareness** – the brain subconsciously denies or represses the existence of the stressor;

☐ **rationalisation** – a subconscious attempt to justify actions that would otherwise be unacceptable, often indicated by a person substituting excuses for certain behaviour rather than logical reasons;

☐ **phantom illness** – to avoid having to face up to reality;

☐ **daydreaming** – staring into space as a means of mentally escaping by creating a fantasy of being in more pleasant surroundings or circumstances;

☐ **resignation** – mentally lost or bewildered, and ready to accept whatever comes, including defeat; and

☐ **anger** – which may range from mild expressions of frustration, such as the use of bad language, to more violent expressions of physical behaviour, such as rough use of the flight controls.

None of these attempts to cope with stress will actually eliminate the problem. Instead, some realistic method of managing the pressure load should be adopted.

Avoid Self-imposed Stress

To some extent, the pilot has some control over the stress level, and can often reduce the pressures. Some ways in which this can be done are:

☐ **Make early decisions** – turn back or divert before flying into bad conditions, or land well before last light if necessary.

☐ **Do not accept** an Air Traffic Control VFR clearance leading into clouds – keep clear of cloud and request a new clearance.

☐ **Do not be distracted** from checklists: request your passengers, flight instructor, or examiner not to interrupt.

☐ **Do not interrupt** or change your usual routines unnecessarily.

☐ **Request ATC to "stand by"** if you are busy coping with an emergency or having trouble handling the aeroplane – flight-path and airspeed always come first.

☐ **Be prepared for delays** – weather may force a delay, as can refuelling and aircraft unserviceabilities; always allow a time buffer, even for the drive to the airport.

☐ **Do not press on regardless.**

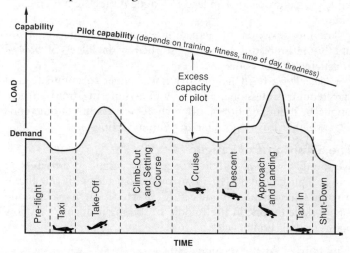

■ *Figure 5-2* **Pilot capability versus workload**

The workload for a pilot during a normal flight is represented by the lower line in the Figure 5-2. High workload levels occur during take-off, and during the descent and landing. They may also occur with an emergency, or poor weather, at any stage of the flight. The ability of a pilot to cope with this workload is represented by the upper line, which can vary in position. Good training, being current, being fit and well rested, will raise the capability line, and increase the safety margin between it and the workload line.

Being fatigued, nervous, under-confident, not current, and feeling unwell, will lower the capability line, diminishing the safety margin, and perhaps removing it altogether.

Under normal conditions, you should be able to operate using only about 50% of your capability, with the other 50% in reserve to cope with unforeseen events and emergencies. During a long and tiring flight, you can expect your capability line to gradually lower.

Keep your capability level above the demand level.

Fatigue

Fatigue is a very deep tiredness that usually comes from:
- [ ] a lack of restful sleep;
- [ ] a lack of physical or mental fitness;
- [ ] excessive physical or mental stress and anxiety; or
- [ ] a desynchronisation of your body cycles (jet lag).

All of the items discussed earlier that cause stress, such as noise and vibration, high temperatures or a lack of oxygen, domestic or work-related problems, can lead to fatigue if they are not checked and resolved.

The most essential immediate cure for *acute* fatigue is *sleep* – and this means restful sleep, not disturbed by the effects of alcohol or caffeine (tea or coffee).

Rest properly.

Chronic long-term fatigue may take longer to eliminate, and may require professional advice. A pilot suffering from chronic fatigue, be it due to physical or psychological reasons, should consider whether it is responsible to continue flying.

The Symptoms of Fatigue
We should always be looking for signs of fatigue in ourselves, in our cockpit colleagues, or in anyone associated with our flight. Aircraft maintenance engineers, for instance, often have to do highly skilled work in the middle of the night during very low points in their body cycles.

Symptoms of fatigue include:
- [ ] **lack of awareness** – radio calls or checklists that go unanswered;
- [ ] **diminished motor skills** – sloppy flying, writing that trails off into nothing as weather reports or clearances are written down;
- [ ] **obvious tiredness** – drooping head, staring or half-closed eyes;

- ☐ **diminished vision** – difficulty in focusing;
- ☐ **slow reactions**;
- ☐ **short-term memory problems** – unable to remember a clearance long enough to repeat it or to write it down accurately;
- ☐ **channelled concentration** – fixation on a single possibly unimportant issue, to the neglect of others and to the neglect of maintaining an overview of the flight;
- ☐ **easily distracted** by trivial matters or, the other extreme, impossible to distract – either extreme could indicate fatigue;
- ☐ **poor instrument flying** – difficulty in focusing on the instruments, fixation on one instrument to the neglect of others, drifting in and out of sleep, diminished motor skills with poor hand–eye coordination;
- ☐ **increased mistakes** – poor judgement and poor decisions, or no decisions at all, even simple ones like "Will I turn left or right to avoid this thunderstorm?"; and
- ☐ **abnormal moods** – erratic changes in mood, depressed, periodically elated and energetic, diminished standards.

Sleep

*This discussion on sleep goes into areas which are of more concern to professional pilots, but it is included here for general information to pilots involved in more-demanding private operations. **All pilots should read the next two pages,** however, before attempting the exercises.*

A lack of properly restful sleep can lead to fatigue, so it is very important that you as a pilot obtain adequate sleep prior to a flight. Being fatigued is different from being sleepy or drowsy – it is being deeply tired to the point of being unable to attend satisfactorily to your flight duties for sustained periods. Fatigue is stressful and damaging for a person.

A flight in itself can be fatiguing, with the pilot being exposed to mental and physical stressors such as noise, vibration, hypoxia, temperature extremes, dryness, physical restraint, navigation problems, bad weather, technical problems, difficulties with passengers, etc. The additional influence of poor sleep and disturbed body rhythms imposed upon the natural tiredness of the pilot can have a very serious effect on the health.

The Purpose of Sleep

Sleep is revitalising, and is necessary.

The purpose of sleep is to revitalise your body and brain in preparation for the activities of the following day. A typical person requires 8 hours of restful sleep in preparation for 16 hours of activity – in very approximate terms, one hour of sleep gives you an energy credit good for two hours of activity.

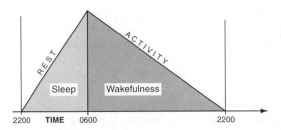

■ *Figure 5-3* **8 hours rest for 16 hours of activity**

Strategies for Getting Good Sleep

There are some measures that you can take to assist you in sleeping well.

☐ **Sleep in a comfortable bed in a dark and quiet room.** Darkness and quietness encourage sleep, whereas bright light and noise have the opposite effect. Maintain a pleasant temperature, with fresh air available if possible.

☐ **Try to maintain a regular sleep schedule.** Going to bed at the same time each night, falling asleep, then waking up eight hours later feeling rejuvenated, will become a habit.

☐ **Keep fit, eat well, and go to bed tired, but not over-tired.** A body that is healthy as a result of exercise and a good diet will not only perform better during the hours of wakefulness, it will also rest better during sleep. Being fit and healthy is natural and desirable. Exercising earlier during the day so that you go to bed 'tired' will encourage sleep, provided you have not had too many naps. A cup of warm milk or some form of carbohydrate before going to bed will also encourage sleep (but avoid stimulants like coffee or tea, and avoid alcohol, animal fats and high protein foods). Exercising or eating a big meal just before going to bed should be avoided.

☐ **Try to turn off mentally.** If you can, avoid excessive mental activity or thinking about emotionally stressful matters before turning in for what you want to be a good sleep. Relaxing with a good book or soft music can sometimes take your mind off the worries of the day.

Sleep Disorders

Insomnia is an inability to sleep, or to obtain restful sleep. There are different types of insomnia. The most common one is 'nervous' insomnia. Most people experience this from time to time, especially when they are anticipating something potentially stressful that is about to happen in the near future, such as an examination or a flight test. Nervous insomnia might disrupt sleep for one or two nights, often to a lesser extent than the person thinks. It is not a serious problem, with a quick recovery from any resulting tiredness or fatigue.

Acute or short-term insomnia resulting from stress or illness, or disturbed body rhythms (jet lag), is also usually not serious, with a quick recovery within days when the cause is removed.

Chronic insomnia is another matter, however, when the person is unable to obtain restful sleep for a period of weeks or months due to long-term unresolved stress, or due to illness. This continued sleep deprivation may require medical attention.

Other sleep disorders besides chronic insomnia that may require medical attention include the reverse problem, that of an inability to stay awake even when well rested, as well as very heavy snoring, and breathing interruptions during sleep.

Sleeping Drugs, or Hypnotics

Avoid sleeping pills.

Drugs used to aid sleeping are called *hypnotics*. They may assist sleep, but some of them also have fairly serious side effects that could affect the skill and performance level of a pilot. They should not be used by a pilot without advice and supervision from an expert aviation doctor.

Pilots should be careful when using medication in case of side effects which may drastically affect flying skills and performance. Subtle effects might also be very dangerous, since it is less likely that they will be noticed. Be cautious with the use of painkillers, decongestants to combat the effects of a cold, antihistamines to treat hay fever, antibiotics to combat infection, stomach tablets, or pills to combat gastro-intestinal infections.

Melatonin

The hormone *melatonin* has received much publicity recently as a 'quick-fix' to jet lag and other forms of sleep disturbance. In the UK melatonin is available only on prescription, but is freely available in the USA and some other countries.

Melatonin is produced by the pineal gland in the brain, mainly in hours of darkness. Its function is not fully understood, but it is related to biological rhythms such as sleep and activity patterns, and ovulation. Secretion of melatonin at night-time lowers body temperature, which helps to bring on sleep. Taking melatonin orally has a similar effect. Clinical trials have not been conducted on melatonin, but laboratory studies have shown that it may be helpful in improving daytime sleep. However, the incidence and extent of side effects are unknown at this stage. Furthermore, use of the substance for a period, followed by withdrawl, can worsen the effects of jet lag. Refer to AIC 25/1998 (Pink 168).

The CAA recommends that pilots should not fly for at least 12 hours after taking melatonin and should not take it while on duty.

Those who do not wish to read further about sleep should complete **Exercises 5** *up to Question 38.*

The Stages of Sleep

The nature of sleep is not the same throughout the whole sleep period. As we all know from experience, being woken at an early stage when we are just drifting off to sleep is quite a different matter from being woken from a very deep sleep, when it may take some minutes to return to full consciousness. Also, just prior to waking up naturally, we often feel in a semi-conscious state, with thoughts running around in our head, and eyes darting around behind closed eyelids – quite different from when we are in a deep stage of sleep, with the body relaxed and mental activity slowed right down.

Your sleep goes through various stages.

The study of sleep is far from complete (we seem to know more of what is going on in outer space than what is going on in our heads); however, we can safely say that there are four different stages in terms of depth of sleep or unconsciousness.

After you drift from wakefulness into sleep, you go down through the four stages into ever-deeper sleep, where you stay for a while, and then rise through the stages, sometimes missing one or two, before sinking back into deep sleep. This occurs in a series of cycles that take about 90 minutes each. In a normal night, you may go through four or five cycles, each one perhaps a little different from the previous one, with some stages missing or lasting for shorter or longer periods. As can be seen in Figure 5-4, the very deep Stage 4 sleep is commonly more predominant in the early cycles than in the later cycles.

Often, after you rise back to an earlier stage of sleep and before you sink back down into a deeper stage (or continue rising into wakefulness), you experience a totally different type of sleep, known as *REM (rapid eye movement)* sleep. This is so different that sometimes the first four stages are known as *non-REM* sleep in contrast to it.

'Rapid eye movement' sleep is vital.

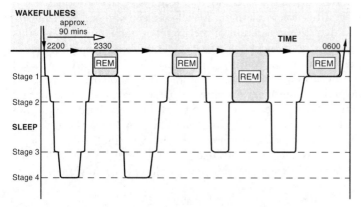

■ *Figure 5-4* **Typical cycles of non-REM and REM sleep in the course of a sleep period**

Stages 1–4 non-REM sleep has fairly low-frequency electrical waves in the brain and so is sometimes referred to as *slow-wave* sleep, whereas the electrical waves in the brain during REM sleep are high frequency and short wave. REM sleep is sometimes called *paradoxical* sleep because, even though the muscles are very relaxed and the person is still asleep, brain activity is similar to a person who is awake.

The Stages 1–4 non-REM sleep and the additional REM sleep are different types of sleep and perform different functions. The non-REM Stages 1–4 sleep revitalise the body, and so is needed in abundance after a lot of strenuous physical activity, whereas the REM sleep restores the brain and is needed after strenuous mental activity. In the course of a long sleep period, you alternate between the two types of sleep, your body and brain organising it so that you obtain sufficient of the required type of sleep each night, according to your needs.

The first onset of REM sleep usually occurs about 90 minutes after commencing sleep, and recurs at about this interval throughout the sleep period as you rise out of deep sleep and sink back into it. Your brain is being rejuvenated during REM sleep, and **it is important that REM sleep is not disturbed.** This can be caused by alcohol, drugs, stress, or being forcefully wakened.

Sleep Patterns

Individual sleep patterns vary – different people require different amounts of sleep and prefer to go to bed and rise at different times. The need for sleep also varies with age, an older person may need less sleep, but on a more regular basis; this can cause problems for older pilots involved in long-haul international operations crossing many time zones. Daytime operations close to home might be easier from the sleeping point of view.

In very general terms, we need around eight hours of sleep in a 24-hour day – eight hours of good rest and revitalisation in preparation for sixteen hours of activity. Some people need only six hours; others need ten.

The average sleep requirement is 8 hours per day.

Some people prefer to retire to bed at 9 p.m. and rise with the sparrows, while 'night owls' prefer to retire at midnight or later and rise late the next morning. For the purposes of our study of sleep patterns, we will consider a person who goes to bed at 2400 hours and, after eight hours of sleep, rises at 0800 hours. You can move these hours forward or back, or reduce or increase them, to suit your own particular case.

Unfortunately, there seems to be a maximum limit on the number of sleep-hours credit you can build up. Once you get to eight sleep-hours credit, that is it! No matter how hard you try to sleep longer and gain more sleep credits, it will not be successful.

In broad terms, we can say that **one high quality sleep-hour is good for two hours of activity.**

Eight sleep-hours will prepare you for the sixteen hours activity of a 24-hour day. After this time of wakefulness, your sleep credits will have been used. Your credits are now zero, your energy level will be low, and you will begin to feel tired and ready for another sleep. If you do not go to sleep, you will go into a sleep *deficit*, which will probably cause a significant decrease in your alertness and performance capability.

An ideal, uninterrupted sleeping pattern for a person with regular habits is illustrated in Figure 5-5.

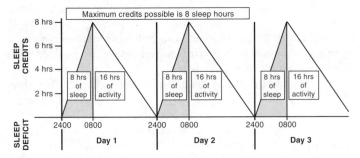

■ *Figure 5-5* **One sleep-hour is good for two hours of wakeful activity**

Disturbed Sleep Patterns

It is not always possible to achieve the desired 8–16–8–16 sleep pattern due to the demands of work, family, illness or social life, in which case compromises have to be made.

If you reduce the sleep-hours credit, then you also reduce the hours of useful wakeful activity available to you before you are due for another sleep, or before you start to slip into a sleep deficit. If you are deprived of sleep you will not perform as well as when you still have some sleep-hours in credit.

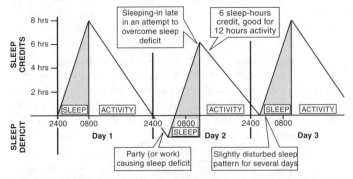

■ *Figure 5-6* **Going into a sleep deficit (beyond 16 hours of activity)**

A very common sleep deficit occurs when you 'party on' late into the night, well beyond your usual bedtime. This can also happen to you if you work through the night and use up all your sleep credits. If you have the luxury of being able to sleep in until late the next morning, then you can recuperate and move out of the sleep deficit fairly quickly, provided your sleep is restful and not disturbed by alcohol and the like.

An **alcohol-induced sleep** gives the impression that it is a deep sleep – but it is not! Your REM sleep will not be normal, your mental rejuvenation will not be as good as usual, you will probably wake earlier than you would otherwise and, most importantly, when you wake you may not feel refreshed. This is an important point to note for pilots who, in the past, may have used alcohol to relax after a stressful flight and to induce sleep.

> Disturbed sleep
> is not as restful.

Trying to build up a store of sleep-hour credits by sleeping long hours the previous night will not work. Once you get to the eight hours credit, you will most likely wake up. Perhaps you could increase your energy level for a party, however, by taking a late afternoon nap after you have used up some of your sleep credits, and raise them back towards eight sleep-hour credits, which should then get you comfortably well into the night.

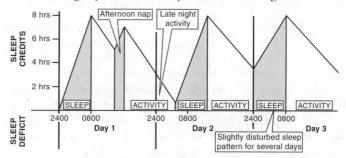

■ *Figure 5-7* **Preparing for a late flight, or a party**

Shorter-than-Normal Sleep

If you are woken following only four hours of sleep instead of your usual eight, then (in very approximate terms, and on the basis that one sleep-hour prepares you for two hours of wakefulness) you have only eight hours of activity available to you before you begin to get tired. If you go beyond this time of wakefulness, then your performance is likely to deteriorate.

> Naps can help overcome
> a sleep deficit.

You may be able to recuperate to some extent by taking an afternoon nap, but this may not be as effective and restful as sleep at a normal time, and your sleep credits may build at a slower rate. With a nap, you also run the risk of sinking into a deep sleep from which it may be difficult to awaken before the sleep cycle runs its full course, the result being that you do not feel rested at all.

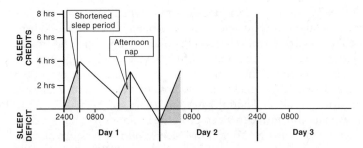

■ *Figure 5-8* **Normal sleep pattern shortened, followed by a nap later in the day**

Irregular Sleep Routine

For a person with a regular lifestyle, the *need* for sleep and the *ability* to sleep generally coincide, and going to bed when tired and falling asleep occurs naturally. This is usual for most of us working normal day shifts, and is also usual for the perennial night-shift worker whose body rhythms have adjusted to his lifestyle. His sleep pattern of 8–16–8–16 may be the same pattern as for a normal day worker, but it may occur at different times of the day.

For the *irregular* night-shift worker, however, or the pilot who has to crawl out of bed at an unusual time to go flying, it can be quite a different matter. The body rhythms are synchronised for the normal eight hours of sleeping between 2400 and 0800 local time, followed by the sixteen hours of wakefulness between 0800 and 2400, and suddenly this pattern is broken.

Irregular shift work is fatiguing.

Going to work in the late afternoon after a normal night's sleep will not feel too bad but, sometime after midnight, fatigue will make its presence felt. This is a similar situation to 'partying on'. A late afternoon nap before work, or a nap in the early morning during a break from work, may prove helpful.

Going to work in the early morning, however, is a different problem. The body is crying out to continue sleeping, but the pilot has to force himself against all of his body rhythms into wakefulness, and head off to what might be quite demanding activity. Trying to get eight hours of sleep at an unusual time prior to commencing work may not be possible.

The *need* for sleep and the *readiness* of the body for sleep depend not only on tiredness due to the time awake, but also on the time of day according to your body rhythms. The intermittent shift-worker may have trouble going to sleep, staying asleep, and then waking and feeling well rested. A few short naps during his period of 'wakefulness' might be necessary to overcome the sleep deficit.

Body Rhythms

The regular 8–16 sleep/wakefulness rhythm is only one of our body rhythms. Others include the rhythm of internal body temperature, and the digestive rhythm with its regular hunger pangs and elimination of waste products.

The body has many rhythms.

These body rhythms usually have a frequency of approximately 24 hours, and so are often called the **circadian rhythms,** from the latin *circa* (about) and *dies* (day). There are many of these circadian rhythms, and they seem to be connected to one another, in that a change in one leads to a change in others, not necessarily at the same rate, nor with the same amount of ease. In fact, it can be very difficult to change some body rhythms and have all body rhythms synchronised normally. Long distance east–west travellers know this from struggling to get their bodies into a new time zone and not fall asleep when everyone else is operating at peak efficiency.

The sleep/wakefulness rhythm is perhaps one of the rhythms that is easiest to change. There are other rhythms, such as internal body temperature, which are very tightly bound into a regular rhythm and which are much more difficult and take much longer to change. Our performance capability and our enthusiasm to perform is closely tied to our body rhythms – especially that of internal body temperature, which rises slightly by day and falls at night.

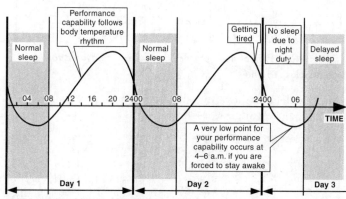

■ *Figure 5-9* **The body rhythm cycle**

The Sleep/Wakefulness Rhythm

Zeitgebers reduce the sleep/wakefulness rhythm to 24 hours.

The sleep/wakefulness rhythm seems to have a natural time span somewhat greater than 24 hours, more in the range of 25–26 hours, but it is regularly pulled back into a 24-hour time span by a succession of time-of-day reminders, known by the German word **zeitgebers.** *Zeit,* pronounced "sight", or more correctly "tsight" (if you can get your tongue around it) means **time,** and *geber,* pronounced "gayber", means **giver** – so that a zeitgeber is a *time-giver* – a reminder of the time of day.

Typical zeitgebers *(tsight-gaybers)* are the rising and setting of the sun, the everyday ringing of the alarm clock, the 8 a.m. breakfast pangs, the need to use the toilet before rushing off to catch the 8:23 train, lunch time, the ever-present wristwatch and clocks, the afternoon tea break, knock-off time, the 6 p.m. evening meal, the 9 o'clock news, and so on. Each person will have their own series of zeitgebers throughout the day pulling their sleep/wakefulness cycle into line, with the sun as a very powerful natural zeitgeber. The rising of the sun is a strong force moving us into wakefulness; darkness is a reminder that sleeping time is coming.

The *natural* length of the sleep/wakefulness cycle can be observed by removing all of the zeitgebers – for instance, by placing a person in a darkened room and removing all time clues. The result is a sleeping pattern that becomes later each day, as shown in Figure 5-10.

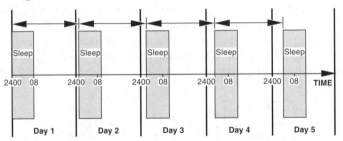

■ *Figure 5-10* **A typical sleep pattern on successive days without zeitgeber clues to time**

With zeitgebers, however, the sleeping pattern will be continually pulled back into the 24-hour cycle.

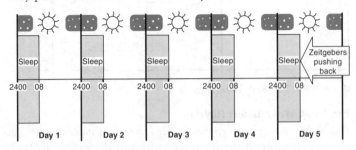

■ *Figure 5-11* **The normal sleep pattern on successive days with zeitgebers**

People who live in high latitudes, such as Scandinavia, Northern Canada and Siberia, have to cope with the loss of the sun as a zeitgeber. In summer they have continual light, and in winter they have continual darkness (or conditions approaching this). Stress levels, sleeping patterns, and fatigue may change with the seasons in some people living in these latitudes.

Body Temperature

Internal body temperature averages at about 36.5°C (98°F), with a regular circadian cycle of fluctuations 0.3°C above and below this. Its natural cycle is about 25 hours, but again zeitgebers pull it back into a 24-hour cycle, as shown.

The natural body temperature rhythm is hard to change.

The circadian rhythm of internal body temperature is a very strong rhythm that cannot be altered easily, as can other rhythms like the sleep/wakefulness cycle. For this reason, body temperature is often used as the standard rhythm against which to compare others.

Alertness is related to natural body temperature.

A high body temperature is linked to alertness and good performance capability; a low body temperature is linked to low mental performance and drowsiness.

Sleep usually occurs at times of low or falling body temperature.

The sleep/wakefulness cycle usually runs in tandem with the body temperature cycle. Your body is usually ready for sleep at a time of falling or low body temperature, and ready to be awake at a time of rising or high body temperature.

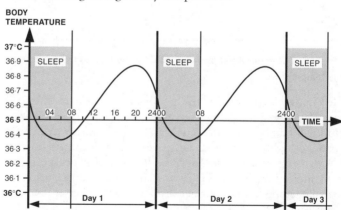

■ *Figure 5-12* **The circadian rhythm of internal body temperature**

The Performance Cycle

Peak performance capability and alertness occurs at the time of a rising or high body temperature, which is when you are usually wide awake; low alertness and performance capability occurs at times of low body temperature, which is when you are usually asleep.

Different types of performance (such as *psychomotor* perform-ance, hand–eye coordination, mental agility, reasoning ability, and reaction time) vary somewhat differently throughout the day; however, we can generalise and say that alertness and performance capability vary with body temperature.

NOTE Even if your sleep/wakefulness pattern is disturbed, the temperature pattern will remain the same. If you are forced to be awake at 4–6 a.m., your alertness and ability to perform well will be impaired somewhat because of the low point in your body temperature cycle that will occur as normal. The lowest body temperature occurs about 4–6 a.m., when you are usually in a very deep sleep and, if you have to work at this time, you may have great difficulty in staying awake.

If you are awake at a time of low body temperature, your performance could be lower.

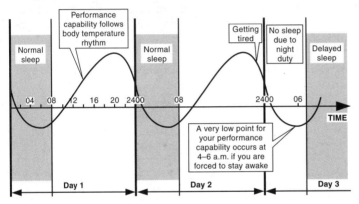

■ *Figure 5-13* **A generalised performance rhythm follows the internal body temperature**

It is possible to modify the performance cycle by lifting it, rather than by shifting it in terms of timing. Your performance graph will be raised if you are feeling well, if you are well rested, if you are highly motivated, and if you are well practised in the skills that you wish to use. Even the low performance points are raised, indicating that, if you are forced to stay awake during the normal sleeping hours, your performance will be better if you are fit and well.

Extroverts and night owls usually have their performance cycle moved slightly to the right, compared with introverts, to match their other body cycles. Similarly, perennial shift workers have their performance cycle moved to match their body cycles, which run to a different body clock compared with daytime workers, but their peak performance may not reach that of a daytime worker because of the inevitable disturbance to the sleeping periods of a night-shift worker caused by normal family life, and sunlight and darkness.

The ability to maintain a high level of performance decreases significantly if you are fatigued or deprived of sleep. This applies in particular to physically passive but mentally active tasks, which is often what a long-haul pilot is involved in when the aeroplane is on the cruise − systems monitoring, maintaining a navigation overview with correct radio communication − while the autopilot handles the physical task of maintaining height and track, and the autothrottle maintains speed.

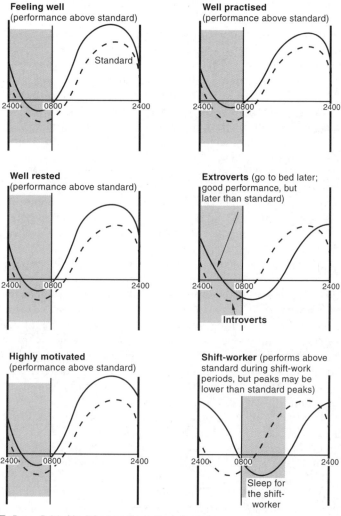

■ *Figure 5-14* **Modified performance rhythms**

Jet Lag – The Desynchronisation of Body Rhythms

The long-haul pilot and the passengers are subject to the normal fatigue of a flight caused by a dry, oxygen-deficient atmosphere, vibration, noise, lack of exercise, and the stresses associated with any flight, plus, on east–west flights especially, the very significant problem of crossing time zones and finding yourself in a place where the local time differs from home time. The rising and the setting of the sun, and the habits of the local population are on local time, and out of synchronisation with your body clock, which is still on home time. You feel like going to sleep just as darkness turns to light with the rising of the sun, and just as everyone else is waking up ready to start the new day. The early morning sounds of garbage collection, milk delivery, trains running, church bells ringing, do not match the way your body feels.

Moving to a new time zone disturbs the body rhythms.

The problem is: do you try to bring your body into the new time zone or not? This usually depends on how long the stay will be. For a pilot who will fly back home the next day, there is no point. For a long stay, such as a holiday, then the attempt is probably worthwhile making.

There are many body rhythms, the body temperature cycle being only one, although perhaps the most important one. Some rhythms can be brought into local time at the rate of about one hour a day, which means that, if the time zone change is four hours, then after four days this body cycle will be aligned with local time.

Different body rhythms, however, change at different rates. Also, any disturbance of one body rhythm may lead to disturbances in other body rhythms. Some body rhythms change at one and a half hours per day, others at only one half-hour a day and therefore take much longer to move into local time – eight days in fact if the time zone change is four hours. This means that as your body attempts to transfer into a new time zone, many of the body rhythms that are normally synchronised are now desynchronised with one another and may be a little abnormal within themselves. This is known as *circadian disrhythmia*.

Each rhythm adjusts at a different rate.

The result could be headaches, poor sleep, disturbed eating patterns, constipation, giddiness, poor mental performance, and even slight depression. Hunger pangs and toilet habits still based on the old home time could also disturb your new sleeping pattern as you try to move your body clock into the new time zone, making you generally tired all day long, and delaying further your move into the new time zone. The time between about 4–6 a.m. on your body clock, irrespective of what the local time is, will also be a period of low alertness and poor performance capability, which could be significant if you are in the middle of an important meeting or taking part in an activity that requires alertness. Accidentally falling asleep is not uncommon.

It may take three weeks or even longer before all the body rhythms are back 'in synch' again, and before you are operating at peak efficiency in the new time zone. Exposing yourself to sunlight, and allowing the powerful zeitgeber which is the sun to influence your body and mind, may speed the process a little.

Adjustment of the Body Clock

The adjustment process of the body clock is easier if you travel west. The time needed for the body clock to adjust if you are crossing time zones by travelling west may be less than if you are travelling east. This is because travelling westwards you are travelling with the sun, and the hours of daylight that you experience will be longer than normal. The day will appear to be longer than 24 hours.

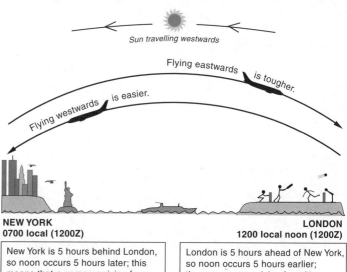

NEW YORK
0700 local (1200Z)

LONDON
1200 local noon (1200Z)

New York is 5 hours behind London, so noon occurs 5 hours later; this means that a person arriving from London experiences a 29-hour day. The body clock is 25 hours, so: **only 4 hours jet lag,** but the 25-hour body clock will tend to close the gap naturally in 4 days, and even less with the aid of 'zeitgebers'.

London is 5 hours ahead of New York, so noon occurs 5 hours earlier; thus, a person arriving from New York experiences a 19-hour day. The body clock is 25 hours, so: **6 hours jet lag,** i.e. 2 hours worse off than the reverse flight. 'Zeitgebers' alone work to remove this by reducing the body clock to less than 24 hours (hard work!).

■ *Figure 5-15* ***Jet lag after travelling westwards is less than eastwards***

Because many natural body rhythms have a period of 25 hours if they are not pulled back by zeitgebers, they have a natural tendency to move towards the new time zone at the rate of about one hour a day.

Conversely, when travelling eastwards, the days are shortened, and the body rhythms have to be pulled back to less than 24 hours, against their natural tendency to lengthen.

Flying east is tougher than flying west.

Although travelling north or south does not mean crossing time zones, there can still be jet lag problems, due to the usual fatigue from a long flight, and also due to the somewhat displaced zeitgebers.

Flying north-south is easy.

In winter, for instance, a Scandinavian or a Scot might be used to the sun rising at 10 a.m. If the northerner travels south to somewhere in Africa, the local time might be the same, but the sun now rises at 5 a.m. This change of time of an important zeit-geber may unsettle some of the body rhythms.

Now complete

Exercises 5 – Stress Management, Fatigue and Sleep.

Information Processing

If you understand how we humans process information, then the learning of a new skill, such as flying, becomes much easier.

The initial feeling of being overloaded and bombarded by sensations from all sides on early flights is quite typical. As the training progresses, however, actions that at first required your full attention, such as manipulating the aircraft, become *motor programmes,* which are also known as *skills.* Your brain is then freed to think of other things, such as maintaining an overview of the flight, handling the radio, and perhaps even conversing with your flight instructor or passenger.

Some information processing is involved with responding immediately to a stimulus – for instance, applying the brakes of a car when the traffic lights ahead turn red. Other information processing is concerned with longer-term items, such as *learning* and *remembering,* where the information processed is stored in the memory for later retrieval and use.

The System of Nerves

The brain is the central decision-maker.

The processing of information occurs within the nervous system, consisting of the brain and the spinal cord; these together make up the *central nervous system.* A series of smaller nerves radiating out through the body make up what is known as the *peripheral nervous system.* The highest-level decisions, i.e. conscious decisions that require consideration, are made in the brain, which is where our so-called 'intelligence' resides.

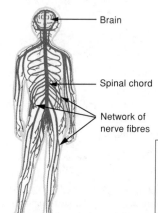

Brain

Spinal chord

Network of
nerve fibres

The brain and spinal chord comprise the *central nervous system.*

The *peripheral nervous system* consists mainly of pairs of nerve fibres leading to and from the central nervous system.

■ *Figure 6-1* **The nervous system**

The individual nerves can be thought of as telephone lines carrying messages to and from the central nervous system, especially the brain. It is more than just a central telephone exchange – more like a massively powerful computer that not only redirects messages, but makes major (and minor) decisions.

The main limitation of our brain as a **central decision-maker** is that it functions only as a *single-channel* computer, which means that we can consider only one thing at a time. Decisions made in the brain are therefore not made simultaneously, but are made consecutively in a series, one after the other.

The brain has only a single channel.

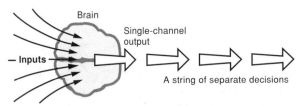

■ *Figure 6-2* **The brain is a single-channel decision-maker**

A Basic Model of Information Processing

How we process information is best explained by the use of a *model* – a hypothetical plan of what we think happens. Some models are simple, others are more complicated. We will consider a fairly basic model that is in accordance with conventional understanding.

The information-handling process involves:
- ☐ a **stimulus**;
- ☐ **analysis** (i.e. thinking or cognition) and decision;
- ☐ **action**; and
- ☐ **feedback**.

Stimulus

All models begin with a stimulus, the information that is detected by our senses in the form of images, sounds, feel, smells, and taste. This sensory information is sent as electrical signals along the appropriate sensory nerves in the peripheral nervous system to the central nervous system for attention. There is so much sensory information presented to us that only a fraction of it is absorbed, or *perceived*.

The brain perceives some stimuli.

Analysis

The perceived sensory information is analysed and considered, along with previously known information stored in our memory, and a decision made. This is the fundamental process of **conscious decision-making**, also known as *thinking* or *cognition*, which occurs between input and action.

The brain analyses the stimuli.

Action

After a decision is made, *action* is taken by the brain sending out electrical signals along small motor nerves to the appropriate muscles, which then move as commanded. *Feedback* on the effectiveness of the decision and the action(s) taken is provided by our perception (senses); follow-up action can then be taken if necessary.

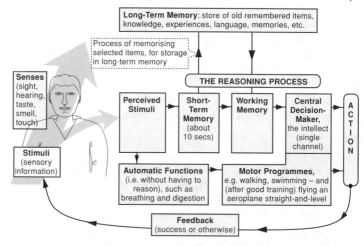

■ *Figure 6-3* **A basic model of our information processing**

Different Levels of Mental Activity

If our brain can only consciously think of one thing at a time, how can we do several things concurrently, such as hold a conversation at the same time as we are walking?

The answer is because there are different levels of mental activity; conscious thinking (or *cognition*) is only the most advanced.

Thinking

Conscious decision-making occurs in a part of our brain known as the *central decision-maker*. This area can concern itself with only one problem at a time. The single-channel central decision-making channel means that only one decision at a time can be taken, although more decisions can follow quite quickly in sequence.

Motor Programmes

It is obvious that there is more than one activity going on within our bodies most of the time. For instance, when playing tennis and consciously thinking about tactics, we are still able to run about. This is because there are other levels of action that occur which may not be controlled by conscious decision-making, but by motor programmes or skills.

Motor programmes control skills that are so well learned that no conscious effort is required to control the actions (or very little conscious effort, and then only on an occasional basis). For instance, walking has been so well learned that it requires little conscious attention; for children or adults suffering brain damage, however, trying to walk occupies them totally.

Signing your name normally does not distract you from other tasks, such as holding a conversation, because you have trained your eye and hand so well that a motor programme controls the task – but try signing your name with your non-writing hand. Now your signature is no longer run by a motor programme but has to be consciously, and probably not too successfully, created. Continuing a conversation simultaneously is almost impossible because your single-channel decision-maker is already occupied.

Motor programmes (skills) are semi-automatic.

Reflexes

At a more primitive level of nervous activity, some actions, known as **reflexes,** occur with little or no involvement of the central nervous system. In this case, the sensory nerve is linked closely to the motor nerve so that action occurs before the signal is consciously processed in the central nervous system. For instance, pricking your finger with a pin, or touching red-hot metal, will cause it to withdraw spontaneously without any mental activity in your brain, and before any conscious thought of pain occurs.

You have natural reflexes.

Conditioned Reflexes

A *conditioned* reflex is not a natural reflex, but a *trained* reflex. A conditioned reflex responds, not to the sensory stimulus that normally causes it, but to a separate stimulus which has been learned to be associated with it. A good example is 'Pavlov's dogs'. Pavlov, a Russian physiologist, trained his dogs to associate the sound of a bell with feeding time, and eventually the association was so strong that their mouths would water at the sound of a bell irrespective of whether food was present or not.

There are trained reflexes.

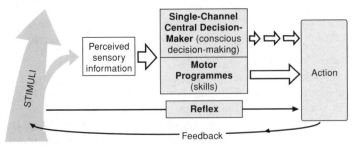

■ *Figure 6-4* **The three main causes of action: conscious decision-making, motor programmes, and reflexes**

Autonomic Activities

Normal bodily functions such as breathing, the heartbeat, the digestive process, maintenance of body temperature, etc., continue under the control of the *autonomic nervous system*, which does not require any thinking on our part. Biological control systems and reflexes do not require learning and/or conscious thought. Many unfortunate children born with a poorly functioning brain still have normal bodily functions.

Thinking and Flying

Learning the basic flying skills initially requires a lot of conscious thought and decision-making (as did walking when you were a child).

Practising the basic skills time and time again allows you to learn the responses needed to certain stimuli so well that, eventually, manipulating the aeroplane can be run by motor programmes. An experienced pilot, for instance, will almost automatically apply back pressure on the control column when sinking below the flightpath, and add power if speed is decreasing. A trainee pilot must think it through before acting, which of course takes a lot more effort.

Flying gets easier as you learn the skills.

Well-learned skills being run by motor programmes leave the central decision-making part of your brain available for other activities, such as navigation, updating fuel calculations, making and receiving radio calls, handling emergencies, making judgements and, in general, just managing the whole flight from start to finish – a task which requires a lot of conscious thought. Using an autopilot can also off-load a pilot from mechanical tasks.

Stimulation, Sensing and Perception

An enormous amount of stimulation from the external world is presented to us in the form of visual images, sounds, smell, taste, and feel. These can be sensed by our so-called *sense organs* – the eyes, ears, nose, taste buds, and feel receptors in the skin and muscles. We can also use receptors within the balance mechanism of our inner ear to sense accelerations and balance, and to determine which way is 'up'.

Not all physical quantities are sensed, however. For instance, whilst our inner ear can detect accelerations, which are *changes* in velocity, it cannot detect velocity itself. Being stationary or travelling at a steady speed of 80 kph feels the same, and with your eyes shut you might be unable to tell the difference, but you would certainly know if you were accelerating from 0 to 80 kph, or vice versa, and decelerating from 80 to 0 kph.

Each of the sense organs is a collection of specialised cells, known as *receptors*. The receptors are capable of detecting particular changes in the environment (either outside the body or within), and triggering electrical impulses in the sensory nerves. The *sensitivity* of the receptors in each sense organ, which is their ability to respond to a stimulus, is different – for instance, those on the retina of the eye are sensitive to changes in light, whereas the receptor cells in the taste buds on the tongue respond to chemical changes, and the receptor cells in the skin are sensitive to heat, pain and touch.

There is a *sensory threshold*, below which the stimuli will not be detected by the particular receptors. For instance, very soft sounds, or sounds outside the frequency range of our ears, may go undetected. Similarly, electromagnetic radiation that does not lie within the visible light spectrum, or that is very faint, will go undetected by the light receptors in our eyes. The sensory threshold is a measure of the sensitivity of our sense organs, and is often tested in pilot medicals, especially for sound and visual images.

If the stimulation is continuous or repetitive, then the receptor cells run the risk of *adaptation*, which is showing a gradually diminishing response to that particular stimulus. For instance, the adaptation of touch receptors in the skin causes the presence of clothes to be no longer felt just a few minutes after putting them on. Similarly, after long exposure to a steady sound, such as an aeroplane engine or wind noise, the pilot may become completely unaware of it.

Sensory nerves, such as the optic nerve from the eyes and the auditory nerve from the ears, carry the sensed information towards the central nervous system (the brain and the spinal cord), where the messages are integrated, i.e. perceived. The sensory information is stored only briefly in a *sensory memory* before it is displaced by new information, unless we decide to absorb it and process it.

Each sense has its own memory, with the time of storage varying between the senses. For instance, a visual image lasts only about one second before it fades – illustrated by waggling a pencil in front of your eyes and noting that the blurred image of where it has just been quickly fades. Movies make use of this memory, enabling you to see a series of individual 'still' pictures as a moving image.

Sounds last considerably longer than visual images – about five seconds – before they begin to fade. This is time enough for us to recognise half way through a sentence that it is being directed at us and recall its beginning, or for us to be able to count back the number of times a clock has struck.

Sensed information is stored only briefly in the sensory memory.

Perception involves the senses receiving some information about the environment, and analysing it to make it meaningful. For instance, a group of sounds may become a sentence with meaning, and a sequence of visual images may become an aeroplane moving

You can develop mental models from sensed information.

across the sky. Your senses are continually collecting new information to enable you to continually update your mental model of what the situation is.

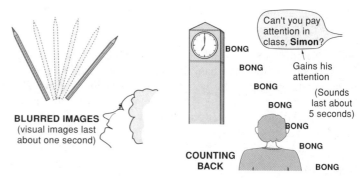

BLURRED IMAGES
(visual images last
about one second)

BONG
BONG
BONG
BONG
BONG
BONG
BONG

Can't you pay attention in class, **Simon**?

Gains his attention

(Sounds last about 5 seconds)

COUNTING
BACK

■ *Figure 6-5* **Sensed information lasts briefly in each sensory memory**

Experience and Expectation

The amount of sensed stimulation that is actually perceived and integrated depends to some extent upon our experience and expectation.

If we recognise the stimulus through previous experience, then we can more readily absorb it and integrate it into a model of the world around us. For instance, through experience we know that red–hot metal can cause pain, and when we feel pain and then see that our finger has just touched a piece of glowing metal, then we have no difficulty in forming a mental model of the situation – hot metal has burnt your finger.

Experience helps perception.

Another example of useful experience is to do with radio messages from Air Traffic Control. Pilots can understand these messages through experience, but no one else can – all they hear is a jumble of sounds and a lot of static.

Do not have mind-sets.

Some radio messages are even difficult to understand for pilots, but an *expectation* of what the message will contain often helps. But we must guard against hearing what we want to hear or expect to hear, rather than what is *actually* said! In the lined-up position on the runway at a controlled airport, for instance, we expect to hear, "cleared take-off", and this is also what we want to hear. We are mentally geared up for the take-off. The actual instruction, however, might be 'taxi clear of the runway'. It can be dangerous if we only hear what we want to hear, and see what we want to see – this is known as having a *mind-set*.

Sensory Confusion

When we hold our hand under a water tap marked 'C' and turn it on, we expect to feel a cold sensation, since we associate the letter 'C' with the word 'cold'. Many travellers to Italy are thrown into confusion, however, when they feel hot water rather than cold coming out of the tap marked 'C'. 'C' in this case represents *caldo*, the Italian word for *hot,* while 'F' for *freddo* would be labelled on the cold tap. This mixing of signals can cause sensory confusion in our brains.

Another example of sensory confusion occurs when our eyes present an image to the brain that does not match up with the signals from our balance mechanism – for instance, after recovering from a prolonged spin, the wings of the aeroplane appear to be level with the horizon (eyes), but we feel as if we are still turning (balance mechanism). In this situation, we need to show sufficient discipline, as a result of good training, to take note of the signals from our eyes and discard those from the balance mechanism.

Anticipation

Anticipating an event or message is good, provided we do not have a *mind-set* that locks out other possibilities and causes us to interpret a stimulus to be what we expect it to be, or want it to be, even though that might not be the case. Pilots are prone to this, especially when under high levels of stress.

During an early cross-country flight, trying to convince yourself that the ground features below match the mental model of your position (i.e. where you think you are), when in fact they do not, is a common feeling, and one which must be resisted. Similarly, hearing ATC clearances that we want to hear ("clear to land") rather than what is actually said ("go around") can lead to disaster.

Expectation and anticipation can help us, but it can also lead us into trouble if we are not disciplined enough to continually reassess the information that our senses present to us.

> Continually reassess sensed information.

Attention and Motivation

Attention refers to the (limited) control that you have over what sensed stimuli you choose to process, which will usually be the stimuli that you consider to be relevant to the task in hand.

You can consciously focus your attention on a particular item – for instance, if you are specifically looking out at night for lightning flashes or for other aircraft, or your attention can be drawn to a particular item by external events – for instance, when you overhear your name being mentioned your attention will almost automatically be diverted from your current activity to what is being said about you in this distant conversation.

Selective attention refers to the sampling of stimuli and the selection of some of them for further processing, the remainder being allowed to fade away. The selected stimuli are usually associated with the subject currently under consideration, which might be controlling the flightpath and airspeed of the aeroplane.

> When stressed, you can overlook important information.

Most of the time, however, if stress levels are not too high, there is sufficient additional capacity to notice stimuli not associated with the current task, such as emergency signals (bells, horns, etc.), your name, or your aircraft callsign.

Selecting what we think are the important stimuli for us to attend to consciously is known as *precoding*, and it usually depends upon what we think is important, how strong the stimulus is, and also upon our mental state (e.g. stress level).

Divided Attention

Learn to divide your attention.

Whilst we often concentrate on one task at a time, it is not possible to devote all of our time to the prime task to the total exclusion of all others. There are often secondary tasks that have to be considered, such as raising the flaps following take-off when your attention has to be diverted briefly from the main task of monitoring and controlling the flightpath, or when making a radio call in the middle of handling an emergency. Switching our attention from one set of stimuli to another is known as *divided attention* or *time-sharing.*

Stress Can Diminish Perception

Usually we can switch our attention between tasks quite quickly, but stress and over-concentration on one task can inhibit this. Calls from ATC often go unnoticed when pilots are dealing with an emergency and their attention is narrowed to this one task.

On some occasions, attention has not been divided enough to monitor the flightpath concurrently with handling an emergency and, even though the emergency was resolved, the aeroplane crashed. Pilots under stress have also failed to hear warning signals, and have landed wheels-up or flown unexpectedly into the ground when warnings were there, but not perceived. Learning to divide your attention and share your time between tasks is an important skill, particularly for a pilot.

Motivation

Too much of a workload may diminish our ability to perceive, but so also may too little stimulus – for instance, when a person is drowsy. Our perception of stimuli, and indeed our overall performance, is generally best with some degree of stress.

Be adequately aroused for the task at hand.

In order to always be ready to respond to important stimuli, pilots must be *motivated* to remain sufficiently aroused – for instance, a pilot should avoid becoming drowsy on the cruise even though the autopilot is plugged in. At the other end of the scale, a pilot should avoid becoming unable to cope with the incoming signals due to being overloaded.

Being under-aroused and half asleep, or being over-aroused and stressed-out or in a panic, can cause you to miss important stimuli, especially stimuli not associated with the prime task, and hence lead to poor performance.

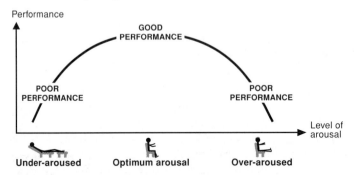

■ *Figure 6-6* **An optimum level of arousal leads to best performance**

Abnormalities in Perception

Perception is the process of receiving information through the senses, analysing it, and making it meaningful. This process is, on occasions, subject to certain abnormalities, which include:

- **hallucinations** – false perception of something that is not really there, i.e. *imagined* and not real, with no actual stimulus, only an imagined one;
- **illusions** – false perception due to *misinterpretation* of the stimuli, e.g. psychological illusions due to misinterpretation of signals from other people, optical illusions due to deceptive qualities in the stimuli received, such as sloping ground when we expect flat ground; and
- **agnosia** – a brain disorder that interferes with the correct interpretation of sensation, and which would disqualify a person from holding a pilot's licence.

Problems in perception also arise when we receive conflicting information from different senses, such as between our eyes and our balance mechanisms during a prolonged turn.

After settling down into a prolonged turn, the balance mechanisms of the ear no longer signal entry to a turn, and it feels (in balance terms) like flying straight; visual information from our eyes, however, such as the relative position of the horizon (real or artificial), indicate a turn. In this case, good instrument training should encourage you to trust your eyes and believe what you see on the real horizon or on the artificial horizon, rather than rely on your sense of balance and 'seat-of-the-pants'.

Memory

Memory is the ability to store information and retrieve it when needed.

Memory is an amazing thing. Events from years ago can be brought immediately to mind, words not used for a long time fit readily into sentences, which are correctly structured according to rules of grammar learnt in schooldays, smells not experienced for decades can be recognised immediately, and so on. Memories of events, and a store of language, appear to be filed away in our brain for use at any time.

The memory has various components.

How the memory functions precisely is not fully known, but it seems that memory consists of electrical signals passing between millions of brain cells, with different sorts of memories, based on the period for which the information is retained, available for use. These different sorts of memory can be thought of as:

- ☐ **the sensory memory** – where sensed items remain briefly (1 second for visual images, 5 seconds for sounds) – also known as the ultra-short memory, and already discussed under 'stimulation', sensing and perception;
- ☐ **the short-term memory;**
- ☐ **the working memory;** and
- ☐ **the long-term memory.**

In some models, the short-term memory and the working memory are considered to be one.

The Sensory Memory

The sensory memory retains images, sounds, and other sensed stimuli, for just a second or two – long enough for us to select which ones to attend to – before they are lost.

The Short-Term Memory

You can remember about 7 new items for 15 seconds.

The short-term memory in the brain is capable of holding only a few items for a brief period, typically seven items for 15 seconds, before they are forgotten. For instance, when you hear a telephone number spoken, or read the number in a telephone book, and then immediately dial it without error, you are using your short-term memory. If you delay the dialling for say 30 seconds, and do not rehearse (i.e. repeat) the number to hold it in your short-term memory, you will most likely dial a wrong number.

Similarly, a message from ATC to *change frequency to one three two decimal one (132·1 MHz)* will remain in your short-term memory long enough for you to select the frequency. Any delay, however, or any excess of additional information, and you will probably select the wrong frequency. Well-trained air traffic controllers pass only a few pieces of information at the one time, especially when they are aware that a pilot is inexperienced or may be under stress.

An ATC *route clearance* may contain four or five or even more items, and so is best written down as it is received. Your short-term memory may not be able to cope, both in terms of number of items and also in time of retention.

ATC clearances must be read back by the pilot to ensure correct understanding. You can try this out by reading the next sentence once, and then repeating it aloud as a read-back. *"Golf Alpha Charlie Delta X-ray, cleared to destination Glasgow, via Ponteland, Wallsend, then flight planned route, initially climb to flight level eight zero, squawk 4206, call 129.5 after departure."* Not so easy is it – hence the need to write clearances down as they are being given.

The seven items for 15 seconds is very variable between people (some might only be able to remember three items for 10 seconds), or for the same person under different levels of stress or tiredness.

It is possible to increase the capacity of the short-term memory, not by trying to remember more items, but by combining several items into one, a process known as *chunking* information, i.e. making chunks of information instead of individual items.

For instance, when you are given a new telephone number, such as 315 3023, it is better to remember it, not as seven pieces of information 3-1-5-3-0-2-3 but as two chunks 315 3023, or three chunks 315 30 23. This still leaves some capacity in your short-term memory, if needed immediately, say, for a name, before the number of items reaches 7 or thereabouts. Similarly, the radio frequency 132.1 could be remembered as one item instead of four.

> *Chunking information aids short-term memory.*

Also, mnemonics can be used to chunk information, such as in checklists. It is a lot easier to remember the mnemonic *PUF* on short final than it is to remember each of the items individually, which are 'Propeller Pitch', 'Undercarriage', and 'Flaps'.

> *Memory 'joggers' also help.*

The Working Memory

The working memory contains the information that we are currently using, and which may be drawn from the short-term memory or the long-term memory, with electrical signals passing back and forth between the memory and the central decision-making part of the brain. The working memory does, however, have limited capacity.

In the working memory, we work on the information that we have chosen to attend to. We either:

- ▢ **rehearse it,** i.e. repeat it a number of times in an attempt to remember it, as in rote learning; or
- ▢ **encode it,** by trying to understand it, or relating it to something we already know.

The working memory works on information, trying to remember it by repetition or by understanding it.

Encoding (understanding) is usually a better way of remembering something over a long period than rehearsal (rote learning).

As mentioned earlier, some models treat the short-term memory and the working memory as one.

The Long-Term Memory

The long-term memory is where information is filed away for later use after being rehearsed or encoded in the working memory. The information may have to be retrieved several minutes later, or as long as several decades later.

Information seems to be stored in two areas, one involving *meaning*, such as the use of language, and the other involving *events*. The information can be reconstructed and brought together in the working memory when needed. Unfortunately, the reconstruction is not always totally accurate, as we all know when comparing our memory of an event with someone else's, or even with our own diary.

The long-term memory stores remembered information.

Items that are encoded (entered) into the long-term memory are thought to stay there for ever, although there may be problems and delays in retrieving the information, especially if it has not been recalled or used for some time. Periodically recalling important information from the long-term memory, i.e. practice, enables it to be recalled more readily when you really need it. For this reason, it is good technique to occasionally practise recalling items that should be known, such as limitations and vital emergency checks.

The information stored in the long-term memory is of value when the brain is trying to evaluate new information that has just been sensed. Usually, the brain will try to associate new data with data already stored in the long-term memory.

Totally new information, bearing no relation to anything previously sensed and stored, will probably take longer to process mentally than familiar information, because the brain cannot associate it with anything. An example of this could be when attempting your first visual approach, with no experience of how the runway should appear, or how the aircraft should feel. You have to think everything through from first principles. With experience, however, you will be able to compare the current situation with previous earlier situations.

The **meaning memory** part of the long-term memory is also known as the *semantic* memory. It is where information is stored in terms of words. Knowledge stored in this part of the long-term memory includes the meaning and use of language, remembered items such as home telephone number and address, vital checklists, and so on.

New material being learned and entered into the meaning part of the long-term memory should be given our full attention. We should try to understand it thoroughly, organising the various pieces of information logically into word messages so that our brain can encode it accurately and then store it. Association with items already in store helps with the encoding process.

Learning in position – for instance, learning checklists in an actual cockpit or simulated cockpit – often helps with encoding, and with the retrieval later on, since the information was learned in a familiar environment. Good encoding into the meaning memory makes later retrieval of the information easier and more meaningful. If the meaning of the information is understood, it can often be retrieved bit by bit through logic.

Meanings are remembered.

The **event memory** part of the long-term memory is also known as the *episodic* memory. Interesting events and episodes are stored here. Unfortunately, they are occasionally stored not all that accurately, sometimes being coloured by our attitudes and expectations, i.e. what we think must have happened, what would have been logical to have happened, or what we would like to have happened.

Accident investigators are often faced with expert witnesses of aircraft accidents, such as pilots, not remembering the event totally accurately. Their knowledge of aviation and their attitude and expectations as to what must have happened, or at least of what possibly happened, interferes with their memory of what actually happened. Non-expert witnesses, with no prejudices or expectations, can often recall the details more accurately, and without interpretation.

Events are remembered, but not always accurately.

Visual images can also be stored in the *spatial* part of the memory.

Sometimes information cannot be retrieved due to poor encoding, and sometimes due to brain damage. *Amnesia* is the total or partial loss of memory following physical injury such as concussion, disease, drugs, or psychological trauma. It usually affects the event (episodic) memory, with the meaning (semantic) memory relatively untouched. A person suffering amnesia or brain damage may be able to speak sensibly with a good use of language, but be unable to remember events.

The Central Decision-Maker

Conscious decisions are made in the so-called *central decision-making* part of our brain. This is where thinking, reasoning and decision-making occur, with electrical signals then being sent out along the motor nerves to activate the appropriate muscles.

Signals come into the central decision-maker from many sources, the sensory memory, the short-term memory, the working memory, and the long-term memory, with messages often being passed back and forth until a decision is made.

Single-Channel Decision-Making

Decisions are made one at a time.

It seems that the central decision-maker is capable of only making one decision at a time, i.e. it is a **single-channel decision-maker.** This means that conscious decisions on separate matters are made consecutively (one after the other), and not simultaneously.

Sequential decisions can be made quite quickly if we switch our attention between tasks, i.e. by **time-sharing,** so that the more complicated tasks move forward in stages. For instance, when attempting to fly straight-and-level at a steady airspeed, we need to monitor three things (at least) – altitude, heading, and airspeed.

☐ If we concentrate on **heading alone,** then we will probably drift off altitude and the airspeed may gradually change.

☐ If we concentrate on **airspeed alone,** then altitude and heading may vary.

In the early stages, when we are still learning to fly accurately and are having to make *conscious* decisions about handling the aircraft, we need to share the time of our central decision-maker between various tasks:

☐ **check altitude** and adjust with a change in pitch attitude if needed;

☐ **check airspeed** and adjust with a change in power if needed;

☐ **check heading** and adjust with a change in bank attitude if needed;

☐ **then return** to check attitude again and repeat the process.

Over-concentration on one specific task to the neglect of others can prevent completion of the overall task.

Divide your attention.

Time-sharing will at first be poor, the result probably being rather late and jerky corrections, or over-corrections. With practice, however, time-sharing between different items will occur more quickly and the resulting corrections be smaller and less noticeable. An experienced pilot will fly much more smoothly and accurately than a beginner, because of spotting deviations sooner and thus making smaller corrections immediately.

The **response time** between perceiving a stimulus and responding to it depends to a large extent upon how much mental processing is required. If the central decision-maker is involved, then the response time will be longer than if the response comes through a reflex or a motor programme not involving the central decision-maker.

Motor Programmes or Skills

A motor programme can run an activity without conscious reasoning. This means that the activity proceeds without the continuing involvement of the central decision-maker, which is therefore freed for other decision-making tasks.

Motor programmes are often the result of well-learned skills, such as walking, speaking, writing, riding a bicycle, driving a car, and (eventually) flying an aeroplane. A child learning to walk, or to ride a bicycle, has the mind fully occupied. Nothing can intrude. Having learned to balance the bicycle, however, the child can navigate a bit better, hold a conversation while riding, or perhaps even juggle balls at the same time.

Flying as a Motor Programme

While a beginning student is concentrating on learning to fly the aeroplane accurately, the central decision-maker will be almost fully occupied. There will be very little capacity remaining for other tasks such as navigation and radio calls.

Once the student has learned the handling skills well, however, and practised them until they are almost second nature, flying the aeroplane will occur with little conscious thought. In this case, the activity is said to be run by a motor programme in the brain, leaving the central decision-maker available for higher-level decisions that require reasoning, such as generally managing the entire flight.

Motor programmes are often *initiated* by the central decision-maker. You might make a decision to get up and walk towards the door, but once this decision has been taken, the central decision-maker can drop out of the picture temporarily and let the motor programme run the activity. As well as *initiating* the activity, the central decision-maker should also return to *monitor* the motor programme from time to time, first to check that the proper motor programme is in use, and second to check progress and decide when to stop.

It is possible that, even though a decision to commence a certain motor programme has been taken, the wrong programme swings into action. This could be walking in the wrong direction, or it could be raising the flaps instead of the undercarriage – something which is especially likely when flying a different aeroplane type in which the position of the two controls has been interchanged. Motor programmes need to be periodically monitored.

Using the wrong motor programme can also be dangerous with respect to movements of the throttle, mixture control, pitch control, and carburettor heat in an aeroplane. More than one aircraft has landed short of the runway because the mixture control

Monitor your motor programmes.

was pulled fully out instead of the carburettor heat, stopping the engine instead of protecting it from ice. Hence the need for the central decision-maker to monitor the motor programme in important cases, even *before* the first action is taken. For instance, when about to raise the undercarriage after take-off, visually check which lever your hand is on before you move it.

Errors due to old habits, such as moving the wrong lever, are more likely to occur when a pilot is tired and under-aroused, or when over-aroused and in a state of near panic. You will remember that there is an intermediate level of arousal where optimum performance occurs. This is another reason why you should never fly when fatigued, and never get into a situation beyond your capacity. Fatigue will lead to *under-arousal* and reduced capabilities; a situation beyond your capacity might lead to *over-arousal* and reduced capabilities.

Practise your skills.

Motor programmes are the result of learned skills. If these skills are not used regularly, however, they may be lost, and an activity that was once run by a motor programme may now have to be controlled by conscious decision-making. This will occupy the central decision-maker and, as a result, you can expect a deterioration in the performance of other tasks. Professional pilots returning from holidays notice this, as do musicians and others who have to perform skilled tasks. Keep your skills well honed!

We can certainly *do* more than one thing at a time, thanks to motor programmes, but we can only *think* about one thing at a time.

Action and Feedback

Action will be initiated by a conscious decision from the brain (a thinking-based response) or by a motor programme that is running (a skill-based response). A series of electrical signals will be sent along motor nerves to the appropriate muscles for the action to commence. It could be speech, body movement, or a decision not to move. The results of the action can then be observed by our senses, with important feedback hopefully being perceived, i.e. noticed, analysed, and made sense of. If the feedback indicates that action is not having the desired result, then we can take further action.

Monitor the results of your actions.

For instance, during the take-off or landing roll, we attempt to maintain the runway centreline by moving the rudder pedals. A student may have to think consciously about this; an experienced pilot may allow a motor programme to run the operation. In both cases, the result as to how good we are holding the centreline needs to be monitored every few seconds, and adjustments made if necessary. In any manoeuvre, there is a continuing process of **action–feedback–action–feedback–action**, etc.

Response Time

The time it takes for any initial stimulus to be perceived, considered, and acted upon can take between a fraction of a second and several seconds, depending upon the complexity of the decision, or decisions, to be made. Responding to a stimulus often requires a series of sequential decisions to be made; this of course needs time due to the single-channel nature of the brain's central decision-maker.

On approach to land, for instance, the undercarriage has been selected down and a horn unexpectedly sounds. Some of the decisions that now need to be made are:

- ☐ **Silence the horn** to remove the distraction now that the warning has been noted, how do we do that?
- ☐ **What does the horn mean?** Is it undercarriage not down, or something else? It means that the undercarriage has been selected down, but is not actually down.
- ☐ **How else can we check** if it is down or not? Check for three green lights, or lack thereof.
- ☐ **Is there time** to rectify the problem and continue with the approach?
- ☐ **Should we initiate** a missed approach immediately?
- ☐ **Should we advise ATC?**, etc., etc.

Throughout all of this decision-making following a very simple unexpected event, we must periodically switch our attention to monitoring the flightpath, and the speed and configuration of the aeroplane.

In a situation like that above, we can remove the time pressure (by making a missed approach, joining a holding pattern, or taking some other delaying action), and so make more time available to solve the problem.

Allow time to respond.

In other situations, we may not have that luxury – for instance, in a take-off that is rejected at a high speed on a limiting runway. This will require a split-second decision and immediate actions.

If the pilot of a large aircraft suspects a problem during the take-off run, especially as the decision speed, V_1, is approached, there is only a second or two to decide what to do, "Stop or go?" Stopping may not be possible if a tyre has blown and reduced the wheel-braking capability. Flying away may not be possible if the problem is with the flight controls, or if the problem is multiple engine failure due to bird strikes. The enormous pressure of limited time between input and a necessary decision can sometimes lead to a faulty decision and response.

Rehearse critical manoeuvres.

A pilot can minimise the risk of making a poor decision, and increase the possibility of a good decision, by maintaining a high level of knowledge, and by practising the manoeuvre frequently. Simulators can play a big role here, particularly when practising critical manoeuvres, such as aborted take-offs from a high speed on a short runway, or engine failure after take-off.

Mental Workload

Best performance is achieved with high levels of skill, knowledge, and experience, and with an optimum degree of arousal. Skill, knowledge and experience depends upon the pilot; the degree of arousal depends not only upon the pilot but also upon others, such as the designer of the cockpit, the air traffic controllers, as well as upon the environment, weather, and so on.

Low levels of skill, knowledge and experience, plus a poorly designed cockpit, bad weather, and poor controlling, may lead to a high mental workload and a poor performance.

If the mental workload becomes too high, then decision-making will deteriorate in quality, or maybe not even occur. This could be the result of concentrating only on one task, sometimes called *tunnel vision*. Conversely, too little workload can lead to under-arousal, with some important stimuli not being noticed, and performance consequently being poorer. A healthy level of workload keeps us aroused.

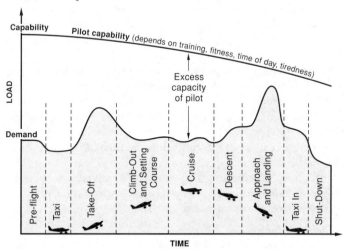

■ Figure 6-7 **Typical workload requirements and capacity**

All pilot tasks designed into the operation need to be tested so that at no time do they demand more of the pilot than what the pilot can give. There should always be some spare capacity left to ensure no overload occurs, and to allow for handling unexpected abnormal and emergency situations.

At the design stage, the pilot to be considered should not be the average pilot, because then half of all pilots would be below this standard, but the weakest pilot who maintains only the minimum required standard. Make sure that this is not you! Many pilots feel that, under normal conditions, they should be able to operate at only 40–50% of capacity, except during take-offs and landings, when that might rise to 70%. This leaves some mental capacity to handle abnormal situations.

You can raise your capability line on the graph in Figure 6-7 by studying and practising, and by being fit, relaxed and well rested.

Increase your capacity.

Mental Overload

Different parts of the brain can be overloaded, in which case mental efficiency will break down. Flying by using well-honed motor programmes will leave space in the brain for strategic thinking, overall management, and airmanship considerations. The student pilot, however, may not yet have reached this stage of skill.

The **sensory memory** can be overloaded if there is too much stimulus, with too many important incoming signals to be perceived. A pilot coping with an abnormal or emergency situation, such as a ringing fire bell, might miss an ATC radio call advising details of conflicting traffic.

The **short-term memory** can be overloaded by excessive information or by time delays. It cannot cope with more than about 7 items, and these will only be retained for 15 or 30 seconds unless rehearsed (repeated). New information coming in will replace these items.

The single channel of the **central decision-making** part of the brain can be overloaded if:
☐ **conflicting information** that cannot be resolved is received;
☐ **too many decisions** are required in too short a time; or
☐ **if the person is overstressed.**

Conflicting Information

Conscious decision-making is easier if all the information coming to the brain is in conformity and matches up. For instance, the clap of thunder that is heard is more easily assimilated if it matches up with a flash of lightning that occurred a few seconds prior.

Unfortunately, the brain often receives *conflicting* information during flight, especially information that comes from the eyes and that which comes from the balance mechanism of the ears and bodily feel. Your balance mechanism and bodily feel might tell you that you are turning, but your eyes will tell you that the wings are level.

Try to resolve conflicting information.

Good instrument training will ensure that you trust your eyes and what the instruments tell you over and above the other information. If, however, the situation is not so simple, say flying in cloud with a toppled attitude indicator or other failed instruments, resolving the conflict may be more difficult, and may lead to some stress.

Excessive Workload

As we have seen in the previous chapter, a high level of demand can adversely affect a person and thereby limit the amount of stimuli that are perceived, as well as limit the degree of attention available to consider the stimulus which is perceived and acted upon. For instance, concentrating on a single task, such as handling an engine malfunction, can lead to neglect of other essential tasks like monitoring the flightpath or responding to radio messages.

Try and avoid mental overload.

The mental overload could be due to an inability to handle the task through lack of knowledge, or because of too much stimulus, with too many items to be perceived, considered and acted upon. Alternatively, the mental overload could be due to lack of time, with too much time pressure to make the decisions required.

Ideally, we need to have sufficient knowledge and skill, and be calm enough and have enough time available, to be able to sit back almost as an observer in all situations and watch our own actions, with enough spare capacity to maintain an overview of the flight. Even in an emergency, we should try to be involved but detached.

Now complete **Exercises 6 – Information Processing.**

Judgement and Decision-Making

Good judgement and the ability to make good and timely decisions are skills that a pilot needs to develop. They can be learned.

Faulty judgement and incorrect decisions or indecisiveness are major causes of aircraft accidents and incidents, rather than poor flying skills. For example, a serious accident is more likely to be caused by a faulty decision to continue visually into poor weather conditions over hazardous terrain rather than by an inability to land the aeroplane.

In some situations the actual decision is not all that important, rather the fact that a decision has been made. Turning either left or right to avoid an obstacle or to fly around a thunderstorm is probably acceptable; not turning, through indecision, is far worse. Similarly, deciding to hold position on a taxiway after having been cleared for an immediate take-off by the tower, due to another aircraft on short final, shows better judgement than going along with the clearance and taking off without being fully prepared.

Learn to make well-judged decisions.

Judgement is the mental process used to make a decision. It can be divided into two extremes:

☐ **Learned skills,** such as landing an aeroplane, where judgement of flare height, rate of descent, and touchdown becomes almost automatic and requires little brain power once learned. This is known as *perceptual* judgement.

☐ **Thinking judgement,** where multiple information has to be assimilated, compared and evaluated, situations have to be responded to, and a series of smaller decisions made en route to an ultimate decision (for instance, whether to continue or to divert, and if so where to). This is a much more complex process involving forming an opinion or conclusion from information presented to the mind. It is a process of risk-analysis and decision-making based on skill, knowledge and experience. It often requires a lot of brain power, and is known as *cognitive* or *thinking* judgement.

There is a range in between the two extremes of semi-automatic skills and thinking judgement. The aim of *training* is to move as many of the situations that initially require a lot of thinking (i.e. requiring *cognitive* or *thinking* judgement) more and more into the learned skill area (or *perceptual* judgement area), so that correct decisions can be made without placing extreme demands on your concentration and thought processes.

Experienced pilots can generally make sound decisions with less difficulty than new pilots, because of their extra exposure to good training and operational experience. It is a lot easier to make a good decision when you have seen the situation before, or have read about similar situations.

As a new pilot, you can look forward to decision-making becoming easier as you gain more experience. Learn from the experience of others by reading widely and listening to other pilots. It is often more comfortable to learn from the experience of others than to make the same mistakes yourself.

When using your judgement, especially if dealing with something that requires serious thinking, you will make use of:

- **your knowledge** (hence the need to keep current with the bookwork);
- **your dedication** to standard operating procedures (SOPs);
- **your understanding** and thinking ability;
- **your practical skills.**

Making a Decision

When making a decision, you need to:

- **recognise relevant information** and evaluate it, comparing it with past events (using your knowledge and experience);
- **separate facts from emotions** and see what the real situation is (rather than what you would like it to be), and identify the problem (if any);
- **consider alternative solutions** taking into account the time available, the aircraft (e.g. fuel situation), the environment (weather, daylight/darkness), and your skill level;
- **balance the risks;** and then
- **make a timely decision.**

Action

Having considered the situation, used your (good) judgement, you then put your thoughts into action. Good judgement and decision-making is valueless if not acted upon.

You need to develop confidence in your ability to judge and decide, and then to act. These skills will develop along with experience. Under-confidence is damaging to decision-making; over-confidence can be dangerous; well-placed confidence is essential! With good training and with good application you can develop well-placed confidence in your ability both to judge and decide, and to act.

Think, decide, then act.

Personality and Attitude

Sound knowledge, a high skill level and experience will help you use your judgement and make good decisions. We must recognise, however, that some deeply in-built characteristics, such as personality and attitudes, play a role in how we think and behave. Some people are cheerful, others are erratic and unstable. Some people are natural extroverts (outgoing, often noisy and confident, and sometimes noisy to cover a lack of confidence), others are introverts (inward looking, often quiet, and perhaps shy).

Both personality types, extroverts and introverts, plus those in between, can make good pilots. Absolute extremes of personality, or an inability to modify behaviour, however, may mean that a person is not suitable to be trained as a pilot.

Some attitudes to avoid are macho show-off behaviour, arrogance, being dogmatic, disrespect for the rules and standard operating procedures, passive resignation and allowing things to just occur, too little respect for others, too much respect for others, complacency and lack of awareness of developing situations ('fat, dumb and happy'), rushed decisions, indecisiveness, over-confidence, or under-confidence.

Some positive attitudes to develop include:

- ☐ **respect for the rules** and standard operating procedures (SOPs);
- ☐ **recognition of your own ability,** especially your ability to handle unusual situations;
- ☐ **an ability to manage the cockpit;**
- ☐ **an ability to manage people;**
- ☐ **calm but timely decision-making;**
- ☐ **an ability to control stress levels;**
- ☐ **an ability to control risk level;**
- ☐ **an adventurous, positive spirit,** but with new tasks approached with careful consideration, risk assessment, and preparation; and
- ☐ **well-placed confidence in yourself.**

Cockpit Resource Management

You, as pilot-in-command, are responsible for the whole flight, and must coordinate the activities associated with your flight. *Cockpit resource management* means using whatever resources are available – and this includes people, equipment and information – to maximise the safety, efficiency and comfort of your flight. Cockpit resource management is often referred to as CRM.

Cockpit resource management in a single-pilot cockpit involves:

- ☐ **a good pre-flight preparation;**
- ☐ **a tidy cockpit** with all equipment possibly required in flight placed in a secure and accessible position;
- ☐ **an orderly approach** to the whole operation, with standard operating procedures being followed in an unhurried but efficient manner;
- ☐ **situational awareness** at all times (position and weather);
- ☐ **time awareness;**
- ☐ **a setting of priorities,** with vital tasks being performed and monitored ahead of less important tasks (for instance, regular monitoring of the flightpath, main instruments, and main systems such as fuel should occur even when other tasks have to be performed);
- ☐ **using all the information** and resources available to you when necessary;
- ☐ **stress management** (avoid becoming overloaded);
- ☐ **risk management** (making well-judged decisions such as whether to continue into doubtful weather or to divert);
- ☐ **well-placed confidence** in your own ability; and
- ☐ **maintaining a good overview** of the flight and managing its progress.

Cockpit resource management involves two-way communication with others, be they fellow crew members, air traffic controllers, flight service staff, a maintenance engineer, or your flight instructor.

Crew Coordination

Crew coordination is the term used to describe the organisation and distribution of tasks associated with a particular flight in a multi-crew cockpit environment.

In a two-pilot cockpit, the tasks should be systematically organised and distributed so that one pilot has the primary task of handling the aircraft, this person being known as the *pilot flying* or PF, supported and monitored by the *pilot not flying* or PNF. The systematic organisation tasks and distribution of duties between the PF and PNF will be found in the Operations Manual of the organisation operating the aeroplane, but the success of the flight will be determined mainly by the strength of leadership exerted by the pilot-in-command, and by adherence to standard operating procedures (SOPs).

Make good use of your crew.

Each person's duties should be clearly defined either by the standard operating procedures, or by the pilot-in-command, with the workload being fairly evenly divided. There must be systematic cooperation between the PF and PNF, with an open flow of information in both directions. The tasks being performed by one must be monitored by the other, in both normal and abnormal situations. Vital tasks, such as the performance of checklists, are usually performed together.

In a single-pilot cockpit, the abilities of a passenger, especially if the passenger happens to be a pilot also, can sometimes be used. Handling the radio and the navigation charts could easily be delegated to such a person, provided the pilot-in-command monitors everything and keeps firm control of the situation.

Make good use of other human resources.

Crew coordination should be used in ground operations as well. The captain can make good use of the many resources available, such as briefing officers, maintenance engineers, refuellers and ground staff. You can make best use of these resources by first of all knowing your own tasks thoroughly and knowing what you want. Having established in your own mind what you want, then request it from the appropriate person in a professional manner. This usually produces the desired result.

The *crew coordination concept* is sometimes referred to as '*ccc*'.

Leadership Qualities

The pilot in a multi-crew cockpit must have leadership skills if the operation is to function safely and efficiently. A good leader will be:

- self-confident;
- understanding of others;
- able to communicate;
- able to listen to the opinion of others and accept their input;
- able to separate facts from emotions;
- able to impart views and opinions clearly;
- able to persuade;
- able to give good briefings;
- able to manage a team, on both technical and emotional levels;
- able to show good judgement and make good decisions that the rest of the team will agree with (or at least accept);
- able to breed confidence in others and enable them to learn and develop;
- able to delegate tasks and responsibilities, but cross-check task performance and accept ultimate responsibility;
- able to set priorities;
- able to maintain a good overview of the flight and manage it to a successful conclusion;
- able to fly well according to standard operating procedures;
- able to show flair and an ability to deal with non-standard and unusual situations (this comes with experience); and
- able to handle him/herself socially.

Leadership Style

When leading a team to accomplish a task, there can be a variation in emphasis between:

☐ **total task orientation,** where completing the task at all costs occurs without regard to the human aspects of the team; and

☐ **total people orientation,** where keeping everybody happy takes precedence over completing the task safely and efficiently.

The ideal leader will encompass both aspects in completing the task safely and efficiently, but in a manner that involves the team and takes advantage of their input and skills. This person will be a captain that is respected and liked by the crew.

Manage both the task and the people.

The totally *task-oriented* captain will be seen as a good pilot (possibly), but as a poor captain. He or she may even be viewed as a bit of a tyrant.

The totally *person-oriented* captain may be seen as weak. Aeroplanes cannot be run by committees. Even though a contribution from team members is required, someone has to make the final decision, and within a suitable time frame. In emergency situations especially, this decision-making person is usually the captain (or should be). The totally person-oriented captain may be well liked – until the time for tough decision-making comes and he is found to be indecisive or weak, or makes serious mistakes.

The captain who is neither task-oriented nor person-oriented will be avoided by all. Such an unmotivated person has no place in a cockpit.

You can become a good captain. By gaining the required skills, which can all be learned, and displaying the leadership qualities listed earlier, you can train yourself to be a good leader – one who encourages confidence, looks like a leader, and is a leader. Being a good captain is also closely linked to being a good person in other aspects of your life.

Develop leadership skills.

Who is in Control?

As pilot-in-command, you must always be in command, even if you have delegated flying duties to a second pilot. Even in a single-pilot cockpit, the problem of who is in command can arise, especially if the pilot acts in a passive manner and allows others to make decisions for him. Domineering and demanding crew members or passengers can sometimes be a problem, and occasionally the pilot-in-command has to exert authority.

Unsatisfactory clearances from ATC (such as: "cleared immediate take-off" before you are fully ready, or a VFR clearance that would take you into cloud) must be rejected with confidence; this will be understood and accepted by ATC. The student pilot must learn what the role of *pilot-in-command* is, and how to act in this capacity.

The Pilot-in-Command

Be in command.

The role of the pilot-in-command is indeed to **be in command.** This means being in control of the whole situation as well as being responsible for the smooth and professional handling of the aircraft. It is as much a task of management as of physically flying the aircraft.

You should **know your aircraft well,** and know how to operate it efficiently according to the laid-down standard operating procedures. You should **plan each flight thoroughly,** and **be well rested** prior to flight.

Arrive early for each flight if possible and plan at a professional pace, making use of the resources available. **Do not allow distractions** to interfere unduly with your planning. This may mean a polite "I am busy right now. I will talk with you shortly."

The pilot-in-command is in command.

Establish your command role on the ground prior to flight. Often your passengers will be people who have a 'senior' position to you in normal life, such as a parent, or the chief of your airline or flying school, but when it comes to achieving a sound and safe flight, you have to be in command. You can do this in a polite manner at the flight planning stage, or even earlier such as on the drive to airport, by acting in a professional manner and setting the pace so that the flight can depart on time.

After planning the flight, you will then probably need to **organise and supervise** the refuelling of the aeroplane, and then the loading of the baggage and **embarkation of the passengers.** An efficient preparation of the aeroplane for flight and clear communication with mechanics, ground staff and other crew will give everyone a feeling of confidence.

Do not allow your walk-around check to be unnecessarily interrupted, since an overlooked control lock, missing fuel cap, or chocks that have not been removed can have unpleasant, embarrassing, or even fatal consequences. Be aware of exactly where you are, what it is you are looking at, and how it should look.

Organise the loading efficiently, according to weight-and-balance requirements, with heavy articles tied down. Organise your equipment in the cockpit so that everything necessary is at hand. Make your passengers comfortable, and **carry out any required briefings** (seat-belts, route of flight, etc.). Doing this prior to start-up shows good airmanship.

Often you will have a passenger with an interest in flying, or who might even be a qualified pilot, and who questions you continuously about aeroplane characteristics, new equipment, navigation procedures, etc., which can distract you from vital tasks. It is good to satisfy a passenger of course, but there are times when you need to say "I really need to concentrate now", or "The workload will increase shortly, so we will finish this conversation later." Passengers, including other pilots, respect this strength of command which does not allow you to be carried along by others who are not in command.

Make your radio calls professionally and with an air of authority (which should be genuine and not just acting). **Handle the aeroplane smoothly and also with authority,** both on the ground and in the air.

If you wish to distribute some tasks to others, then do so in a sensible manner, and retain control of the situation by providing clear guidance and then monitoring the actions. Do not allow any confusion to be present in the cockpit. If a second pilot is assisting by operating the radios or some of the controls, such as the flap control or the undercarriage (or landing gear) lever, then be especially careful.

Informal assistance without overall control from the pilot-in-command can be dangerous. Do not allow uncalled-for assistance, even from a more experienced pilot, as it may interfere with your operation and how you want to run it. This is not to say that you should not listen to advice as part of a normal learning process, but as pilot-in-command you must **set the pace.** In a training situation the situation is a little different, since you will normally have to defer to your flying instructor, but even then, you should think independently and express any difference of opinion.

Remember that your flying instructor is training you to be a pilot-in-command. In fact, even in a two-pilot cockpit with both pilots fully trained and operating as a team, they should be thinking independently and informing each other of any differences of opinion. When flying with a more-experienced pilot who, in your opinion, has chosen a course of action that might endanger the aircraft, *always* express your doubts! In a two-crew cockpit, always be certain who has physical control of the flightpath of the aeroplane by using the phrases "I have control" and "You have control" appropriately.

Remaining in Command

To stay in total command of the flight, you must ensure that you do not get into situations for which you are not prepared or trained for, or for which the aeroplane is not equipped (such as night flight, or instrument flight). You should know your own limitations and capability, and you should assess the expected workload on this basis.

You should be able to operate safely right up to the point where the workload meets your capability, but if the workload exceeds your capability at any time, due to increased workload or to diminished capability, then you are a candidate for an incident or an accident. If you feel that the workload at any point in the

Know your limits.

flight could exceed your current capability, then do not perform the flight. Say "No."

For instance, the workload associated with normal take-offs and landings at your home airport has always been well within your capability, but today you feel tired (diminished capability) and there is a gusty crosswind (increased workload). In this situation, you need to make a rational *go/no-go* decision. This could be the most important decision of the whole flight.

Keep in practice.

Sometimes the workload imposed by individual items are within your current capability, but a combination of factors (such as an unfamiliar airport, a radio communications failure, and difficult weather conditions including rain and a gusty crosswind) might add up to a total workload beyond your capability. Be prepared for this by keeping yourself current so as to maintain a high capability, which will enable you to keep something in reserve for emergencies.

The best advice for a new pilot is:
- **gain the knowledge** and learn the skills to be a good pilot;
- **have well-placed confidence** in yourself;
- **know your limitations** and the limitations of the aeroplane;
- **exert command** over your flight from the planning stage to the signing-off stage; and
- **approach each and every flight** with total professionalism.

*Now complete **Exercises 7 – Judgement and Decision-Making.***

The Flight Deck

Ergonomics and Flight Deck Design

A visit to the flight deck of any recently designed aeroplane will convince you that cockpit design is an improving art. Beautiful instrumentation, well-designed and well-positioned controls, good lighting, and comfortable seats, are a vast improvement over earlier cockpits – at least in most cases. As with all things, there is still room for improvement.

Cockpits are usually at the front of the aeroplane, with large windscreens to give the pilots a good view of the surrounding environment. In some aircraft, the pilots sit a little back from the nose – for instance, in the *Boeing 747* where the pilots up on the flight deck actually have passengers on the lower deck ahead of them. The *Tiger Moth* is flown solo from the rear cockpit for weight and balance reasons, creating vision problems during the flare for a three-point landing, and during taxiing.

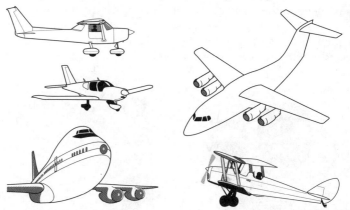

■ *Figure 8-1* **Most cockpits are at the front, but not all**

Early Cockpits

Some early cockpits were draughty, smelly places, often with poor forward vision and poor internal lighting. Instruments were spread around the panel in a haphazard and cluttered manner, placed wherever there happened to be space, often in different places in different aeroplanes of the same fleet, and often widely displaced from their associated control. Some displays were so small, or poorly lit, or poorly placed, as to be almost impossible for the pilot to read.

Many aircraft currently used in general aviation training have a design that is over twenty years old. These designs, despite some limitations, have served their purpose very well, and continue to do so. They were certainly a big step forward in their time, and brought safer aviation to ordinary people. Many of these aircraft have been modified to accommodate newer and better instrumentation, and do operate quite efficiently in the modern aviation environment.

The Pilot and the Machine

The pilot and the aircraft form a very important combination that depends on a good pilot, good controls and good cockpit displays. The pilot–aircraft combination is a *closed-loop* system, in that the pilot makes a control movement, observes the effect as displayed on the instruments (or through the windscreen), decides if the response is what is desired, and then makes further control inputs to bring the *actual* even closer to the *desired*. It is a closed loop of: *pilot–control–display–pilot* repeated again and again.

The pilot and aircraft form a closed loop.

When controlling the aircraft, you, the pilot, decide where you want it to go and then manipulate the flight controls to achieve this desired flightpath. You then observe the effect of the control movement on the flightpath by reference to the instruments and/ or the outside environment. Next, you decide if any further action is needed – any *fine-tuning* – and then make further movements on the controls, check their effect, etc., etc.

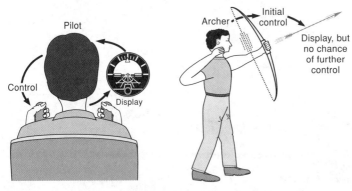

■ *Figure 8-2* **A closed-loop system; an open-loop system**

Good pilots have the skills to make the closed-loop system work so quickly that flightpath and airspeed, for instance, are kept within tight limits. For beginning pilots, however, the closed-loop may take a little longer to operate, and so flightpath and airspeed are not controlled as tightly (but will be with practice and determination!).

Another example of a closed-loop system is a radio-controlled glider which the operator can control from the ground. A glider *without* radio controls, however, is out of the control of the operator once the glider is launched. There is no means of altering its flightpath, even though the glider is visible to the observer. In this case, the loop is not closed. Similarly, an archer has no further control over the path of an arrow once it has left the bow, even though it is apparent where the arrow is going.

There are many closed loops in the cockpit – for instance, when controlling cabin temperature, the pilot adjusts the control then checks the cabin temperature gauge; or when adjusting the cockpit lights at night, the pilot dims them and then sees charts are readable, then makes further adjustments if necessary. Action, feedback, and further action is a continual process in the cockpit.

In automatic flight, the pilot shares the tasks with the automatics to a certain extent, but there are further closed loops in this relationship, since the performance of the automatics must be monitored.

Designing the Work Space of the Flight Deck

In designing the cockpit or flight deck, account has to be taken of the limited space available, the size of the pilots, their need to reach and operate the controls, their need to see both the internal displays and the external environment, preferably while strapped into a comfortable seat.

Good ergonomics is important in aircraft design.

Improving the efficiency of people in their work place is called **ergonomics,** from the Greek words *ergon* meaning work and *nomos* meaning natural law. In aviation, the term ergonomics refers to cockpit design and the improvement of the pilot–machine interface, taking into account human factors such as expected human behaviour and performance which, as we all know, is a variable – not only between people, but also within the one individual at different times.

The cockpit or flight deck has to be designed to cater for us human beings, allowing for our foibles and weaknesses, and encouraging us to operate safely and efficiently. The first thing a well-designed cockpit has to provide a pilot with is a good view.

The Design Eye Position

Adjust your seat properly.

The pilot needs to be seated with the eyes in a position so that, with as little head movement as possible, there is:

- ☐ an unobstructed view of the **main instruments** in the cockpit; and
- ☐ a good view of the **outside environment,** not only the general area ahead for traffic avoidance reasons, but especially the area forward and down from the nose to assist in judging the final stages of the approach and landing.

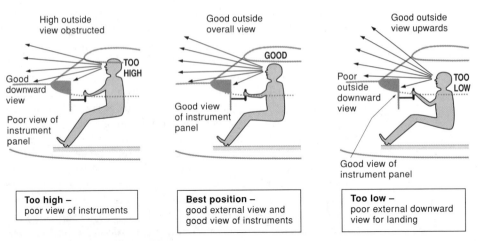

Too high –
poor view of instruments

Best position –
good external view and
good view of instruments

Too low –
poor external downward
view for landing

■ Figure 8-3 **Sitting too high, just right, and too low**

Pilots Come in All Shapes and Sizes

Having determined the design eye position for the pilots who are going to fly the aeroplane, the designer now needs to plan other aspects of the cockpit or flight deck, and this will depend to a large extent on the size of the pilots.

People vary a lot in size and shape, with some very short people in a given population and some extremely tall people, but with most of us somewhere in the middle. Race and gender are also significant, with the average Japanese female likely to be shorter than the average European male. The task of the flight deck designer would be complicated if it was necessary to cater for 100% of the population, and it is generally accepted that the small number in the 5% at either end of the size-and-shape range may be neglected. The designer therefore plans for those who lie in the range from 5% to 95% of the population.

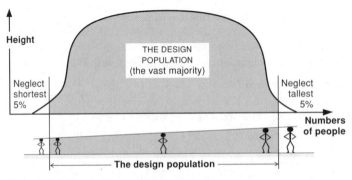

■ Figure 8-4 **The design population**

Seat Design

The seat should be able to be positioned fore and aft, up and down, and the backrest tilted if desired, so that the design criteria for operating the aeroplane are achieved: the eyes in the design eye position, and all vital controls within reach and capable of being moved to the full extent of their travel without undue stretching by the pilot.

Adjust your seat, and lock it.

The seat, having been designed to be moved and altered in shape to suit a wide range of pilots, must then be capable of being locked into position so that it cannot move in flight. Some accidents have occurred as a result of the pilot seat slipping back on its rails during the take-off acceleration – the tendency is for the pilot to pull himself forward again using the control column, perhaps causing the aeroplane to become airborne prematurely with the pilot in no position to control it. You should **check that the seat is securely locked** prior to every take-off and landing.

Adjust the rudder pedals.

With the seat adjusted so that your eyes are in the design eye position, you should now adjust the rudder pedals. You can do this while parked, but you may not be able to check full left and full right movement until taxiing, since in many aircraft moving the rudder pedals not only moves the rudder but also the nosewheel. The control column should be checked for full movement to ensure that it will not strike your knees or stomach. In some aircraft, other controls may also have to be positioned – for instance, a control column that may have to be swung over from right seat to left seat, or moved forward or back, although this is rare.

The Seat-Belt

The harness or seat-belt is a major protector of the pilot in turbulence, during aerobatic manoeuvres, or in an emergency, such as during heavy braking or (and let us make sure that it never happens) during an impact with the ground or some other object.

There are different seat-belt designs, but for any of them to be effective they must be fastened correctly. The simplest is a lap belt, often used for airline passengers, where the belt should be fastened firmly over the hips with the buckle kept away from the soft abdomen if possible, so that bone structure and not soft body parts carry the strain. The belt should be flat and not twisted, so that it will not cut into the body under the pressure of deceleration or turbulence.

Fasten your seat belt.

Many light aircraft have a lap belt for the occupants of the pilot seats, with an inertial reel shoulder strap that comes across one shoulder and fastens into the buckle, which should be positioned to the side of the hip and not over the soft abdomen. The inertial reel allows the pilot to lean forward under normal conditions, but under conditions of rapid acceleration or deceleration, such as in turbulence, the shoulder strap locks and holds the upper body of the pilot very firmly in position. Usually pilots lock the shoulder strap before commencing aerobatics or before entering unavoidable areas of known turbulence. You should test the inertial reel prior to use by pulling sharply on the shoulder strap and checking that it locks.

Larger aircraft usually have lap belts for the pilots, with a groin belt to hold the lap belt down and also to prevent the pilot from slipping under the lap belt, plus an inertial reel shoulder harness over each shoulder. During turbulence the shoulder strap can be locked. It is common during normal cruise in smooth flying conditions to remove the shoulder harness, but to have it fastened during take-off and climb-out, and during descent, approach and landing.

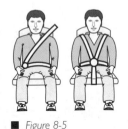

■ *Figure 8-5*
Seat-belt designs

Checks of seat-belts in the cockpit should include:
☐ **belts attached securely** to aircraft structure;
☐ **no fraying** or chemical attack on the belt, as this will weaken it;
☐ **inertial reel locks** when tugged;
☐ **no twisting** of the belt, to prevent it to cutting into the body;
☐ **belt fastened,** with buckle correctly positioned.

Remember to check that your passengers have their seat-belts fastened during take-off and landing, and whenever you expect turbulence. Use the seat-belt sign if you have one, or inform them verbally.

Design of the Controls

The cockpit contains many controls, such as the flight controls which are manipulated by the pilot to control the flightpath of the aeroplane, the engine controls, the flap control, the undercarriage control, the knob to adjust the pressure setting in the subscale window of the altimeter, radio frequency selectors and a transmit button, heating and cooling controls, switches for the electrical system, lighting controls, and many more.

Getting used to the controls can be quite a handful for a beginning pilot or a pilot converting to a new type, but by using a certain degree of standardisation and good design, the task is made somewhat easier. There has to be some flexibility of design available to the aeroplane manufacturer, however, otherwise there would be no progress.

Some general principles of control design for all aeroplanes are:
☐ **controls should be within reach** of the pilots and capable of being moved to their full extent without obstruction or without undue force being required;

- [ ] **controls should be standardised** where possible, so that controls in one aircraft resemble those in another, and are placed in similar positions;
- [ ] **controls for different functions** should be different enough to avoid confusion, so that the throttle is not confused with the propeller pitch control, or the flap lever with the landing gear lever;
- [ ] **controls should be logically designed** and placed, especially when they are to be used simultaneously or sequentially; and
- [ ] **controls should not be prone to failure.**

The Control Column

Most aircraft have a fairly standard control wheel placed centrally in front of the pilot. It is used to manipulate the elevator for pitch control by fore-aft movements, and to manipulate the ailerons for roll control by rotational movements. The standard control wheel is also known as the control column or yoke, and may have additional features in more advanced aircraft as mentioned before, such as a radio transmit button, a trim control, and an autopilot disconnect button.

There are other designs, however, involving totally different shapes such as the ram's horn in the *Concorde,* the joystick in older aeroplanes and some aerobatic aeroplanes, and the sidestick in the *Airbus 320* and *340* placed not directly in front of the pilot, but to the side as its name suggests. The sidestick is not just the province of modern airliners – the *Victa Airtourer* (and later development, the *CT-4*), a light aircraft designed in the 1960s, had a sidestick placed between the two pilots seated side-by-side; however, it was mechanical rather than electronic.

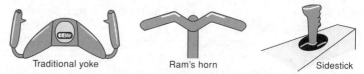

Traditional yoke   Ram's horn   Sidestick

■ *Figure 8-6* ***Some variations in design for the same control***

Converting from one type of control to another as you change aircraft types will take a little time, but is made much easier by the fact that all operate in a logical sense – fore-and-aft for pitch, and sideways or rotation for roll.

The Throttle

The throttle (or throttles, on multi-engined aircraft) controlling engine power, is usually placed forward and to the right of the pilot occupying the captain's seat, which is traditionally on the left.

The throttle is designed so that a forward movement will add power, and a rearward movement will reduce power.

Similarly, on aircraft with a constant-speed propeller, the rpm control (or pitch lever) is moved forward to increase rpm, and rearward to reduce rpm. The idea of moving a control forward for increase, and rearward for decrease, is a general design principle.

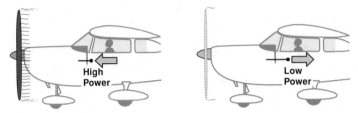

High
Power

Low
Power

■ *Figure 8-7* **Forward to increase, back to reduce**

Other Engine Controls

Aircraft with piston engines and constant-speed propellers have quite a few engine and propeller controls: throttle, propeller rpm (pitch) lever, mixture control, carburettor heat control (or alternate air control, if fuel injected), and cowl flaps control. On the four-engined *DC-4* (now rare), this meant 20 levers, plus an assortment of fuel control and fire switches.

It would be nice if there was an industry standard with respect to relative position of the engine controls, but unfortunately there is not, and sometimes you will find the rpm levers to the left of the throttles, and sometimes to the right. You must become very familiar with the control positions in any new aeroplane that you fly. On modern jets, an engine that is running is controlled by the throttle alone – much easier!

Fuel Tank Controls

Fuel tank switching has a notorious history, with many engines having stopped through fuel starvation while there was still plenty of fuel remaining. Faulty switching is often a result of poor design, and if you look at a variety of light aircraft you are sure to see a variety of fuel tank switches. Some aircraft have all tanks in use at the one time, others have left, then right, some have all tanks off with the switch forward, others with it aft. Always make sure that you know how yours works, as you may have to reach down and operate it at a stressful time in a darkened cockpit while you are trying to control the aeroplane.

Know your fuel system.

It is good airmanship to check that the fuel distribution system is indeed working correctly before setting out over an ocean where fuel from various tanks might be required. If an engine on a twin fails, the aeroplane will slowly go out of lateral balance limits unless cross-feeding from the tanks occurs. Fuel starvation could eventually be the result, even though the tank in the opposite wing contains fuel.

■ *Figure 8-8* **Different designs of fuel tank switches**

Control Functions and Differentiation

Controls used for associated functions should be grouped together – for instance, the engine controls (throttle and pitch lever) should be near each other, but in an unambiguous manner that does not lead to confusion as to which control is which. Associated instruments should be nearby and, where possible, aligned with the control.

If certain controls are used for associated but different functions, and especially if they are located near each other, they need to be differentiated one from the other as much as possible. For instance, the throttle must look and feel different from the pitch lever, as must the mixture control and the carburettor heat control. This differentiation can be designed into the controls by using different shapes and different textured-surfaces (to provide a different feel), and different colours (but this may not be all that effective, especially at night). Throttles often have a rounded black knob, propeller pitch controls are often blue, mixture controls are often red, and carburettor heat controls are often white.

Know your cockpit.

Two controls that have been frequently misused by pilots in the past are the landing gear lever and the flap lever – a 'pilot error' to be sure, but one induced by poor design. In some older aircraft, the two controls were of similar shape and size, placed side by side, with the different colours not seeming to help fatigued pilots in darkened cockpits late at night.

Raising the flaps in flight immediately after take-off (reducing lift) instead of raising the landing gear (thereby retaining high drag instead of reducing it) sometimes had disastrous consequences. An unexpected loss of lift instead of an expected reduction in drag is not conducive to a safe climb-out. There were also embarrassing moments on the ground following a successful landing when the pilots retracted the landing gear instead of the flaps.

In more modern aircraft, the flap lever and the undercarriage lever are easily distinguishable, and are not placed side by side. The undercarriage (or 'gear', for landing gear) lever has a knob that resembles a wheel, and is moved up or down; the flap lever has a knob that resembles a flap, and may be moved through a series of slots to select the desired flap position.

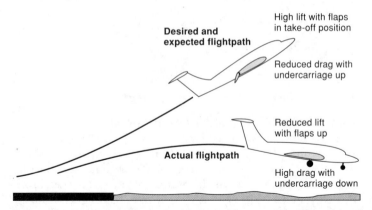

■ *Figure 8-9* **Results of poor design leading pilots to misuse controls**

The use of logically associated symbols – such as a wheel for the undercarriage – both in controls and on displays, can help a pilot significantly.

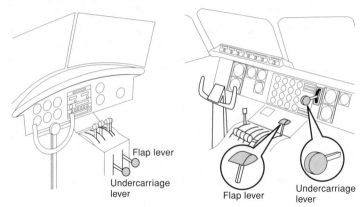

■ *Figure 8-10* **Design – the old and the new**

NOTE Be very vigilant if flying a mixture of different aircraft that you do not confuse the controls of one with the controls of another. Some pilots fly several types on the one day.

Some cockpits are well designed to enable a pilot, having a limited number of hands and feet, to perform more than one function simultaneously. The rudder pedals, for instance, allow the pilot to move both the rudder and the nosewheel, and apply differential braking. Some advanced yokes, as well as controlling movement of the elevator and ailerons, allow a pilot (still using only the one hand) to operate the elevator trim control, a radio transmit button, or the autopilot disconnect button.

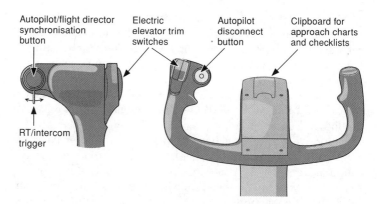

Autopilot/flight director synchronisation button

Electric elevator trim switches

Autopilot disconnect button

Clipboard for approach charts and checklists

RT/intercom trigger

■ *Figure 8-11* **Simultaneous operation of various controls made easier by good design**

Design of Cockpit Displays

The function of cockpit displays (or instruments) is to pass information to the pilot. This information needs to be presented in a clear, unambiguous manner, where it can be easily seen. A well-designed display needs to be:

- □ **easily seen;**
- □ **placed in a logical position,** ideally near any associated control;
- □ **standardised;**
- □ **reliable,** and not prone to failure, but clearly indicating when it has failed;
- □ **easy to interpret** (and difficult to misinterpret).

These points will now be discussed with reference to flight instruments, engine instruments, and others, with comments on new developments which are helpful to pilots, and which we may soon see in basic training aeroplanes.

NOTE The coverage of cockpit displays includes some detail on more advanced features; whilst these are not examined in Private Pilot *Human Performance and Limitations,* the discussion is not complicated and will be of interest to many newer pilots who may be planning on making their career as professional pilots.

Standardisation of Displays

If particular displays are standardised in design and have a standard position in all cockpits, it helps a pilot. Of course this is not totally desirable if it rules out further development and improvement. We therefore have to expect some variations from the ideal.

The 'Basic-T' Layout of the Flight Instruments

In the old days, instruments were scattered around the cockpit, sometimes in a haphazard manner, as if providing information to the pilot was an afterthought. Critical instruments, such as the attitude indicator (AI), were placed in out-of-the-way positions, difficult to see and well away from associated instruments such as the airspeed indicator (ASI), the altimeter, and the compass or heading indicator (HI).

The basic-T is standard.

It was a big advance when designers decided to arrange the main flight instruments in a standardised pattern, known as the *basic-T* pattern, on the panel in front of each pilot. The aim was to place the very important attitude indicator in a central position, since this is the instrument which pilots spend most time looking at. The other important flight instruments are placed to either side of and beneath the attitude indicator, forming a T-shape. Slightly less important flight instruments are placed diagonally beneath it.

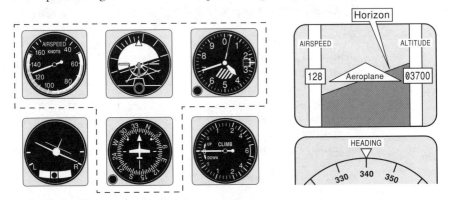

■ *Figure 8-12* **Basic-T – old-style and new-style**

The Attitude Indicator

The attitude indicator (AI) goes under various names including *artificial horizon* (AH) and *attitude direction indicator* (ADI). It is a most important display, since it informs the pilot of pitch attitude and roll attitude relative to the horizon. It should therefore always occupy a central position on the instrument panel. It is an analog (pictorial) display, showing the attitude of the wings and nose of the aeroplane relative to the horizon.

■ *Figure 8-13*
Attitude indicator

Often the sky above the horizon is represented by the colour blue, and the ground beneath the horizon by black or brown. Usually the blue of the sky is above the brown of the earth, indicating that the aeroplane is flying right side up. In a good instrument, the reverse would be the case if the aeroplane was inverted – and this can happen even in airliners, in extreme turbulence or following mishandling.

Less-than-perfect AIs topple when the angle of pitch or bank is too great, but a really good AI would give correct indications even when an aeroplane is in an unusual attitude. Unfortunately, many lives have been lost in the past when pilots have followed AIs that have toppled.

Modern instruments are more reliable, but never forget that indications from one instrument, if doubtful, can usually be confirmed or contradicted by indications from other instruments. Instrument-rated pilots will be familiar with the additional training that goes under the name of *limited panel*, which is necessary to cope with failure, complete or partial, of the primary flight instruments.

The same attitude information that is shown on a standard AI could be presented on a digital (numerical) display, but a pictorial representation of attitude seems to convey the information more efficiently and more quickly to a pilot than just numbers. 'P+3 R25L' is not as informative as a picture of the nose pitched 3° up, indicated by '**Pitch +3**', and the wings banked 25° to the left, indicated by '**Roll 25 left**'.

Analog display   **Digital display**

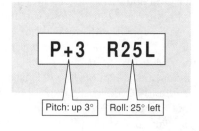

Attitude indicator showing
3° pitch up, 25° left bank

■ *Figure 8-14* **Analog versus digital – which do you prefer?**

Personally, I prefer analog displays, with one exception – the altimeter. There is more to follow on this shortly.

The AI is closely linked to the control column that the pilot uses to change pitch attitude and bank attitude, and so the AI is usually positioned directly in front of it. In normal flight, moving the control column back raises the nose; moving it to the left rolls the aeroplane to the left – movements relative to the horizon that are replicated on the AI. However, there are different AI designs that display the pitch and bank attitudes in quite different ways. It seems that once pilots get used to a certain attitude display, it is quite difficult to train them off it onto another.

On the standard AI, the artificial horizon moves, while the index aircraft remains fixed within the instrument. As the aircraft pitches up, the index aircraft and the AI dial move with it, and the artificial horizon moves down within the instrument to stay aligned (symbolically) with the real horizon. As it rolls from wings-level into a left bank, the index aircraft and the AI dial move with the real aircraft, and the artificial horizon remains horizontal in space and aligned with the real horizon. Bank angle can be determined from the angle that the wings of the model aircraft make with the artificial horizon, or from the bank pointer at the top of the instrument. The AI can be thought of as a porthole through which the attitude of the aircraft in relation to the horizon can be seen.

Know your instruments.

Unfortunately, even within the basic standard design of the AI there are variations. For instance, some designs of bank pointers give a clearer picture than others. Although we are used to a basic standard design of the AI, with its fixed index aircraft and moving artificial horizon, there are AIs in which the artificial horizon remains fixed in the instrument, and the model aircraft moves. This gives the pilot a view of the aircraft's attitude as if standing upright behind it as an observer.

In this instrument, however, the artificial horizon does not remain aligned with the real horizon in a banked turn, nor does the wing of the model aircraft remain aligned with the wing of the real aircraft. This sort of AI is common in Russian-designed aircraft, and the pilots like it. I have recently experienced the difficulties that pilots used to this instrument have had in converting onto standard Western AIs; this is very significant, considering how vital the AI is.

On other AIs, not only the model aeroplane moves, but also the artificial horizon — the index aeroplane moving quickly to indicate the change of attitude, and the horizon moving a little later to indicate the change of flightpath.

Most pilots seem to like the attitude indicator that they were trained on.

The AI is perhaps an instrument which may be replaced in the future, possibly by a predictive flightpath vector. At present, to determine the flightpath you have to integrate in your mind information obtained from the attitude indicator, the altimeter and VSI, the airspeed indicator and the direction (or heading) indicator — quite a task, as instrument trainees know.

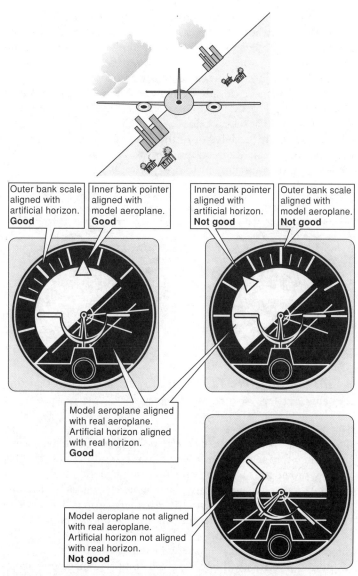

■ Figure 8-15 **Differently designed AIs all displaying a 45-degree banked turn to the right**

Heading Indicators

The modern heading indicator (HI) (also called *direction indicator*, DI, *gyro horizon* or *directional gyro*, DG), which is placed directly beneath the attitude indicator in the basic-T layout, is an easy instrument to interpret and to use instinctively (or intuitively).

It is obvious to most pilots that to change heading from 360° to 340°, and further to 320°, a left turn is required. The desired heading is to the left of the current heading, both in reality and on the HI.

The heading indicator is based on a gyroscope which maintains its direction in space (ideally having been aligned with magnetic north by the pilot), and gives an accurate indication of heading during turns and accelerations.

> *Periodically check the alignment of the HI against the magnetic compass.*

In contrast, the predecessor of the modern HI pictured in Figure 8-16, the original directional gyro (DG), was not an instinctive (or intuitive) instrument to use (Figure 8-17).

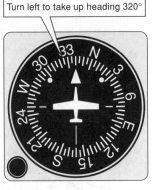

Turn left to take up heading 320°

Turn *left* to take up heading 320°; ... but indication of 320° is *right*

■ *Figure 8-16* **The modern HI is an easy instrument to use**

■ *Figure 8-17* **The older DG display**

The Magnetic Compass

The magnetic compass is the *primary* heading reference in an aeroplane, therefore it is the magnetic compass, and not the HI, that initially provides us with the direction of magnetic north.

Why then do we not just use the magnetic compass for heading information, and do away with the HI? The reason is that, because of its design, the compass has certain indication errors, and also a non-instinctive relationship between its display and the necessary direction of turn to take up a new heading.

Indication errors will occur on the compass during any acceleration, deceleration or turning, with the degree of error being different on different headings, and reversed in the northern hemisphere compared with the southern hemisphere. Instrument pilots know the frustration of having to apply "undershoot when turning through north, overshoot when turning through south", by greater amounts at higher latitudes compared with lower latitudes near the equator, and then totally reversed when in the southern hemisphere. As if the pilot did not have enough to think about!

■ *Figure 8-18*
**The magnetic
compass has a non-
instinctive display**

The non-instinctive display of the magnetic compass derives from its construction, and the fact that the pilot is really viewing the compass card from behind, and not from ahead or above. The card remains oriented in space, and the pilot moves the aeroplane around it, the pilot's view being confined to viewing the most rearward face of the compass card.

On heading 360°, 340° will be to its *right* on the compass card, even though a *left* turn is required to take up heading 340°. This requires some thinking activity from the pilot if the intention is to turn in the correct direction – brain time that could perhaps be used on other problems.

Mental gymnastics are required from the pilot if wanting to turn in the correct direction (due to the non-instinctive display), and then roll out exactly on the correct heading (having allowed for turning errors during and shortly after the turn). For this reason, the usual technique of using the direction instruments is to:

☐ **allow the magnetic compass to settle down** in steady straight-and-level flight; then

☐ **align the HI with it,** and adjust heading according to the HI.

Modern instruments on some aircraft have heading indicators that *automatically* align with magnetic north, but in *all* aircraft, including the most sophisticated modern airliners, you will find an old-fashioned magnetic compass as a standby – it needs no power other than the earth's magnetic field, and has few moving parts that can fail.

Even though it is a simple instrument, the magnetic compass is difficult to use well, and pilots used to flying on the most modern glass instruments need practice to use the old, but faithful, magnetic compass (the same could be said of the practice needed to use the simple ADF well).

The Airspeed Indicator

Aerodynamic performance depends on indicated airspeed.

The airspeed indicator (ASI) displays the very important aerodynamic quantity *indicated airspeed* (IAS), upon which the flying capability of all aeroplanes depends. The pilot often needs to check IAS with a quick glance – for instance, when on approach to land – the indication must be clear and unambiguous.

Traditionally, IAS has been displayed on a circular dial, with the pointer moving clockwise to indicate an increasing airspeed, and anticlockwise to indicate a decreasing airspeed. Colour codes for various limiting airspeeds, such as maximum operating speed, stall speeds, and flap speed, are shown on the ASI, but only for maximum weight.

Some older ASIs may be graduated in mph or km/hr instead of the usual knots – always check this when flying a new aeroplane.

Flying at 80 km/hr (50 knots) because you are used to seeing 80 knots in your familiar aeroplane could be dangerous.

Recent advances with 'glass' instruments (i.e. on small TV-like screens) have made it possible to display airspeed on a vertically oriented *speed tape* that moves behind a fixed pointer. Limiting speeds and advisory speeds can be shown on the electronic tape for the actual weight and configuration, such as flap limit speed, stall speed, and buffet boundary.

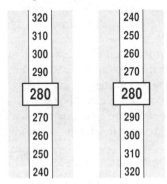 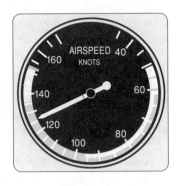

■ *Figure 8-19* **Two designs of the speed tape, plus a traditional ASI**

There is a design choice to be made with regard to the speed tape: should the high speeds be at the top of the tape (as would be traditional), or should the high speeds be at the bottom of the tape, encouraging a pilot to lower the nose of the aircraft to increase speed? Both designs are in use, even though a common standard would be preferable. It seems that pilots get used to the speed tape that they use consistently. Some older pilots even admit to referring to the traditional airspeed indicator that is often included in modern aircraft as a standby, and neglecting the tape.

A disadvantage of the speed tape is that the whole speed range is not always in view, but a compromise can be achieved in the glass cockpit by having vital speeds that are out of range printed above or below the tape until they come into view – for instance, the 'V$_2$' safety speed that is set for take-off by the pilot.

The Altimeter

The altimeter is a vital instrument, and misuse of it, by failing to set the correct pressure setting in the subscale or, more commonly, by failing to read its indications accurately, has led to many tragic accidents.

Setting Mean Sea Level Pressure (QNH)

With the current QNH pressure setting on the subscale, the altimeter reads altitude, the height above sea level (at least approximately). QNH is therefore the correct setting when operating at low altitudes where terrain could be a problem. It is set for take-off and landing, and when operating below what is called the transition altitude.

The mean sea level pressure varies from place to place, and from hour to hour, as pressure patterns move across the earth, so a pilot has to be aware of the current value of QNH, and have it set in the subscale, for the altimeter to provide good information.

Flying above the transition altitude, the standard pressure 1013.2 millibars (or hectopascals, hPa) – (or 29.92 inches of mercury in the USA) is set on the subscale (on the assumption that terrain is no longer a problem). Aircraft operating in the same airspace, however, need to have the same altimeter pressure setting to ensure vertical separation from one another. The level at which this change in pressure setting is made varies from country to country (3,000 feet at most UK aerodromes; 18,000 feet in the USA; 10,000 feet in Australia). Unless pilots are orderly and carry out consistent cross-checks, the wrong pressure can sometimes be set on the altimeter subscale, significantly reducing air safety for themselves and others.

In Figure 8-20, one pilot has 1013 mb set and is flying so that 11,000 feet (Flight Level 110) is indicated on the altimeter. The other pilot has mistakenly set 990 mb instead of 1013 mb, and is flying with 10,000 feet indicated on the altimeter. With 990 mb set instead of 1013 mb, this mistake of 23 mb will translate into a height indication error of 23 × 30 = 690 feet. He is 10,000 feet above the 990 mb pressure level, which means he is 10,690 feet above the 1013 mb pressure level. He *thinks* he is 1,000 feet below the first aircraft, but in fact is only 310 feet lower. This is a dangerous situation for both aircraft, and for the people on the ground beneath them!

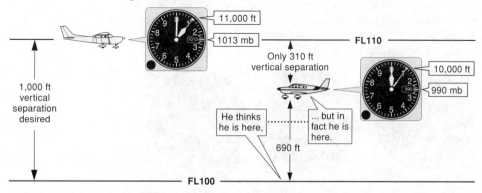

■ Figure 8-20 **Vertical separation compromised by an incorrectly set altimeter**

Flying a precision instrument approach to a decision height of 200 feet above ground level (agl) when the altimeter pressure window has not been reset from standard pressure 1013 to the current QNH could be lethal. If the QNH was in fact 1006, but this value had not been set in the pressure window, the altimeter would indicate 210 feet agl when in fact the aeroplane was **at** ground level (assuming 1 mb to be equivalent to 30 feet).

A pilot not becoming visual before reaching what is expected to be the decision height of 200 feet agl would most likely make unexpected contact with the ground. This potential for serious error must be addressed by each pilot, who must maintain adequate discipline and ensure that standard operating procedures are followed and checklists completed.

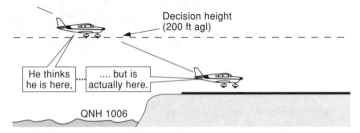

■ Figure 8-21 **Flying an ILS with an incorrect QNH set is dangerous**

Another aspect of the altimeter that can trap a pilot is caused by poor design on some instruments. We expect that clockwise rotation of a knob will bring an *increase* in the subscale reading, and that the scale bearing the pressure-setting numbers will move in the same direction as the nearest part of the knob. This is not the case for all altimeters – on some, a clockwise rotation of the knob brings a *decrease* in the pressure setting, something that many of us would consider a design weakness. Check your altimeter, and always check and recheck that you have the correct pressure setting for your current stage of flight.

■ Figure 8-22 **Good and poor designs for the altimeter subscale and setting knob**

There has not been an altimeter designed that can automatically set the pressure subscale to 1013, or to current QNH, because of all the variations, but there are some devices that can help avoid altitude problems, such as:

☐ **the altitude alert system,** a light or sound that activates as you approach or depart a selected altitude, and that helps prevent incorrect altitudes being flown;

☐ **the radar altimeter,** or radio altimeter, and the associated *ground proximity warning system* (GPWS), that warn of impending ground contact;

☐ **the traffic alert and collision avoidance system (TCAS),** that shows potential conflicting traffic on your map display.

Reading or Misreading the Altimeter

Misreading the altimeter has led to many fatal accidents. Why should such a simple instrument as the altimeter be so dangerous? There is no doubt that the traditional three-pointer altimeter, whilst it works well technically, is often difficult to read correctly. Accidents caused by misreading it could be judged, at least to some extent, to be *design-induced errors*, even though the human pilot made the final mistake.

One safety magazine, in an attempt to improve the performance of pilots, showed a series of photographs of three-pointer altimeters, and challenged pilots to read them all correctly – and remember, just *one* mistake could be fatal! The pilot performance was not all that good, but the truly disturbing feature was that when the answers were published in the next issue of the magazine, some of them were wrong and had to be corrected. And these were answers that were prepared by people sitting in cosy offices and not in the cockpit of an aeroplane in flight. This is an indictment of the three-pointer altimeter!

Many errors have occurred with the 10,000-foot pointer – the altitude being misread by 10,000 feet or more – making it a particularly dangerous instrument for high-flying pilots descending in cloud or at night.

Know your instruments.

Some pilots have hit the ground at 3,000 feet when they thought that their altimeter was reading 13,000 feet – the altimeter was in fact reading 3,000 feet – they just did not know how to read it. It cannot be emphasised too much that any pilot who uses a three-pointer altimeter must really know how to use it – know which is the 10,000-foot pointer, which is the 1,000-foot pointer, and which is the 100-foot pointer – it is not obvious from the design.

A   B   C

■ Figure 8-23 **Can you read these three-pointer altimeters?**
(Answers shown below.)

NOTE On three-pointer altimeters, to assist pilots to know whether they are above or below 10,000 feet, designers incorporated a small striped sector which appears below the centre of the altimeter when the reading is less than 10,000 feet. This is labelled in Figure 8-24.

Some Better Designs

A *digital* altimeter read-out consisting only of numbers is a possibility. 13,430 feet is quite easy to read, and difficult to misread as 3,430 feet (as has occured with three-pointer *analog* (pictorial) altimeters).

Disadvantages of a pure digital read-out, however, show up when climbing or descending; it is easier to judge the *rate* of altitude change from a moving pointer on an analog altimeter than from a series of changing numbers on a digital read-out. It is also easier to maintain a constant altitude using a pointer and keeping it fixed rather than just by numbers!

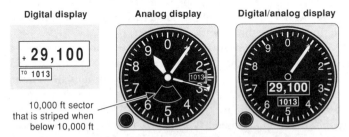

Digital display   Analog display   Digital/analog display

10,000 ft sector
that is striped when
below 10,000 ft

■ Figure 8-24 **The digital, analog, and combined digital/analog**
altimeter displays

A well thought-out design improvement on older style altimeters was to keep the 100-foot pointer, where one complete rotation around the dial equals 1,000 feet, and to replace the 1,000-foot pointer and the 10,000-foot pointer with digits. This retains

Figure 8-23   **Altimeter A** 7,300 feet   **B** 2,900 feet   **C** 11,750 feet

the advantage of the pointer for maintaining altitude or estimating rate of climb or descent, but removes the possibility of misreading altitude by 10,000 feet. This modification has resulted in a successful and easy-to-use instrument.

Instrument design is improving.

It is also possible to have a vertical altitude tape rather than the traditional altimeter dial, and this is often the case in 'glass' cockpits, with higher altitudes towards the top as is logical, and lower altitudes towards the bottom.

Rate-of-change of altitude can be judged by the speed at which the tape is moving behind the index mark (as well as from the VSI, of course), and *actual* altitude can be read from the numbers behind a pointer or displayed in an altitude box.

Important altitudes or flight levels, such as selected cruising level, can be displayed digitally above or below the tape as appropriate until it comes into range.

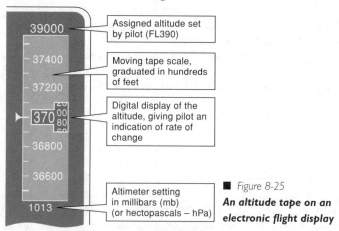

Assigned altitude set by pilot (FL390)

Moving tape scale, graduated in hundreds of feet

Digital display of the altitude, giving pilot an indication of rate of change

Altimeter setting in millibars (mb) (or hectopascals – hPa)

■ *Figure 8-25*
An altitude tape on an electronic flight display

The Vertical Speed Indicator

The typical VSI is an analog display, with a pointer indicating rate of climb or descent against a static scale. On a glass display, the VSI may sometimes be associated with the altitude tape. It is easy to read, and has been a design success.

The traditional VSI is operated by static pressure, but often lags or shows a move initially in the wrong direction when altitude is changed, before settling down and indicating correctly.

A small accelerometer removes the lag in modern instruments, known as the *instantaneous VSI* (IVSI).

■ *Figure 8-26*
Traditional VSI display

Vertical speed indicators in very expensive airliners are operated, not by variations in static pressure, but by vertical accelerations measured by laser gyros.

The Turn Coordinator

The turn indicator in most modern light aircraft shows the wings of an index aeroplane which can move only in a rolling sense, with the nose fixed. Whilst the real aeroplane is rolling into a turn, the wings of the index aeroplane move in the appropriate direction to indicate *rate of roll*.

Once the aeroplane is in a steady turn, the position of the wings indicates the *rate of turn*. The scale is marked with a '1' to indicate a rate-1 turn of 3°/second (360° in 2 minutes), and possibly with a '2' to indicate a rate-2 turn of 6°/second. Rate 1 is usual in instrument flying.

There is also an older instrument, the turn and slip indicator, which uses a 'bat' to indicate rate of turn – it does not indicate rate of roll.

The turn coordinator is an instinctive instrument for a pilot to use. It can be used in a turn to maintain the desired rate of turn – for instance, by keeping the indication on rate 1, and it can be used when straight-and-level to keep the wings of the real aeroplane level by not allowing any roll rate to develop, i.e. by keeping the wings of the turn coordinator's index aeroplane level, while keeping the balance ball centred. Normally, of course, the attitude indicator would be used for this purpose, but (on rare occasions) the AI has been known to fail. In such a situation, the turn coordinator is very useful.

It is very important not to confuse the index aeroplane of the turn coordinator with the index aeroplane on the typical attitude indicator, which remains fixed while an artificial horizon moves behind it to give an indication of pitch attitude and roll attitude. To remind you of this, many turn coordinators are marked with the words 'no pitch indication', or something along these lines. Having to remind a pilot what the instrument does *not* do is a design weakness – any suggestions?

The coordination ball which is usually found with the turn coordinator is a simple pendulum-type indicator that lets a pilot know if the aeroplane is flying efficiently, with the tail following the nose, or if it is skidding or slipping. If the aeroplane is coordinated, or *balanced,* then the ball is in the centre. If not, it is out to one side, and the pilot can remedy this by applying same-side rudder pressure to centralise the ball.

The coordination ball is a very good and simple instrument, and is found in all aeroplanes, even the largest and most modern. These aeroplanes, however, may not have a turn coordinator, its functions having been taking over to some extent by a *flight director* incorporated into the attitude indicator.

■ *Figure 8-27*
The turn coordinator (top), and the older turn indicator

Know your instruments.

Some instruments are simple and good.

The Flight Director

The flight director (FD), sometimes called the *flight director indicator* (FDI), is a device superimposed over the attitude indicator display to provide the pilot with guidance in pitch and bank attitude. It does not tell the pilot what the pitch and bank attitude is (which is the function of the underlying ADI), but what should be done with pitch and bank attitude to achieve the desired flightpath. It can therefore be used as a *predictive* instrument. By placing the aeroplane in this attitude, you should achieve the desired flightpath.

The flight director receives inputs from various sensors, and integrates them into a simple guidance indication for the pilot. Some features are automatic and the pilot can program some in according to how it is desired to use the flight director. It can also be selected off, so that its symbology disappears from view and the basic attitude indicator remains.

Two typical designs of flight director are:

☐ **flying wings:** the pilot manoeuvres the aeroplane so that the index aeroplane on the ADI is tucked into the flying wings of the flight director; and

☐ **crossbars:** the pilot uses the controls to place the nose of the index aeroplane directly beneath the intersection of the two crossbars.

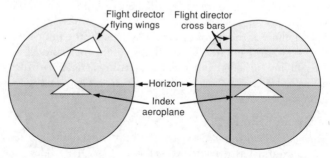

■ *Figure 8-28* **The two types of flight director presentations**

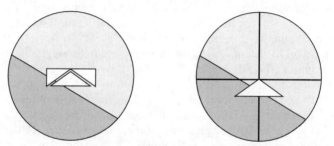

■ *Figure 8-29* **Instrument indications when the pilot has positioned the aeroplane attitude according to the flight director commands**

The flight director commands as shown in Figures 8-28 and 8-29 could be for an entry to a climbing left turn. How the instrument responds to the pilot (or autopilot) control input depends upon its design but, in the typical ADI found in most aeroplanes, the index aeroplane remains fixed in the ADI and the artificial horizon moves to remain aligned with the real horizon outside. The flight director command indicator moves within the instrument and, when the pilot has achieved the commanded pitch and bank attitude, it then overlies the index aeroplane.

The pilot can usually program the flight director indicator to provide many types of commands, as desired, such as:

- **maintain or change heading** (by connecting the flight director to a bug on the direction indicator which the pilot can move);
- **maintain or achieve a selected airspeed** (by connecting the flight director to the airspeed system);
- **maintain altitude,** or achieve a selected rate of climb or descent (by connecting the flight director to the altitude system); and
- **maintain a localizer track and a glideslope** (by linking the flight director to the electronic *instrument landing system,* ILS).

Modern flight directors are so good that a pilot can easily become dependent upon them, but, like everything, they can fail. Many strenuous flight simulator exercises have resulted from the simulated failure of the flight director. As a result, the pilot has to revert to basic instrument attitude flying, using the basic AI and other flight instruments, and the basic radio navigation instruments, instead of relying on the flight director. This is known as flying on *raw data.*

Be prepared to revert to basic instruments.

The ADF and the RMI

The *automatic direction finder* (ADF) is simply a needle that points towards a ground-based *non-directional beacon* (NDB). Older style ADFs have a fixed card to indicate relative bearing to the NDB, such as 30° left of the nose; this meant that a pilot had to use the heading indicator (or magnetic compass) in conjunction with the ADF if wanting to intercept and maintain a particular track to or from an NDB. Mental gymnastics were required, especially in strong winds when drift became a factor.

A major design advance was made when the two instruments, the ADF and the HI, were combined, with the ADF pointer (or pointers in a twin-ADF installation) now placed over a compass card. This instrument is called the *radio magnetic indicator* (RMI). An earlier version has the ADF pointer backed by a manually rotatable card and aligned with the compass or heading indicator.

Combining instruments sometimes improves them.

The RMI combines the
ADF and HI.

Another improvement for the instrument pilot is the ability to select either needle of the RMI to point to a VOR station tuned on the VHF-NAV. This enables the pilot to have a better idea of the position in relation to a VOR without having to alter the course selection on the VOR display itself. The tail of the RMI needle indicates the aircraft's radial from the VOR, irrespective of the aircraft's heading.

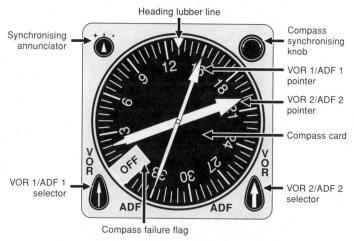

■ *Figure 8-30* **A 'two-needle' radio magnetic indicator**

Two illustrations on page 156 show tracking to an NDB on a simple ADF indicator (Figure 8-32) and on an RMI (Figure 8-33).

The VOR and the HSI

2 dots right of the 062
radial from the tuned
VOR station
(no heading information)

■ *Figure 8-31*
**The early VOR
display, or course
deviation indicator**

The original VOR display that almost every pilot uses shows angular deviation from a selected VOR radial, but it is *not* heading sensitive. If you have the inbound course selected on the *omni bearing selector* (OBS), and you are flying inbound to the radio beacon on a heading close to that track, the course deviation information from the aid is instinctive.

Similarly, if you have an outbound course (known as a *radial*) selected, and you are flying outbound from the beacon on a heading close to that course, the information is again instinctive. If these conditions are not met, the older style VOR, while still being usable, is confusing to a beginner because it is not instinctive, i.e. CDI needle left – so course is left.

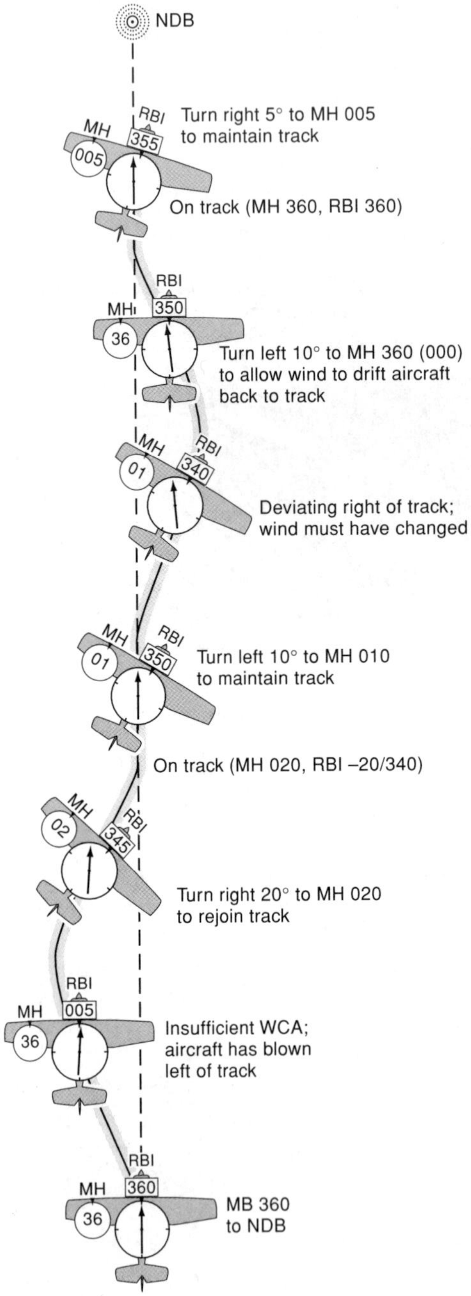

■ *Figure 8-32* **Tracking to an NDB with a fixed-card ADF and HI**

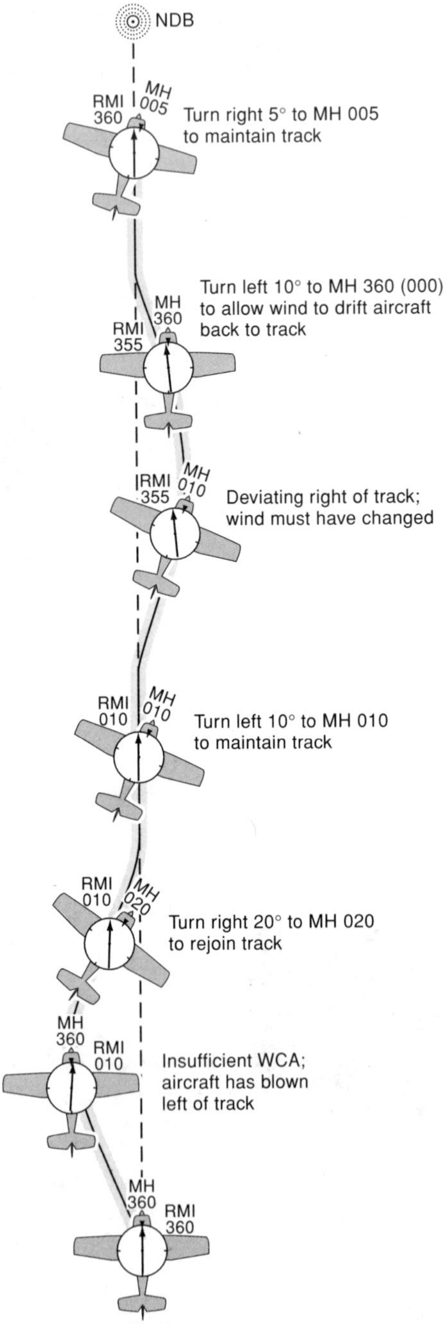

■ *Figure 8-33* **Tracking to an NDB with an RMI**

*The HSI combines the
VOR and HI.*

A big design advance was made when the VOR display was superimposed upon the heading indicator, the new instrument being called a *horizontal situation indicator* (HSI). This means that the VOR display is a command instrument at all times, and the graphic design of the HSI makes it a very good instrument. As well as VORs, you can also select ILSs onto the HSI, and a glide-slope needle will appear as well as the course bar. (When flying an ILS, you also use the marker lights and sounds to check the glide-slope altitude at particular points along the localizer track.)

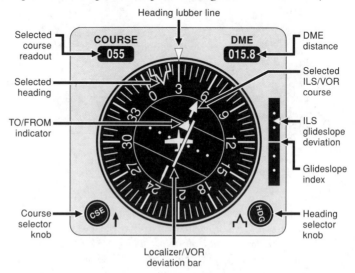

■ *Figure 8-34* **A horizontal situation indicator**

Modern navigation displays in 'glass' cockpits usually can be switched into a VOR or ILS mode for instrument approaches, with the familiar HSI design appearing – proof that it is a design success.

The 'Glass' Navigation Display

Electronic flight instrument systems (EFIS) are usually two small cathode ray tube monitors that display attitude and navigation information.

*Map displays make
visualisation easy.*

The navigation display can be used in various modes, including VOR and ILS, but is generally operated in MAP mode whilst en route. In this mode, it shows the programed route between waypoints in magenta, the track being made good in white (which should overlay the desired route), the heading, and the wind. Some displays are *heading-up* (with the direction of the nose of the aeroplane at the top), others are *track-up* (with the direction of travel relative to the ground at the top).

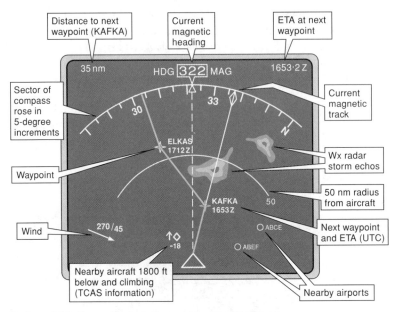

Distance to next waypoint (KAFKA)

Current magnetic heading

ETA at next waypoint

Sector of compass rose in 5-degree increments

Current magnetic track

Waypoint

Wx radar storm echos

50 nm radius from aircraft

Wind

Next waypoint and ETA (UTC)

Nearby aircraft 1800 ft below and climbing (TCAS information)

Nearby airports

■ *Figure 8-35* **Example of an electronic navigation display**

Many other items can be brought up if desired, including nearby adequate airports, VORs, ETAs at waypoints, a weather radar display, and TCAS information (potential collision threats detected by the *traffic alert and collision avoidance system*). Predictions of horizontal (turning) performance and vertical (climb or descent) performance can also be displayed, as shown in Figure 8–36.

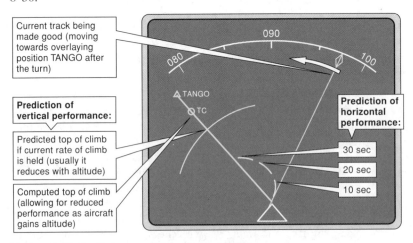

Current track being made good (moving towards overlaying position TANGO after the turn)

Prediction of vertical performance:

Predicted top of climb if current rate of climb is held (usually it reduces with altitude)

Prediction of horizontal performance:

30 sec

20 sec

10 sec

Computed top of climb (allowing for reduced performance as aircraft gains altitude)

■ *Figure 8-36* **Predictions on the navigation display**

Head-Up Displays

A head-up display (HUD) is an instrument display that is projected ahead of the pilot so that instrument indications can be read while viewing through the windscreen. This is in contrast to the conventional head-down display, where the instruments are down on a panel, forcing the pilot to direct the eyes downwards from the windscreen to read them.

HUDs generally use a transparent screen, or block of transparent material, placed between the pilot's eyes and the cockpit window onto which images are projected to indicate various flight parameters to the pilot, such as airspeed, attitude, altitude and rate of change of altitude.

The original idea was to focus the images at infinity, on the basis that this was the natural focal length of the eyes as they looked out the window (a faulty assumption), so that refocusing to read the instruments was not necessary.

There have been problems with HUDs, such as affecting the natural focal length of the resting eyes (which is much closer than infinity) and causing distortions of the outside view, as well as with finding suitable symbology to represent clearly the flight parameters.

HUDs are good, but not yet generally used.

Most applications for HUDs are in military aeroplanes, but a French civil airline has used them for many years with great success in achieving landings in very limiting meteorological conditions of low cloud and poor visibility. Similar success is now being achieved by conventional head-down instruments with good autopilots capable of performing autolands and roll-outs, and this seems to be the current trend. HUDs, however, could re-emerge in the future.

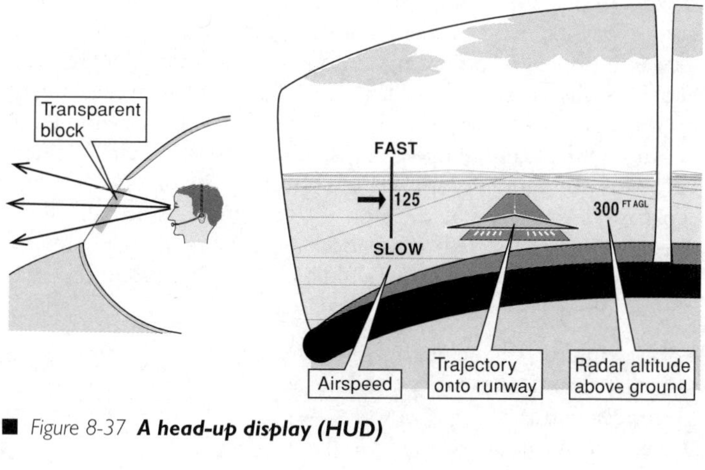

■ Figure 8-37 *A head-up display (HUD)*

Cockpit Checklists

Checklists are a vital part of modern day operation. In the old days, it was possible to commit to memory the few checks that were needed, including normal checks, such as the *Pre-Take-Off* and *Pre-Landing* checks, as well as *Emergency* checks to cope with engine fires and other emergencies. Nowadays, the complexities of aircraft, as well as the fairly intense operating environment and the ever-changing crew members, make checklists very important. Having a good checklist to assist in performing a certain task should reduce the difficulty of that task.

Humans are often better at remembering the generalities whilst forgetting the particulars. It is easier to remember the general rule to do the *Downwind* checklist on the downwind leg than it is to remember the particular items on the Downwind checklist for that particular aeroplane type.

Checklists ensure that the particulars are indeed actioned. In some drills, forgetting one item can have very serious consequences, both in emergency checklists and in normal operating checklists. For instance, some years ago an aircraft was destroyed because fuel was not cut off to a burning engine as the checklist required; and more than one aeroplane has landed wheels-up because the '*gear down*' item on the Final Approach or Pre-Landing checklist was not actioned.

Checklists are vital.

Checklists, if properly used, ensure that particular items are not missed.

One human characteristic that we need to guard against when using checklists is to not see what we want to see, but to **see what really exists.** For instance, with the '*gear down*' or '*wheels down*' call, we all want to see three green lights to confirm normal operation. On occasions, pilots have been known to respond, "Three greens", when in fact that was not the case, resulting in an unwanted wheels-up landing. Never respond to a checklist item automatically; always consider your response before giving it, even if it is an everyday, routine checklist that you are completing.

Actually check your response.

Another human failing with checklists is to skip items accidentally. This can happen with written checklists if you let you finger slip past one or two of the items – easy to do especially if the checklist is interrupted. It is good airmanship *not* to interrupt checklists unless absolutely unavoidable – this often requires cockpit discipline.

Do not interrupt checklists, or skip items.

For maximum efficiency, checklists should be:
☐ **easily found and easily read;**
☐ **concise; and**
☐ **very clear.**

All checklists should be located handily. Many checklists are contained in booklets or on cards located conveniently in the cockpit. Often, normal checklists are placed on a plate attached to the control column, allowing the pilot(s) to use them with very little distraction from instrument monitoring and scanning outside. Other aircraft have checklists that can be raised from the coaming panel, with small plates that can be moved across or down to cover the items as they are actioned.

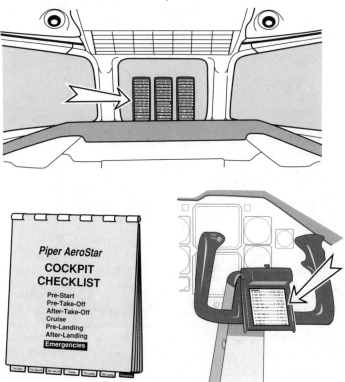

■ Figure 8-38 **Checklists should be accessible**

Checklist booklets should have thumb tabs alongside the index to simplify and speed up location of the precise checklist, bearing in mind that you might have to do this in a smoke-filled cockpit or in extreme turbulence (or both). Some aircraft also have electronic checklists that can be displayed on a screen, but this is often backed up by a conventional written checklist in case of electrical failure.

Some good and bad examples follow. These are taken from a multi-crew cockpit where one pilot monitors the action of the other. In a single-pilot cockpit, you have to monitor your own actions.

Checklists should be very easy to read. This means large, clear lettering, but not necessarily capital letters, as these are often more difficult to read than lower case.

Checklists should be written so that the meaning of each item is very clear, not only in the challenge, but also in response. Challenge-and-response checklists are one of the foundations of the well-functioning multi-crew cockpit. Some vital items need the response of both pilots, sometimes before the action is taken. Good checklists are written so that vital items are checked by both pilots before they are actioned; others are written in a manner that can lead to some confusion – so always be cautious when actioning checklists.

Checklists must be clear.

Fuel Cut-Off Switch – Off; Both – Confirm
  – this sequence may lead to the wrong engine being
    shut down before the second pilot has a chance to
    prevent it; whereas:
Fuel Cut-Off Switch – Both confirm correct engine
  – followed by:
Fuel Cut-Off Switch – Off, both confirm
  – could prevent this.

Figure 8-40 **Checklists need careful attention**

Fire Switch – *Pull* or, not as good: **FIRE SWITCH *PULL***

Figure 8-42 **Checklist items should be easy to read**

It is important also that the items on a checklist are concise, something which is usually achieved by having short, sharp challenges with short responses. Long explanations of the 'whys and wherefores' should be confined to other documents which the pilot can read at leisure, such as in the aeroplane flight manual. These explanations are important so that the pilot understands the logic underlying the checklist, but in the cockpit, say during an emergency, is not the time to read through this information for the first time – the well-trained pilot will have read through it during initial training, and at periodic intervals thereafter.

Checklists must be concise.

The Scan Approach to Checklists

Many operators complete a check in two stages:

☐ **a scan** where the eyes and hands follow a flow pattern around the cockpit, noting and actioning the appropriate items; then

☐ **reading** the checklist to verify the items.

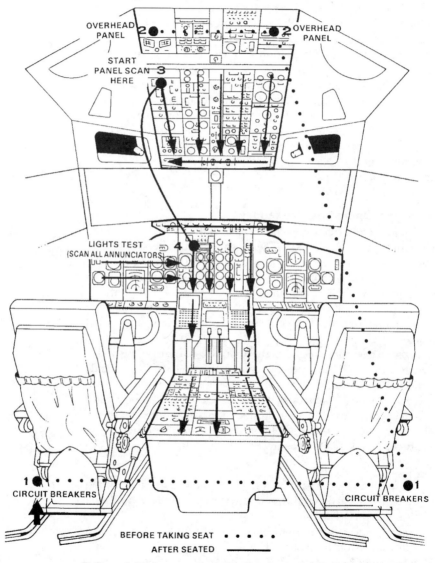

■ *Figure 8-43* **A scan pattern for the initial acceptance check (Boeing 737), which would be followed by completion of the appropriate checklist**

Manuals

Most of the information that a pilot needs to operate the aero-plane is found in a manual. A common problem in even the newest manuals, however, is that the information is often difficult to find, is often spread around various parts of the manual, and is often written in engineering terms. Bearing in mind these difficulties, it is vital that a pilot becomes familiar with the manuals for the aircraft type.

Know your manuals.

The requirements for a good manual, or set of manuals, are similar to the requirements for a good checklist, other than that there is no need for a manual to be concise. The manual is the place for clear and full explanations and additional information, both for new pilots and for experienced pilots, whereas the checklist is a challenge-and-response action list for the qualified pilot. For maximum effect, manuals should be:

- easily found;
- easily read; and
- very clear.

Standard Operating Procedures

In a multi-crew situation, each member of the crew should know what the others are doing, or what they should be doing. This means that the *standard operating procedures (SOPs)* specified by the company should be adhered to whenever possible, which is generally pretty well all of the time. This is not to say that pilots are locked into a totally rigid system, but rather that they participate in an easily controllable operation with no sudden unexpected happenings.

Adhere to standard operating procedures.

Most airline operators have a way out for pilots to improvise if they feel they need to, often by using words such as "Non-standard, I intend doing .....", which may be a slightly unusual visual pattern to avoid a known area of turbulence, or it could be a faster and steeper descent to circuit altitude to make up time, and so on. The main thing is that each pilot knows what the other has in mind before it actually happens.

External Visual Aids

There are many external visual aids designed to assist the pilot, some which do so admirably, and others which are less successful. Typical external visual aids are:

- taxiway and runway markings and lighting;
- wind direction indicators;
- aerodrome beacons;
- approach slope aids;
- parking aids;
- aerodrome notices and signs.

Aerodrome Notices and Signs

Signs should be large, with colour or lighting being used to distinguish them. Often they will use contrasting colours, such as black against a yellow background, for good contrast. Typical signs include: runway entry points (e.g. **Runway 27 Taxiway G**), parking positions (e.g. **B23**), or taxi guidance information (e.g. **Runway 27** ↑, and **Taxiway F** →).

Taxiway Markings and Lighting

Taxiway markings usually consist of yellow painted lines (as against white painted lines on runways), with the yellow standing out well against the dark bitumen of the taxiway, but maybe not quite so well against the white of a concrete taxiway. Dashed lines mean you can cross, full lines generally mean you should not cross without some prior thought (e.g. obtain a clearance to enter a runway).

The markings may be used to show the extent of the taxiway so that you do not allow the wheels of the aircraft to roll onto a soft surface, or they may run along the centre of the taxiway as guidelines for a pilot, which is particularly useful when manoeuvring large aeroplanes around corners or into a parking position; this is accomplished by keeping the lines beneath the pilot's eyes – the lines being positioned so that the aeroplane's wheels follow a safe path.

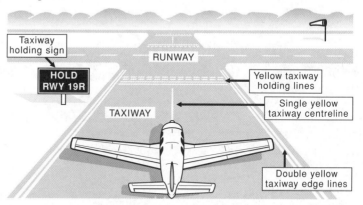

■ *Figure 8-44* **Taxiway markings**

Taxiway lighting usually consists of either blue sideline lights, green centreline lights, or a mixture of both.

With a complicated network of taxiways – for instance, at a large international airport – the pattern of blue lights seen from an angle may appear quite confusing, and you need to taxi slowly and check that you are indeed going between the intended two rows of blue lights.

Green centreline lights are in general easier to follow – just keep your eyes above them and the wheels should follow a safe path. Limits should be shown by red or amber lights, or well-lit signs.

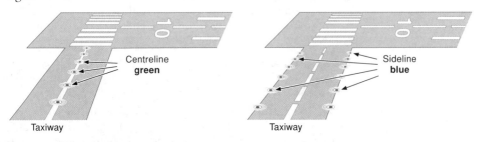

Centreline
green

Sideline
blue

Taxiway   Taxiway

■ *Figure 8-45* **Taxiway lighting**

Now complete **Exercises 8 – The Flight Deck.**

Section **Two**

Safety, First Aid
and **Survival**

Safety and Care of Passengers

The pilot is responsible for the safety of the aircraft and its passengers. As well as being properly prepared for the flight, the pilot must also ensure that the passengers are adequately briefed on safety matters.

Pilot Awareness

Passengers must have confidence in their pilot, and you, as pilot-in-command, can generate this. Passengers will feel more comfortable and less anxious if you, as their pilot and with their lives in your hands for the next few hours, are professional and confident both in your appearance and as you go about your duties. A scruffy looking pilot, running late, and agitated, will not inspire confidence; a well-dressed, well-organised pilot will.

No matter who the passengers are (parents or prime ministers), the pilot is in command during the flight, and the responsibilities of command begin well before the flight. Be aware of this, and conduct yourself in a manner that will inspire confidence.

As pilot-in-command, you are in command.

The normal order of authority may have to change during this period. A person who has authority on the ground, whether a parent or the boss or some dominant person, must subject himself or herself to the authority of the pilot-in-command once a flight commences – and a flight commences well before the aeroplane takes off. In reality, the sense of already being under way may commence much earlier, during the flight planning stages the night before, or on the drive to the airport.

It is important for you to be aware of this, and to assume the mantle of command right from the beginning, no matter how young or inexperienced you are. Passenger safety and the feeling of well-being should commence a long time before the flight.

Flight plan carefully.

Advise your passengers that you will need ten minutes without interruption to consider the weather forecasts and the other paperwork. They will respect this, and feel much better than if their proposed pilot bent to their every whim and did not pay attention to the other duties. Passengers will be aware of how you consider the preflight information and reach your 'go/no-go' decision; you should do this carefully, efficiently, and confidently. You should set the pace.

Prior to Boarding

As pilot you should inform the passengers that at various times throughout the flight you will have important duties to perform which will require your full attention. For this reason, you may occasionally request that there be no interruptions and no excessive conversation during the periods while you are concentrating on 'vital actions'.

Correct clothing is important to passenger comfort. Most aircraft cabins can be kept warm (or cool) in flight. Overcoats and other very heavy clothing need not be worn, although they should remain accessible in the event of an emergency evacuation. Passengers are forbidden to fly when drunk and should not fly if sick or affected by an upper respiratory complaint such as a cold.

Pressure changes will occur as the aeroplane climbs and descends and, if the ears do not automatically adjust, chewing, yawning or holding the nose whilst blowing with a closed mouth may assist. Blocked nasal passages can hinder this process. The higher noise level and possible turbulence may be a little disconcerting. Passengers should be reminded that there are no toilet facilities on board.

Baggage should be checked to ensure that it is not overweight and does not contain dangerous goods such as aerosol cans, pressurised cigarette lighters and matches, none of which should be carried.

Always check baggage.

It is inadvisable to smoke or have any naked flame near aircraft, especially if refuelling is in progress. Normally, passengers should remain well away from the aeroplane as a precaution while refuelling is in progress, since the fire risk is somewhat greater. It is advisable to wash your hands after refuelling because the smell of fuel or oil, or indeed any other unpleasant smells, in the cockpit can be annoying.

Passengers should be warned to remain well clear of propellers, since even a stationary propeller can spring to life, and a rotating propeller may hardly be visible. For this reason, children must be very closely supervised. The safest approach to an aeroplane is from the left and behind with passengers remaining in a single group under the supervision of the pilot.

Supervise your passengers.

Various attachments on the aeroplane, such as the pitot tube and radio aerials, are fragile and should not be used for support. Care should be taken when entering the aeroplane not to step where the wing or any part of the aeroplane structure could be damaged.

Preflight Check of Emergency Equipment
A vital part of any preflight check by the pilot is to ensure that the required emergency equipment is on board and serviceable. The emergency equipment carried will of course vary according to the nature of the flight about to be undertaken, the requirements for a trip across the Sahara being different from those for a trip over northern waters in the middle of winter.

Check emergency
equipment.

The basic emergency equipment, such as emergency checklists and safety belts, will of course be on board at all times. Additional emergency equipment carried may include such items as a torch, fire extinguisher, emergency locator transmitter (ELT), life-jackets and life-raft for long overwater flights, survival kits, emergency flares, first-aid kit, and so on.

On Board

Make your passengers
comfortable.

Ensure that your passengers are comfortably seated and confirm that the front-seat passenger will not restrict full movement of any control with bags, cameras or legs. Any metallic or magnetic objects should be stored well away from the magnetic compass.

Seat-belts will consist of a lap-strap and sometimes a shoulder harness. The lap-strap should be fastened and adjusted until it is firm but comfortable, followed by the shoulder harness if one is fitted. The passengers must be shown how to fasten, adjust and release their seat-belts.

The passengers should know how to close, lock and then open the **doors and windows** or canopy. Once a door is closed by the pilot, the position of the lock and handle should not be altered.

Aircraft cabins can become stuffy, so ensure that there is **adequate ventilation** and each passenger knows how to adjust the appropriate vent to maximise personal comfort.

The **intercom,** if one is to be used, should be explained. The radio volume should be adjusted to a comfortable level.

Passengers need not be passive, but can actively assist in some aspects of flight, such as maintaining a good **look out** for other aircraft and for landmarks, as well as passing the sandwiches around!

Passenger Briefing

An important duty in taking care of your passengers is to brief them on the use of their safety belts, and on any relevant emergency procedures. This would form the basis of your *standard passenger briefing*. Additional items could be added to this standard briefing when appropriate.

Brief your passengers
professionally.

If about to fly over an expanse of water, for instance, you would include in your briefing an explanation of how to don the life-jackets. If the expanse of water was great enough for you to be carrying a life-raft, then you would also brief on how to remove the raft from its pack and inflate it, making sure it does not drift away from the aircraft. If you were about to fly at high altitudes, you would also brief on the use of the supplemental oxygen system.

If you give the briefing in a friendly but confident manner, the passengers will be impressed by your professionalism, and be more relaxed. **A typical standard briefing follows.**

STANDARD PASSENGER BRIEFING

Seat-Belts

Remove any sharp articles from your pockets (such as keys, pocket knives, nail files, cigarette lighters).

Position your seat and ensure it is locked in position so that it cannot move.

To fasten your seat-belt, lengthen the strap if necessary, insert the belt link into the belt buckle, and tighten the belt by pulling the free end until you have a snug fit across your hips. If it is too tight, you will be uncomfortable; if it is too loose you may not be held firm enough in your seat if we meet unexpected turbulence.

To release your seat-belt, pull upward on the top of the buckle.

The shoulder harness can also be fitted into the buckle. It has an inertia reel that allows you lean forward, but will lock you firmly in position with any sudden deceleration.

Your seat-belt must be fastened for every take-off and landing, but I recommend that it remain fastened throughout the flight.

Emergency Exits

In the rare event of having to leave the aircraft quickly, the exit to use is
_____.

Move away from the aircraft, and keep well clear of the propeller at all times.

Smoking

You must not smoke on the tarmac area, nor during take-off or landing.
I would prefer no smoking in flight, because we also have non-smokers aboard and because it introduces the unnecessary risk of fire.

Radio

If you wish to listen in to the flight radio, we can use the cockpit speaker or you may use a headset which should make the communications clearer. The volume control is here _____, and we can also use the intercom (test if possible).

Planned Route

We will taxi out and use Runway _____, which means a take-off into the (N, S, E or W), followed by a (right/left) turn.

We will be tracking overhead _____ and _____ to our destination _____.

The weather we expect en route is (good/may be a little bumpy).

STANDARD PASSENGER BRIEFING

Doors, Windows and Ventilation

Ensure your seat-belt is not hanging out, then close the door firmly and lock it.

The window may be open for additional ventilation while taxiing.

Normal vents are located _____, and you can adjust them by _____.

If you happen to feel unwell in flight, which I do not expect to be the case, advise me early on so that I can try to avoid bumpy areas or tight manoeuvres.

Now we are ready for engine start and radio communication.

End of passenger briefing.

Keep your passengers informed.

If you change your plans in flight, or if you have to carry out any unusual manoeuvres, then a quick briefing to your passengers will put them at ease.

Handicapped passengers may need special attention, and a modified briefing to explain how they should leave the aeroplane in the case of an evacuation.

Life-Jackets

Before flying over any expanse of water (e.g. the English Channel) in a single-engined aircraft, all occupants should don **life-jackets.** There are various types and the pilot must be familiar with their use. Most life-jackets are designed to be worn uninflated inside the aeroplane so that their bulk is minimised, both for comfort and for ease of departing the cabin.

The pilot should explain how to don the life-jacket, which is usually by fitting it over your head with the main part of the jacket in front of your body, then passing the straps around your back and tying them in front. Some jackets may require a different fitting technique for children.

Passenger knowledge of life-jackets is necessary for overwater flights.

The passenger must understand how to inflate the life-jacket and use any attached items such as a light or whistle. It should be emphasised that it is best to inflate the life-jacket *after* having exited from the cabin so that the evacuation is unhindered.

Inflation is generally achieved by pulling a release on a small gas cylinder attached to the front of the life-jacket. If the gas pressure provides insufficient inflation, there is a tube through which the passenger can blow and further inflate the life-jacket.

Uninflated while in aircraft

Inflate after exiting

Follow the instructions in donning

■ Figure 9-1 **Follow the instructions in use of a life-jacket**

Life-Rafts

Immersion in the seas surrounding the UK could result in death within a few hours – within a few minutes in extreme temperatures and winds. Whilst life-jackets are useful for flotation, they will not protect the body from icy water. For this reason, it is prudent, on overwater journeys, to carry a **life-raft** in which the occupants can be sheltered from exposure and remain fairly dry.

If you carry a life-raft, know how to use it.

■ Figure 9-2 **A covered life-raft affords greatest protection in the open sea**

Most life-rafts suitable for light aircraft are stored in a small bag and weigh 10–15 kg. The raft must be inflated outside the aircraft, usually by removing it from its bag, ensuring that its cord is firmly held and placing or throwing the uninflated raft into the water. It may be advisable to swim a short distance from the aircraft before inflating the life-raft to avoid any danger of holing it.

Pulling the release cord should then activate the gas cylinder and inflate the raft. A sea anchor (bucket) can be used to prevent the raft drifting too far from the aircraft, which will assist in the search.

The raft will have associated equipment such as paddles, a canopy (very important in minimising exposure) ropes, knife, dyes, flares, light, first-aid kit and possibly emergency rations.

If necessary due to space constraints (and for faster evacuation of the aircraft), passengers should be instructed not to take luggage with them into the raft.

The Air Navigation Order (ANO), Schedule 4, Scale K lists the equipment that a life-raft should contain.

Oxygen Equipment

For high-altitude flights, brief your passengers on oxygen masks.

If you are going to be flying at high cabin altitudes, then the passengers should be briefed on the use of the on-board oxygen equipment. This will involve instructions on:

- ☐ **removing** fatty materials from facial areas exposed to the oxygen (such as face cream or cosmetics) since they could be combustible;
- ☐ **no smoking** when oxygen is being used because of the risk of combustion;
- ☐ **how to don the mask** and achieve a satisfactory oxygen flow; and
- ☐ **the time of useful consciousness,** which is only a few seconds at very high cabin altitudes, but longer at lower cabin altitudes.

The use of oxygen should be considered at cabin altitudes over 10,000 feet.

Fire

Fire is a hazard to aviation and is to be avoided at all costs. Three things are necessary for a fire to occur:

- ☐ **a fuel** (e.g. Avgas, oil, papers, fabric, cabin seating, etc.);
- ☐ **oxygen** (present in the air);
- ☐ **a source of ignition** (cigarettes, matches, electrical sparks, etc.), but bear in mind that once a fire is burning it is itself a source of ignition.

Prevent fires.

Prevention is by far the best cure, and pilots are advised to pay attention to items and situations that are a potential cause of, or contributor to, fire. Any possible **fuel** and any possible source of **ignition** should be kept separate. For example, when refuelling ensure that no person is smoking in the vicinity, that the aeroplane and refuelling equipment are adequately grounded to avoid the possibility of a static electricity build-up causing a spark, and that no fuel is spilled. As a precaution when refuelling, a suitable fire extinguisher should be readily available.

Cigarettes can cause fires.

In flight, if the pilot permits any passenger to smoke, then he must ensure that no hot ash or cigarette butt comes in contact with papers or even the cabin seating, which may smoulder or burn, possibly unnoticed for some time.

The risk of fire, as well as the detrimental effects of carbon monoxide in the blood, is another reason to discourage smoking in aircraft.

Cockpit fires can also be caused by faulty electrical circuits, which can often be recognised by a peculiar smell. Further development of an electrical fire may be prevented by switching off the electrical power (master switch OFF, or pulling the appropriate circuit breaker).

Extinguishing a Fire

The usual method of extinguishing a fire once it is burning is to eliminate one or more of these items (fuel, oxygen, source of ignition), e.g. blanketing a fire with dry chemical from a fire extinguisher to starve the fire of oxygen. If it appears that a fire has not yet started but is imminent, and the fuel and ignition source cannot be separated, it may be advisable to starve the area of oxygen by using an extinguisher.

Extinguish any fire quickly.

Fire Extinguishers

The CAA requires that Public Transport aircraft carry fire extinguishers; however, for Private Category aeroplanes this is only a recommendation and not a requirement.

Many light aircraft are indeed fitted with a small fire extinguisher that is securely stowed where the pilot may reach it in flight. The usual extinguishants contained in these are BCF (halon) and dry chemical, both of which are capable of handling most types of fires. Other extinguishants in use include carbon dioxide, water and foam.

Know your fire extinguishers.

There is a standard graphic code to differentiate between the suitability of fire extinguishers in fighting certain types of fire, and this is usually displayed on the extinguisher with an indication of its suitability for the specific categories.

Typically, a stored gas pressure discharges the extinguishant when a trigger is pressed. Each particular brand of fire extinguisher may have special requirements (such as to break a seal by twisting a handle, or by releasing a handle, or by breaking a lockwire), so the pilot should read the instructions and become familiar with the extinguisher that he might have to use at short notice. Some of the more common types of fire extinguishers are discussed below.

Some fire extinguishers are re-usable either by recharging the cylinder or by placing the trigger and head mechanism onto a new cylinder, whereas others may have to be discarded once used.

A serviceability check of the fire extinguisher may require checking pressure on a gauge which may be colour-coded, or on an indicator disc which, if it can be pressed in, indicates that the pressure is low and the fire extinguisher unserviceable.

Paper,
wood,
textiles

Inflammable
liquids
& gases

Live
electrical
equipment

■ *Figure 9-3*

Graphic code in use
on many fire
extinguishers

There may also be a weight check to determine that no extinguishant has been lost, but this check is more likely to be done by a maintenance engineer during the periodic inspections.

BCF (Halon)

BCF extinguishers contain Halon 1211 (**b**romo**c**hlorodi**fl**uoromethane), and are often found in light aircraft. BCF is a very versatile extinguishant and is capable of combating most types of fires, including fuel, fabric and electrical. BCF is stored as liquefied gas, which comes out as a fine jet of fluid and develops into a spray. Its toxicity is low (so will not poison the pilot or passengers) and can be safely used in the cockpit, although it is advisable to avoid inhaling excessive amounts of fuel and smoke.

Bearing in mind that the BCF extinguishant gas will exclude oxygen to some extent, **the cabin should be well ventilated once the fire is extinguished.** A significant advantage of BCF is that (unlike *dry chemical*) it does not leave any residue, and so the cabin and instruments will not require cleaning after its use.

Dry Chemical

A dry chemical fire extinguisher contains dry powder and carbon dioxide. It is very effective against most types of fire, including electrical and fuel, but is less effective than BCF against material fires (paper, textiles, wood).

Unfortunately, dry chemical has several disadvantages. During its use it may restrict visibility in the cockpit and cause breathing difficulties, so **ventilating the cabin is important once the fire is out.** After it has been used, a powdery residue will remain which is corrosive to aluminium alloys and can be damaging to instruments, so thorough cleaning is necessary after dry chemical has been used.

CO₂ Fire Extinguishers

Carbon dioxide fire extinguishers contain liquefied CO_2 which can be discharged as a gas and used to combat electrical fires, engine fires on the ground and other fires. When sprayed at the base of the fire, the CO_2 blankets the fire and starves it of oxygen.

A typical CO_2 fire extinguisher will have a trigger with a lockwire that must be broken before use (an intact lockwire is also a check for serviceability), and a nozzle that should be raised before the CO_2 is discharged with the trigger. The nozzle pipe should not be held with the bare hands, since it will become extremely cold as the gas vaporises, and skin could be frozen to it. CO_2 will cause breathing difficulties and is best not used in the cockpit unless oxygen masks are available.

Water Fire Extinguishers

'Wet' water fire extinguishers generally contain distilled water with an anti-freeze agent to retain serviceability at low temperatures and a 'wetting' agent. Water is suitable for extinguishing material fires (e.g. a smouldering cabin seat), but definitely should not be used for electrical fires or fuel fires.

Foam Fire Extinguishers

Foam fire extinguishers are generally designed for outside use. One common type is inverted just prior to use, causing chemicals to mix and form foam under pressure which can then be directed at the base of the fire.

Using a Fire Extinguisher

The instructions on how to use a particular fire extinguisher will normally be found on it, but in general the procedure is:

- ☐ **hold** the extinguisher by its handle in a vertical position;
- ☐ **remove** any safety locks or safety wires;
- ☐ **from a distance** of about 1 to 1.5 metres, direct the nozzle at the base of the fire, depress the trigger and hold it down;
- ☐ **release** the trigger when you want to stop the discharge.

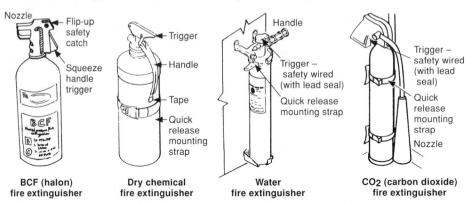

■ *Figure 9-4* **Typical fire extinguishers in aviation use**

Now complete **Exercises 9 – Safety and Care of Passengers.**

First Aid

First aid is what its name suggests – the initial care of the sick or injured. It can preserve life, protect the unconscious, prevent worsening of a condition and promote recovery. First aid lasts until medical aid (doctor, nurse or ambulance officer) arrives or until the casualty recovers.

First aid knowledge can be very useful.

First aid is useful knowledge for all citizens, but is especially useful for those who may find themselves in remote areas well away from medical aid (e.g. following a forced landing in an aircraft). The St. John's Ambulance Association specialises in first aid and is highly recommended for its manuals and courses.

Minor Problems that may Occur In Flight

Minor medical problems may occur in flight and can often be handled without difficulty. It is most important, however, that this does not distract you from flying the aeroplane and adequately controlling its flightpath, which is your principal responsibility.

Airsickness and Nausea

Airsickness (also known as *motion sickness*) may occur in flight, especially if the person is passive, in a hot stuffy cabin and is experiencing unusual motion, such as in manoeuvres or turbulence. Generally, passengers are more passive than the pilot, although it is not unknown for a pilot to become airsick. The affected person may feel poorly, 'hot and cold' and nauseous, but will often feel better after having vomited.

To manage a person who feels airsick (ensuring that you, as pilot, do not neglect your prime responsibilities in controlling the flight path of the aeroplane):

- loosen clothing;
- ensure plenty of fresh air;
- lay the patient down or recline the seat;
- place a cool cloth on the forehead;
- comfort and reassure;
- have a 'sick bag' handy in case of vomiting.

Fainting

Insufficient blood reaching the brain may cause a person to faint and possibly lose consciousness temporarily. A temporary disturbance of the nervous control of the blood vessels can be caused by nervous shock (such as a fright or a horrifying sight), an injury, being passive in a hot stuffy environment or by a sudden postural change (like standing up after having been sitting for a long period).

A person who is about to faint may feel weak and giddy, 'hot and cold', and have a pale, clammy skin, experience blurred vision and have a desire to yawn.

To manage a person who has fainted, or is about to faint:
- lay the casualty down if possible, with the legs raised; otherwise recline the seat;
- loosen clothing;
- ensure plenty of fresh air;
- allow the casualty to rest;
- have a sick bag handy in case of vomiting;
- place a cool cloth on the forehead; and
- if hyperventilating, have them breathe into a paper bag.

Nose Bleeding
Nose bleeding may result from injury, high blood pressure or excessive blowing of the nose. It usually occurs from just inside the nose on the central cartilaginous partition below the bone.

Instruct the casualty:
- not to blow the nose;
- to breathe through the mouth;
- to apply finger and thumb pressure on the flaps of the nostrils (just below the bony part of the nose) for at least 10 minutes;
- to sit up, with the head slightly forward and loosen any tight clothing; and
- to keep cool with a good supply of fresh air and with cold towels on the neck and forehead.

More Serious Problems that may Occur In Flight
Anything that prejudices the health and well-being of the pilot in flight may end in disaster. **Food poisoning,** for instance, can totally disable a pilot quite quickly, even though symptoms may not appear until several hours after an ill-prepared meal. Also, the onset of symptoms, when they do appear, can be quite sudden! Diarrhoea is certainly not helpful to safe flight. Passengers, as well as the pilot, can experience medical problems (fainting, heart attack, stroke, etc.).

Eat carefully to avoid food poisoning.

It is up to the pilot to decide how to manage the problem, either in flight or on the ground following a landing (ideally at an aerodrome, but in a nearby field if urgency demands it).

First Aid Following an Accident
The pilot is responsible for the safety of the aeroplane and its occupants at all times. On rare occasions, accidents do occur and the pilot must be capable of managing subsequent events adequately. The welfare of the group must take precedence over that of any

individual and, if possible, the safety of the flight (whilst it lasts) should not be prejudiced.

Prevention is the Best Cure

Preventing an accident or incident is of course best. Food poisoning, for instance, can be avoided by careful choice of food. Pilot welfare is best achieved by staying on the ground if someone has diarrhoea or nausea, or if an upper respiratory or hearing complaint is being experienced.

Some good points of airmanship (common sense) in *prevention* are as follows:

☐ **have the seat-belts fastened;**
☐ **do not allow careless smoking;** and
☐ **guard against fumes and carbon monoxide** in the cabin by ensuring a good supply of fresh air.

If an Accident Occurs and Passengers are Injured

In the event of an accident actually taking place do everything in your power to stop the situation worsening. Secure the aeroplane and evacuate uninjured passengers, taking any useful emergency equipment and supplies. Consider the welfare of injured passengers and whether or not they should be moved. Do not forget the welfare of the non-injured members of the party.

■ *Figure 10-1*
The coma position

If an unconscious passenger is evacuated, then it should be done gently and firmly, with the casualty being placed in the **coma position.** This is a comfortable position that aids blood supply to the brain and allows any vomit to escape without blocking the breathing passages.

Head Injuries

Head injuries are potentially very serious as they can result in brain damage, altered consciousness, spinal injury, bleeding, breathing difficulties, vision and balance difficulties. Even mild head injuries should be treated seriously.

Indications of head injury may include headache, nausea, memory loss, blurring of vision, weakness on one side of the body, wounds, bleeding, bruising, clear fluid escaping from the nose or ear, twitching, noisy breathing, incoherent speech, congestion on the face, vomiting, dilated pupils or pupils becoming unequal in size, strange behaviour and abnormal responses of the injured person to commands and to touch.

Treat someone suffering head injury the same as for being unconscious. Consider placing the victim in the *coma position* so that any bleeding, discharge or vomit can drain away. An open airway is vital. Ensure that the tongue or dentures do not obstruct the passages. Breathing should be monitored and assisted if necessary. Be alert for possible concussion.

Bleeding

Bleeding is loss of blood from the blood vessels and may be either internal or external. In either case blood is lost to the circulation and the ability to carry energy-giving oxygen around the body and to the brain is reduced. Blood loss can lead to faintness, dizziness, nausea, thirst, a weak and rapid pulse, cold and clammy skin, and rapid breathing.

Fortunately, bleeding will often stop of its own accord but, if it does not, severe bleeding can lead to shock and eventually to death. Severe bleeding, therefore, is extremely serious and must be controlled before less serious injuries are attended to.

External bleeding is best controlled by placing a bulky dressing (or your hand if nothing more suitable is available) over the wound and applying firm pressure to it for 10 minutes or more. Raise the injured part and rest it to decrease the blood flow.

Profuse bleeding may be reduced by pressing the sides of the wound together or by applying a constrictive bandage or hand pressure to block the blood flow through the arteries (say above the elbow or knee). This should be a last resort and the pressure should be released every 10 minutes or so to ensure some blood supply to the area.

Bleeding from the palm of the hand may be serious and can best be treated by clasping a firm pressure pad (e.g. a bandage roll, a handkerchief wrapped around a stone, or two or three fingers of the other hand) and elevating the hand above the head to reduce the blood flow to it.

Internal bleeding may result in pain, tenderness, tight stomach muscles and the above-mentioned signs of blood loss. To manage internal bleeding, rest the casualty completely. Elevate the legs comfortably (if not broken), loosen tight clothing and allow no food or drink. Seek urgent medical assistance.

Fractures

A fracture is a broken or cracked bone. There will be bleeding, either internally or through an open wound, causing a loss of blood to the circulation. The area where the break has occurred may be painful, tender, mis-shapen or swollen, bruised and unable to be used normally.

In managing a casualty with a fracture:

- **Control bleeding and cover wounds** with a sterile or clean dressing.
- **Immobilise and support the fracture** with a sling, bandage or splint, and preferably support the injured limb in an elevated position.

- **Splints:** use any suitable material that is long, wide and firm enough to give support and to immobilise the joints above and below the fracture. Use can be made of the upper body to splint a fractured arm and of a good leg to splint a fractured leg.
- **Padding:** may protect the skin and bony points and may allow the splint to fit snugly.
- **Bandages:** in general should be broad and supportive.

☐ **Check frequently** to ensure that blood circulation to a fractured limb is not impaired, that bandages have not loosened, and that splints are still supportive, and look for signs of shock.

Burns

Burns are a serious injury. Extensive burns to the body or to the respiratory tract (due to breathing hot air or fumes) are potentially dangerous and may be fatal.

To manage a casualty with burns, first extinguish the fire if possible and/or remove the casualty from danger, making sure that you do not become a burns casualty yourself.

☐ **Put out burning clothing** by smothering with a non-inflammable blanket or jacket, or possibly a dry chemical fire extinguisher (directed away from the eyes).

☐ **Remove or cut away any clothing** near the burnt area unless it is stuck to it, in which case leave it alone. Remove any rings, bracelets, watch bands, etc., before swelling starts. Cool the injured area if possible under cold, gently running water − (cooling make take up to 10 minutes).

☐ **Do not prick blisters and avoid touching** the burnt area. Do not apply any lotions, ointments, oily dressings or fluffy material. Apply a sterile non-stick dressing and bandage lightly.

A conscious casualty seriously burnt should be given frequent small amounts of water, weak tea or milk (about ½ cup every 10 minutes) to minimise the effect of fluid loss from the burnt tissues. Do not give alcohol. Seek medical aid urgently.

Deep Shock

Shock can range from fainting (nervous shock) to deep shock following serious injuries and illnesses, especially where there is severe bleeding, pain or loss of fluid from burns. Deep shock can be a life-threatening condition. Insufficient circulation of blood to the brain and other body tissues may lead to a collapse of the circulatory system and death.

Shock is progressive and may take some hours to become obvious and the symptoms should be carefully watched for. A casualty experiencing shock may be faint or dizzy, restless and apprehensive, nauseous and thirsty. The pulse may be very weak and rapid.

The face and lips may be pale and the skin pale and clammy, the extremities becoming bluish. Breathing may be rapid and the casualty may become dull, drowsy, apathetic, confused or unconscious.

To Treat a Person In Shock:

☐ **Increase the blood supply** to the brain if possible by laying the patient down with the head low.

☐ **Control any external bleeding,** dress any wounds or burns, immobilise any fractures and loosen any tight clothing.

☐ **Keep the casualty warm,** but do not overheat him as this draws blood away from the vital organs.

☐ **If thirsty,** moisten the lips or allow the casualty to suck an ice cube.

☐ **Monitor breathing and pulse.**

☐ **If breathing is difficult,** or vomiting likely or if consciousness is lost, lay the casualty on the side with the mouth slightly down.

☐ **Seek urgent medical assistance.**

First-Aid Kits

Although aeroplanes flying for a purpose other than public transport (e.g. for training or for private flights) are not required to carry a first-aid kit, (whereas public transport aircraft are required to do so), it is good airmanship for the operator of the aeroplane to provide one.

Keep your first-aid kit well-stocked.

Scale A

(iii) First-aid equipment of good quality, sufficient in quantity, having regard to the number of persons on board the aircraft, and including the following:

Roller bandages, triangular bandages, adhesive plaster, absorbent gauze, cotton wool, (or wound dressings in place of the absorbent gauze and cotton wool), burn dressings, safety pins;

Haemostatic bandages or tourniquets, scissors;

Antiseptic, analgesic and stimulant drugs;

Splints, in the case of aeroplanes the maximum total weight authorised of which exceeds 5700 kg;

A handbook on first aid.

■ *Figure 10-2* **Air Navigation Order (ANO) Schedule 4, Scale A provides a guide to the contents of a suitable first-aid kit**

Now complete **Exercises 10 – First Aid.**

Survival

Before venturing over dangerous terrain or over water, especially if well away from civilisation, it is good airmanship to consider survival aspects in case an unplanned landing or ditching becomes necessary, and to carry additional survival equipment. The basic aims in survival are:

☐ **let people know where you are** so that rescue time can be shortened; and

☐ **have sufficient emergency equipment** and supplies on board and sufficient knowledge to sustain life until rescue is achieved.

Lodge a Flight Plan

If the territory you plan to cross is dangerous, then you should **submit a flight plan** with Air Traffic Control so that you receive a high level of search and rescue protection. This is advisable if you plan to fly:

☐ **more than 10 nautical miles from the coast;**

☐ **over a remote or hazardous area** (e.g. Northern Scotland, or the west coast down to Cornwall); or

☐ **in an aircraft not fitted with a suitable radio.**

Survival chances are greater if people know where you are.

Quick and effective response by search and rescue organisations can be vital in an emergency, and this is best achieved by you protecting your flight by filing a flight plan. The chance of surviving a ditching in the icy-cold North Sea, for instance, diminishes with every passing minute.

Maintain Body Core Temperature

Maintaining body temperature is critical to survival. Normal body core temperature (core temperature being that of the inner body) is slightly under 37°C, and any change of more than about two degrees, either up or down, can seriously affect bodily functions, including brain function. Unconsciousness will occur if body core temperature falls about 4°C to 34°C. Temperatures above 37°C are called a *fever,* and in a high fever where the core temperature rises about 4°C to 41°C, delirium and convulsions might occur. The brain needs to be functioning well if people are to act to survive, and so body core temperature control is vital.

Keeping body core temperature up, since the environmental temperature is usually more than 10°C cooler, uses most of the energy produced by the body. This production of heat energy is fairly constant, with body core temperature being controlled by heat loss, mainly convection as air carries excess heat away from the skin.

In *low* environmental temperatures, heat loss from the skin by convection is reduced by clothing. This insulates the body from circulating air by trapping a layer of air that is warmed by the body but not carried away. If body temperature still drops, extra heat is generated by muscular contractions that we call *shivering*. Shivering uses a lot of energy and can lead to premature exhaustion.

Keep warm ...

You can be exposed to a severe heat loss:
- **following sudden cabin depressurisation** at high altitude;
- **in extremely cold conditions** on land or at sea; or
- **during immersion in water** below 20°C following a ditching.

In *high* environmental temperatures, light and loosely fitting clothing allows the circulation of air across the skin to carry heat away. If this heat loss by convection is insufficient, the body sweats, and the evaporation of this sweat from liquid to vapour absorbs additional heat energy from the skin. Sweating of course means that the body is losing fluids, and these have to be replaced by drinking if dehydration or overheating is to be avoided.

... but not too warm.

Survival Equipment

The survival equipment to be carried will of course depend upon the nature of the terrain or water to be crossed, and upon the climate and expected weather conditions. Some survival equipment is useful in all conditions (including your communications radio, an *emergency locator transmitter* (ELT), optical signals such as signal mirrors and flares, waterproof matches, a compass, a large knife, rope, a whistle, etc.), whereas other survival equipment (such as a life-raft) is more specific.

The Radio and the Transponder

If a forced landing or ditching is imminent, then you should make use of all means at your disposal to inform someone who can activate the search and rescue organisations. You could:
- **broadcast a Mayday call** on the frequency in use or on the emergency frequency 121·5 MHz which is continuously monitored by ground stations and by many aircraft; and
- **squawk 7700 on your transponder** – this will bring attention to and emphasise your aircraft on any radar screen (provided you are within radar coverage).

Most airliners will be using one VHF-COM set for normal air traffic control purposes, and will be listening out on 121·5 MHz on their second VHF-COM, enabling them to pick up any voice messages transmitted on this emergency frequency or any signals emitted by an ELT. If you ever find yourself in trouble and out of radio range from a ground station, transmit a voice message on

121·5 MHz — some other pilot or ground station may hear you and may be able to pass on your message to the authorities or provide some other sort of assistance.

Communicate your emergency:
• radio (frequency in use or 121·5 MHz)
• transponder (7700)

If you transmit early enough while you are still at altitude, an airport with *VHF direction-finding* (VDF) capability may have time to determine the direction from which your voice signals are coming, which will considerably simplify search procedures.

The Emergency Locator Transmitter (ELT)

The emergency locator transmitter is one of the best means of locating a downed aircraft. It is an electronic, battery-operated transmitter which emits a very distinctive radio signal.

Activate your ELT.

When activated, either by impact following hard contact with the ground or water, or by pilot-activation following a successful forced landing or ditching, the ELT transmits a *wailing* signal on the international emergency frequencies (civil 121·5 MHz, military 243 MHz). Other aircraft and ground stations will be listening out on these frequencies.

Land and sea survival beacons known as *emergency position indicating radio beacons* (EPIRBs) also transmit on 121·5 MHz.

The ELT is also known as the *emergency locator beacon* (ELB), the *radio beacon,* the *VHF survival beacon* (VSB), and by various other names.

Receiving Stations

Aircraft and ground stations monitor the emergency frequencies 121·5 and 243 MHz. The intensity of the ELT signal gives an indication of the proximity of the listening station to the downed aircraft. Searching aircraft can measure variations in signal strength as they fly a search pattern, with strengthening signals leading them towards the downed aircraft.

There is now a global satellite system known as COSPAS/SARSAT (C/S) which uses four near-polar orbital satellites to detect and localise signals from ELTs. In the UK, a local user terminal at Lasham processes C/S satellite information and passes it to the UK Mission Control Centre which is co-located with the Plymouth Rescue Coordination Centre (RCC).

The maximum waiting time between ELT activation and satellite detection should not exceed 90 minutes, and will usually be shorter.

Listen out for others in trouble.

It is good airmanship to listen out on the emergency frequency 121·5 MHz if you have a second VHF-COM radio set. Any ELT signals that you hear should be reported — it could be from a downed aircraft (although on rare occasions it could be a false alarm caused by a pilot accidentally activating the ELT).

Your report should include your position and altitude, and:

☐ **when you first heard,** and last heard the signal; and

☐ **any bearing obtained.**

It is also useful to advise when the signal was at maximum strength.

Activating an ELT

Most ELTs will be activated by impact in the case of heavy contact with ground or water. In the case of a successful forced landing or ditching where no significant impact occurs, some ELTs are activated by a switch, and others are activated by insertion in water or some other fluid. The antenna, if fitted, should be extended vertically for best transmission. Instructions will be found on the ELT unit itself.

The ELT may be activated in its installed position in the aircraft, or it may be removed, depending upon the situation. It is more important for the ELT to be with the survivors, who might be drifting in a raft or hiking through the jungle, than to remain with an abandoned aircraft.

After a ditching, a buoyant ELT with its antenna vertical should be attached by a lanyard to the raft so that the ELT does not become separated from the survivors, and a searching aircraft locate the ELT but not the survivors. The water surface will act as a reflector and effectively increase the ELT's transmitting strength. Hoisting the ELT up a mast would degrade the transmission, since it would eliminate reflection of the signals from the water surface.

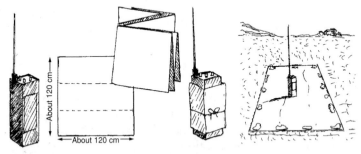

1. Prior to departure, join strips of household aluminium foil, to make a 120 cm (4 feet) square 'earth mat'.

2. Carefully fold the earth mat to a convenient size.

3. Tie or tape the folded earth mat to your ELT.

4. If you need to activate your ELT clear of the aircraft, unfold the earth mat and place it on the ground in a clear area away from obstacles, with rocks or earth to hold it down.

5. Turn the ELT on and place it on the mat so that the aerial is vertical.

6. Remain clear of the ELT.

■ *Figure 11-1* **Operating an ELT**

After a forced landing on land, the ELT can be activated in its installed position in the aircraft, or it can be removed and operated on the ground or on an *earth mat,* which is simply a reflecting surface made from something like household aluminium foil formed to the size of small sheet. If the ELT is removed from the aircraft, place it in a clearing on high ground near the survivors, away from trees, rocks, etc., which could distort or weaken the signal. Some ELTs need to be inserted in a fluid to be activated, even on the ground, and this can be achieved by placing it in a plastic bag containing fluid, and making sure that it remains upright with the antenna extended vertically. Placing the ELT on the wing of the aircraft or some other reflecting surface will also increase its effectiveness.

If possible, secure the ELT in a position so that its antenna remains vertical, using tape, rocks, sticks, etc. Once the ELT is activated, you should keep persons and objects clear of it since they could distort its signals.

When Should You Activate the ELT?

Following an impact, the ELT will activate immediately. Following a smooth touchdown, however, it will not activate automatically, and the pilot-in-command must decide *when* to activate it.

If you are near a ground station or within 100 nautical miles of a busy air route, or if you have already alerted others to your predicament (say with a Mayday call and by squawking 7700 on your transponder), then activate the ELT *immediately.* Also, if anyone is injured or if conditions for survival are poor, then switch it on immediately.

Some ELTs can be switched off and used only intermittently, others operate continuously until their batteries run flat after 48 hours or more. Some can be temporarily deactivated with a switch, others can be deactivated by removing them from their vertical position and laying them horizontal.

If you are in a remote area with no air routes within 100 nautical miles, then you might decide to conserve the ELT and activate it at a time when you think someone might hear it. This could be at or after your expected arrival time when Flight Service, or friends and family, might be starting to question your overdue arrival. It might be appropriate to switch it on at dusk, or at first light the following morning, or whenever you think it might be heard.

Optical Signals

Know your safety equipment.

There are various devices that can be used to help search aircraft to visually determine your position, including signal rockets, hand flares, flashlights, signal mirrors, and sea dye markers.

Signal Mirror

The signal mirror (or *heliograph*) is a small, light and cheap device that can be extremely useful in sunlight. Reflecting sunlight towards a search aircraft, which will probably see it as a series of very bright flashes, can be most effective at distances up to 25 nautical miles. The signal mirror is simply a metal or glass reflecting surface.

One way of using a signal mirror is:

1. **Hold it close** to your face so that you can look through the small hole in the reflecting surface (but not at the sun, which would do damage to your eye).

2. **Hold a** *target* at arms length (the target could be attached to the mirror, or it could be your finger or a pencil) and align it visually between your eye and the aircraft you want to alert.

3. **Move the mirror** so that the sun's rays are reflected onto the target, which means that they will be directed at the aircraft.

Another method of using the mirror, as illustrated in Figure 11-2, involves viewing the aircraft through the mirror and adjusting the angle of the mirror so that the spot of light from the sun that falls on your face, hand or shirt disappears through the hole while you have the aircraft in view through it.

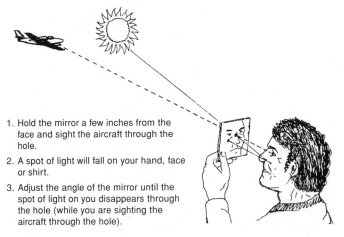

1. Hold the mirror a few inches from the face and sight the aircraft through the hole.

2. A spot of light will fall on your hand, face or shirt.

3. Adjust the angle of the mirror until the spot of light on you disappears through the hole (while you are sighting the aircraft through the hole).

■ *Figure 11-2* **Using a signal mirror**

The target aircraft will spot a *flashing* signal more easily than a steady signal, however there is no need for you to rock the mirror to cause flashing – the natural movement of your hand will be sufficient. If no aircraft or ship is in sight, continue to sweep the horizon using the signal mirror, just in case.

Signal Rockets (Parachute Flares)

There are some signal rockets available which can shoot up a red fireball which then sinks slowly beneath a small parachute. This should only be used when you think that someone will spot it, with the fireball being most effective at night.

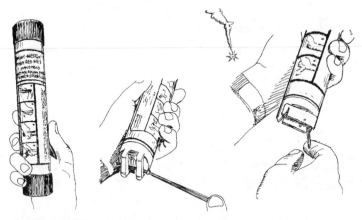

1. Unwrap when ready for use.
2. Read instructions.
3. Remove top and bottom caps.
4. Firing mechanism is in the base.
5. Pull string to remove safety pin.

6. Firing lever falls down.
7. Point rocket.
8. Bend lever up alongside and parallel to the firing tube, and squeeze.

■ *Figure 11-3* **Firing a signal rocket**

The instructions should be read carefully. They will advise that the signal rocket tube should be held firmly, well away from the body, and pointing in the shooting direction, which should be near-vertical in a downwind direction to avoid any contact with your body or anyone else's, before the mechanism is activated.

Hand Flares

Hand flares provide a coloured flare or smoke that lasts for 30 seconds or more, which can draw the attention of searchers to your position.

You should read the instructions carefully before using a hand flare. They will probably advise you to hold the hand flare firmly, well away from the body, and pointing in the shooting direction, which should be near-vertical in a downwind direction to avoid any contact with your body or anyone else's, before ignition. Flares that produce a flame (usually red) are effective at night or in daylight; those that produce smoke (usually orange) are only useful by day.

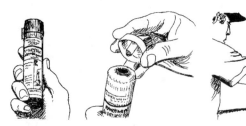

1. Unwrap when ready for use.
2. Read instructions.
3. Unwrap top sealing tape.
4. Remove top card and discard.
5. Unwrap bottom tape.
6. Remove bottom cap incorporating striker.

7. Ignite by grinding striker across top of flare.
8. Hold clear immediately ignition occurs.
9. Smoke is locally dense but is dispersed with the breeze.

■ *Figure 11-4* **Igniting a hand flare**

Flashlight or Spotlight

A strong flashlight can be used both to assist you getting organised at night, and also to send emergency signals in the direction of anyone who might see them. Typical signals that can draw attention are:

☐ a wide circling motion; or

☐ the SOS emergency signal: 3 short flashes, 3 long flashes, 3 short flashes – and then repeated:
(· · · − − − · · ·   · · · − − − · · ·   · · · − − − · · ·   etc.)

Sea Dye Marker

Sea dye marker, when released into the sea, spreads out and forms a very brightly marked area (usually bright green) that can be seen for many miles in daylight hours. It lasts for several hours. The bag containing the dye should be fastened to the outside of the raft so that the dye is released in the vicinity of the raft. In strong winds, the raft might drift away from the dyed area, so it would be advisable to delay the use of the dye until a search craft is in sight.

Ground-to-Air Visual Signals for Search and Rescue

The following ground-to-air visual signals can be used, as appropriate, to inform searchers with whom you have no radio contact what your needs are and what your actions will be. Make the symbol as large as possible (preferably 6 metres or so long, but at least 2 or 3 metres), using materials that contrast with the background. The materials could be clothes or sleeping bags which are held in position by stones, or you could use tree branches, etc.

You could also lay out a large **SOS** signal. It has been known for airline passengers to spot SOS signals on the ground, whereas they may not have understood the significance of the other ground-to-air visual signals.

STANDARD GROUND-TO-AIR SEARCH AND RESCUE VISUAL SIGNALS		
No.	Message	Symbol
1	Require assistance	V
2	Require medical assistance	X
3	No or Negative	N
4	Yes or Affirmative	Y
5	Proceeding in this direction	↑

Flags
Flying anything in the form of a flag will help attract attention. If possible, fly a ball or something resembling a ball directly beneath the flag or above it, which is an *international distress signal*.

Fires and Smoke
Fires can be seen well at night, and dense smoke can be seen well by day. Lighting two or three fires 20 metres apart, and possibly in the shape of a triangle, may help draw attention to your position. Using dry wood at night will produce the brightest flames; using damp wood with lots of green leaves by day will produce lots of smoke, as will adding engine oil. **Waterproof matches** are worthwhile having in any survival kit.

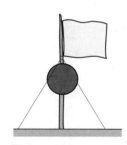

■ *Figure 11-5*
Fly a flag and ball

Acoustic Signals
If the aircraft has some down in a jungle or heavily wooded area, it may not be visible from the air or from the ground. Ground searchers may be assisted in wooded areas or at night if you can make a lot of noise, by blowing whistles or by calling out. The Australian bush call 'coo-ee' has saved many lives.

Written Notes
If for any reason you leave the vicinity of the downed aircraft, then leave a written or scratched note stating your intentions, in case searchers find the aircraft before they find you.

Survival at Sea

A forced landing into water is known as a *ditching*. Some ditchings have been made into lakes, dams, and wide rivers, and others have been made into oceans.

The initial problem following a ditching is to ensure that everyone leaves the aircraft safely, and is able to float and avoid drowning. This is achieved by the use of life-jackets and/or rafts.

The next, and major, problem is to avoid death or injury by exposure. Some oceans are quite warm, for instance those surrounding Hawaii and Northern Australia, where survival might have less to do with water temperature and more to do with sharks. In and around the UK, however, where water temperatures are very cold, the major factor in surviving a ditching is **avoiding hypothermia.** Hypothermia is caused by a loss of heat, leading to a reduction in the core temperature of the body, i.e. not just the skin temperature, but the internal temperature of the body and its organs.

The early stages of hypothermia can lead to a serious reduction in mental and physical performance; a *severe* case of hypothermia can result in death. Therefore, time is of the essence in rescue following a ditching! Rescue must occur before hypothermia sets in.

Fit Life-Jackets before Touchdown, and Fasten Seat-Belts

It is good airmanship to wear life-jackets when flying for extended periods over water in a single-engined aircraft, because you may not have time to fit them in an emergency situation. In the case of a ditching, make sure that everyone has a life-jacket on, and that seat-belts are fastened firmly. Instruct the passengers not to inflate the life-jackets prior to leaving the aircraft, as this could hinder, or even prevent, exit.

Use your life-jackets.

A quick briefing is appropriate, warning everyone to brace for one or two impacts following touchdown on the water surface, possibly with very strong deceleration forces.

Cushions and other soft materials may be used to protect some of the passengers from the impact forces, but they must not interfere with the controls. In some aircraft, the cushions also act as flotation devices.

If Possible, Ditch Close to Rescuers

Ditching is usually a last resort, and it should be performed as close to a shore or to a ship as possible to reduce the time needed for rescue.

Ditch In Smooth Water if Possible ...

Ditching in calm seas is of course preferable, but this option is not always available. On a calm water surface, it is probably best to touch down into-wind to have the lowest groundspeed on contact with the water.

The wind direction can be determined from your drift angle over the surface, or from wind streaks on the surface. There could be sufficient smooth water on the lee side of a ship (i.e. out of the wind).

... Otherwise on the Crest or Back Side of a Swell

In water that is not calm, it is advisable to avoid landing into the swell (i.e. the rows of widely-spread waves coming from a long distance away); it may be better to land along the swell, even if you have to accept some crosswind, preferably touching down on the crest or on the back side of the swell. In a confused sea, try to land on the crest or on the back side of a wave, and *avoid* landing in its face.

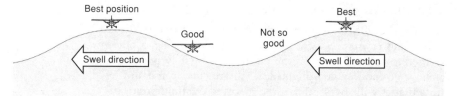

■ Figure 11-6 **Suggested ditching places in water that is not calm**

The wind direction in a confused sea can be determined from wind streaks on the surface and from *whitecaps* which fall forward with the wind, but are then over-run by the wave producing the effect that the foam in the whitecap is sliding backwards.

Touchdown should be as slow as is possible, with a low rate of descent, and with the nose held in a high attitude. Flying at about 10 knots above the stall, power can be used to hold a low height until a smooth patch of water is found, and touchdown can be made near stalling speed on the crest or back side of a swell.

Do not stall the aircraft before touchdown, as this could lead to a heavy drop into the water if you have misjudged the height, which is easy to do above water, especially if it is smooth. There may be one or two impacts, but the slow speed should prevent the aircraft from bouncing back into the air and coming down for a second and less-controlled touchdown. After impact with the water, there is little that the pilot can do to control the aircraft.

If the ditching is as a result of the **loss of power,** then you do not have the luxury of holding off until you find a relatively smooth stretch of water. In this case, glide down at slightly higher than normal approach speed, and then flare early, leaving you some airspeed to bleed off as you feel for the surface. Preferably touch down on the crest or back side of a swell.

Vacate the Aircraft and Enter the Raft

The time the aircraft may float for is quite variable, so plan for an immediate evacuation, using a life-raft if available, and with everyone having their life-jacket inflated before entering the water.

The welfare of the raft occupants will depend upon the skill, knowledge and leadership qualities of the raft leader (usually the pilot-in-command unless incapacitated). Items of importance are:

- ☐ **strengthen the will** to survive;
- ☐ **issue clear orders** in a calm but firm manner;
- ☐ **account for all the survivors** – those in the water can best be brought on board backwards by lifting them under the armpits;
- ☐ **take as much emergency equipment** on board as possible in the time available (ELT, drinking water, flares, flashlights, survival kits, first-aid kits, clothing, blankets, sleeping bags, etc.);
- ☐ **assign a person to maintain watch** for possible search aircraft or for ships or fishing boats.

Disconnect the raft from the aircraft in case it sinks quickly, and move a short distance away. Deploy a sea anchor (e.g. a bucket attached to the raft) to avoid the raft being blown away from the ditching position, which might delay the rescue. Search and rescue activities will always start at the reported ditching position.

Delegation of Duties

Assign tasks to others to offload yourself, and to keep them busy, which will increase their initiative and their will to survive. Initially the tasks can be immediate survival ones – look for survivors, collect emergency equipment, wring out wet clothing, bail out the raft, etc. Later, it can be the more long-term tasks, such as taking duty with the signal mirror, keeping watch, shading sleeping occupants, etc.

Organise the survivors.

Prevent Hypothermia

The colder the water, the faster the body loses heat. Being immersed in water at 20°C, the body would lose a critical 4°C in about 2 hours, probably leading to unconsciousness. In water at 5°C, such as in the northern waters surrounding the UK in winter, this could occur in a few minutes. Also, the extremities, such as the hands, will cool very quickly, making climbing into a raft or grasping anything much more difficult. It is vital to leave cold water quickly and climb into a raft. It is even better if you can **enter the raft directly from the aircraft** and avoid immersion completely.

After coming on board a raft following a ditching, wear dry clothing and stay out of the wind. If possible, wet clothing should be removed and replaced with dry clothing, otherwise wrung out

Keeping warm is vital.

and put on again in a drier state. The evaporation of water absorbs a lot of heat, and could speed up the onset of hypothermia.

Any wind will also increase the rate of evaporation and will lower body temperature, so try to shelter all occupants from the wind, or use warm blankets if available. Some food and drink will provide a source of energy to help in internal warming. Alcohol should definitely *not* be used, since it dilates the vessels near the skin and leads to an even greater heat loss.

The symptoms of hypothermia are skin that is cold to touch, and a slow pulse with slow and shallow breathing. Elderly people and children are especially vulnerable to hypothermia.

Seasickness

If seasickness tablets are available, try to distribute them immediately after things have settled down on the raft, as a preventive measure. Even people not prone to seasickness under normal conditions can become sick quite quickly in a raft. Being seasick causes a loss of food and fluids, wastes a lot of energy, and can weaken the will to survive. Typical dosage is two tablets immediately, and then every 12 hours until rescue.

Emergency Signals

The raft leader should determine when the emergency signals should be used. Normally the ELT will be activated immediately if the raft is near land or near a shipping lane or air route, but it may be advisable to delay using flares, pyrotechnic signals, or sea dye until a ship or aeroplane is in sight, or unless they can possibly attract the attention of people on land. The signal mirror should be used continuously in sunlight. Whistles and other loud noises may attract the attention of people on nearby ships or land, especially at night.

Frostbite

Avoid frostbite.

In cold climates, the extremities with large surface areas (toes, fingers, ears, nose) are subject to frostbite (freezing). The affected parts become pale and numb, possibly appear shiny, and sometimes blisters will form. Ice forms in the tissues and may destroy them, making later amputation necessary.

As a preventive measure, the body should be kept warm, by wearing sufficient clothing and gloves or by placing the hands in the warm area under the armpits, or by the occupants huddling together on the floor close to each other and with their legs pulled up in order to warm each other. The body can be kept warm by light exercise to stimulate blood circulation, but **suspected frostbitten parts should not be rubbed,** since there will be no blood circulation in the tissues – warming using tepid water, if available, is preferable.

Skin Irritation

Exposure to cold and salty water for long periods can lead to skin irritation, stiffness, swellings, and sores. This can be prevented by keeping the body covered and as dry and warm as possible in the circumstances. Bailing out the raft and keeping its floor dry is a priority. The body can be kept warm by light exercise to stimulate blood circulation.

Sunburn

Sunburn is a distinct risk if the sun is shining, even if there is some cloud cover and even if the temperature is low. Use some sun-protection cream and sunglasses if available, and keep in the shade where possible. If temperatures are high, then heat exhaustion or hyperthermia (exceptionally high body core temperature) may occur, causing weakness, dizziness, vomiting, and possibly unconsciousness. Applying moist cloths or shirts to the body may increase cooling.

Avoid sunburn.

Emergency Rations

A person can survive for 30 days or more without food, but only for a day or two without water, so the rationing of water is top priority for long-term survival.

Water should not be rationed out until there is a distinct need for it, which may be after 24 hours, or earlier if a person is in distress or injured. Until then, the body will be functioning on previously consumed fluids. Drink only in small quantities to avoid vomiting up the precious water, which can happen if a large amount is gulped down after a prolonged period of thirst.

Fresh water is vital.

Take every opportunity to collect rainwater, using plastic sheets, plastic bags and buckets if available.

Never drink sea water – it causes vomiting, diarrhoea, and possible mental damage. Do not drink alcohol, but keep it for possible disinfection purposes.

Food rationing could commence after 24 hours. Fishing is a possibility, but only eat raw fish if plenty of drinking water is available, since the salt in fish will increase the need to drink fluids. Do not throw food scraps overboard, especially in warm waters, as this may attract sharks.

Raft Hygiene

Try to keep the raft as clean as possible, with the floor dry.

Behaviour On Board When Rescue Is Imminent

Raft discipline must be maintained until the rescue is complete. Occupants should not leave the raft and swim towards the rescue ship, but should remain on board and await orderly rescue by the crew of the ship or boat.

Maintain survivor discipline.

If found by a search aircraft, the most likely happening will be the dropping of additional equipment, such as locator buoys, food, water, and medical supplies, and the dispatch of a rescue ship. The retrieval of these items must be very orderly to avoid upsetting the raft. There could still be some hours before rescue.

Immersion In Water

If no raft is available in the aircraft following a ditching, then immersion in water for a long period is a possibility. The time for which a person can survive depends to a large extent upon the water temperature. People with a layer of fat and people used to being in water for long periods generally have a greater tolerance and can last a bit longer. Immersion times that people can survive vary greatly, but as a guide, if the water temperature is near 0°C, about 1 hour or less (even a lot less – maybe just a few minutes) is all you can expect. With 12°C, the time could be 4 hours; with 20°C, it could be 12 hours or more.

Heat loss can be prevented by wearing a flotation device that eliminates the need for muscular movement (and hence heat loss) to remain afloat. Clothing, even though wet, will slow the rate of cooling, although the weight of it may prove a disadvantage.

Bunching up under the water will also protect the chest, groin, and arms, and reduce heat loss from these areas. A group of survivors could huddle together to reduce heat loss, and provide mutual support (mental and physical).

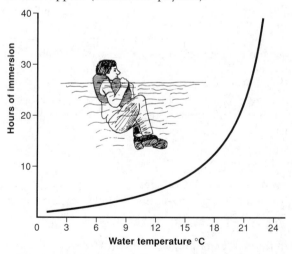

■ Figure 11-7 **Bunch yourself up (or huddle together in a group) to preserve heat**

Survival in Very Cold Climates

If flying in remote icy regions, then a *polar* survival kit should be carried to assist in immediate survival, which has mainly to do with keeping warm in a very hostile environment.

Wear Warm Clothing and Shoes

It is essential to survival in a very cold climate that the body is kept warm and dry, hence the wearing of sufficient clothing, shoes, gloves, and a **head cover** is important. The head is in fact where most heat loss occurs because there are many blood vessels near the surface of the head. Thick layers of loose, dry clothing will provide the best insulation and help retain body heat, with the outer layer of clothing acting as protection against the wind.

Wear the clothing loosely. Clothing that is too tight may hinder blood circulation and lead to frostbite later on. Do not wear too many socks or tight shoes that may hinder blood circulation in your feet. If wearing oversized shoes, however, then they can be packed with handkerchiefs or dry grass or some other stuffing to provide insulation. If shoes are not available, then wrap the feet in clothing. If gloves are not available, do the same, or keep the hands in pockets.

Avoid sweating if possible, as it could lead to frostbite later when you have finished the activity. If working hard, temporarily open the clothing at the neck and wrist, or remove some, but return it to the full warmth position after the work is done and you are cooling down a little.

Keep warm, but avoid sweating.

Keep the clothing as dry as possible. Snow should be brushed off before entering a shelter or approaching a fire which could melt the snow and make the clothes wet. If the clothes are very wet, say from falling in water, rolling in dry snow will help dry them. The dry snow will absorb a lot of the moisture like blotting paper. Wet clothing should then be dried at a fire if possible, but make sure that clothing and shoes do not burn.

If possible, use additional clothing around the shoulders and hips when sleeping, for comfort and warmth.

Gather Survivors and Allot Duties

The leader (normally the pilot-in-command unless incapacitated) should allot duties to fit survivors, such as:

Organise survivors.

- ☐ **gather other survivors;**
- ☐ **assemble emergency equipment,** first-aid kits, rope, etc.;
- ☐ **activate the ELT** if so decided, or fire off flares if help is nearby;
- ☐ **have a person stay by the aircraft** and use the radio if possible;
- ☐ **prepare ground-to-air signals;**

- collect **warm clothing** and food and water supplies;
- **commence construction** of a shelter;
- **search for firewood** or other combustible material (such as oil from the engine) and start a fire;
- **prepare hot drinks;**
- **select a toilet area** some distance from the proposed shelter, but itself sheltered if possible;
- **have a person maintain watch** for possible search aircraft;
- **rotate duties periodically** to provide some variety, to maintain interest, and to ensure that everyone is involved and getting some exercise.

Take Shelter

Immediate shelter in a polar environment is vital. If there is no risk of fire in the aircraft (i.e. no fuel vapours, etc.), then it may be used as shelter against wind, rain, snow, and low temperatures. If the aircraft cannot be used for shelter, then other shelter has to be quickly found or constructed.

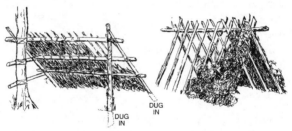

■ *Figure 11-8* **Construct a shelter (or use the aircraft)**

Injured survivors can rest on seat cushions as insulation while fit survivors construct the shelter.

Take shelter.

In a polar environment, construct a shelter near trees if possible, or somewhere that is naturally sheltered against wind and snowdrifts, such as mounds or small hills. Keep away from areas where snowfalls or avalanches are possible, such as the base of high cliffs.

Canvas sheets supported by tree branches or the wing of the aircraft and held down by rocks can provide good shelter. In the long term, a snow hut or snow holes will provide good shelter, but ensure that someone remains on watch for searchers, because snow is a very good sound insulator and may muffle the sound of search aircraft.

Ensure that there is sufficient ventilation for smoke and other fumes to escape from the shelter, and reduce the risk of carbon monoxide poisoning. Drinking water can be obtained from melting ice or snow – ice is better, since it is often cleaner and it also produces more water for less heat input.

■ *Figure 11-9* **Excavating a snow cavity against a small hill for shelter**

The toilet area, some distance from the main shelter, should be the only area used for these purposes for reasons of hygiene. Personal cleanliness can be maintained by wiping the body with a damp cloth. Teeth can be kept clean with a small amount of water or a damp cloth.

If the environment is not icy, for instance in a tundra region in summer, then flies, mosquitoes, and other insects may be a significant problem. Construct the shelter in an elevated and windy position away from bushes, and preferably near a water supply.

Avoid Frostbite

Frostbite is a possibility in icy and windy conditions that remove more heat from the body than it can produce. Reduced blood flow in the extremities can lead to frostbite, even at temperatures above freezing if the clothing is wet.

Prevent frostbite by keeping the extremities warm with clothing if possible, or by covering them with warm hands. Exercise lightly by doing such things as moving, chewing, and contracting muscles.

Neighbours should observe each other for signs of frostbite, such as pale, cold and unfeeling skin, the tip of the nose becoming red, skin turning blue or black (a final stage). **If frostbite is suspected, do not rub the area** or try to remove frozen gloves or shoes; this may do further damage to the skin, as would muscular movement. Try to gradually warm the area with body heat from other people, or use warm water or clothing.

Snow Blindness

Snow blindness is caused by glare from very white and reflective snow. It causes inflammation and burning in the eyes, tears running from the eyes, headaches, and reduced vision.

Prevent the onset of snow blindness by wearing sunglasses or by making improvised eye protectors, say by using cardboard strips with small slits to restrict the amount of light entering the eyes.

Fires and Other Signals

Alert rescuers.

Signal fires should be lit on a solid base (e.g. rocks) to prevent the fire melting the snow or ice and extinguishing itself.

Rescue signals can be laid out in the snow using canvas sheets held down by rocks, or by digging shallow trenches in the snow and laying branches or grass in them, or around the edges of the trench to enlarge the signal and make it stand out.

■ *Figure 11-10* **Prepare visible ground-to-air signals**

The aircraft itself may be very visible from the air if you can keep its upper surfaces clear from snow, especially if the aircraft is brightly coloured. For this reason, many aircraft that regularly operate in Arctic or Antarctic environments are painted bright red or orange.

Survival in a Hot, Arid Climate

Survival in a desert region depends mainly upon the body retaining and obtaining sufficient fluids to avoid dehydration and overheating.

After touchdown and coming to a stop, it is important to remove water and other rations and the emergency equipment from the aircraft as quickly as possible because of the increased risk of fire, and then to find cool and shady protection. As many articles as possible should be taken from the aircraft, including seat cushions and blankets (to be used as cooling insulation from the hot ground by day and for warmth at night).

When the environmental temperature is above 30°C, the greatest loss of water is caused by sweating, which is the natural cooling mechanism of the body when heat loss by convection is insufficient. The evaporation of moisture on the skin absorbs heat (the latent heat of vaporisation), and so cools the skin and the rest of the body. The initial aims of survival in very hot and dry weather are therefore to:

> *Minimise sweating.*

- ☐ **reduce body heat** and minimise sweating; and
- ☐ **find water** (possibly in the cool of the night).

Gather Survivors and Allot Duties
The leader (normally the pilot-in-command unless incapacitated) should allot duties to fit survivors, such as:

> *Organise survivors.*

- ☐ **gather other survivors;**
- ☐ **assemble emergency equipment,** first-aid kits, rope, etc.;
- ☐ **activate the ELT** if so decided, or fire off flares if help is nearby;
- ☐ **have a person stay by the aircraft** and use the radio if possible;
- ☐ **prepare ground-to-air signals;**
- ☐ **collect clothing** (desert areas can be cold at night);
- ☐ **gather food and water supplies** (especially water);
- ☐ **begin construction** of a shady and open-sided shelter;
- ☐ **search for firewood** or other combustible material;
- ☐ **select a toilet area,** some distance from the proposed shelter; and
- ☐ **have a person maintain watch** for possible search aircraft.

Activate the appropriate emergency signals, or plan when to activate them. If the radio in the aircraft is usable, and there is no risk of fire, then it can be used to broadcast Mayday calls, either on the local frequency most likely to be used, or on the emergency frequency 121·5 MHz. Conservation of the battery should be considered, and the radio only used at times when it is likely to be most effective.

Fires laid out in a clearing can also generate a lot of smoke by day that will be visible for many miles by day, and with flames that may be visible by night. Perhaps three fires laid out 5 or 10 metres apart in an unusual and unnatural triangle would attract attention more easily than just one large fire. Oil drained from the engine could also be added to increase the amount of smoke.

Fires should be lit in a cleared and open area – away from over-hanging trees – as the risk of setting fire to the entire area of veg-etation around you would be high in hot and dry climates, espe-cially if it is windy.

Clothing

Light clothing is the best protection against sunburn and heat exposure, especially if all parts of the body can be covered, including the back of the neck and the head. This will also reduce the need for water, especially if sweating is kept to a minimum, and provide protection against sand and insects. A single layer of loosely worn clothing will minimise any heat gain, and maximise the amount of heat lost through sweating.

The cooling benefit of any sweating will be maximised by light clothing worn loosely.

Good shoes should be worn as protection against the hot ground and also as protection against insects, spiders, snakes, scorpions and other inhabitants of desert regions. Shoes and clothing should be shaken and checked clear of insects, spiders, etc., before being put on.

If there is a lot of dust or sand in the air, which will be the case in duststorms or sandstorms, use a handkerchief or shirt to protect the mouth, nose and eyes.

Find Shade and Set Up Camp

It is important to minimise the increase in body temperature and the loss of fluids. Finding a cool and shady place is vital! Solid shade is better than leafy or intermittent shade.

Do not consider travelling by day unless a copious water supply is guaranteed. Set up camp near the aircraft of possible (i.e. within some hundreds of metres from it), since the aircraft will probably be very visible to search aircraft. If you move further away than this, leave arrows indicating the direction of where you have gone to set-up camp. There have been cases where abandoned aircraft and cars have been found, but no survivors – they had wandered away and perished in the desert.

Any enclosed space such as the cockpit of the aircraft, even though it may provide shade, will very quickly heat up due to heat soaking in the sun, and may even become much warmer than the outside air temperature. A naturally shaded area, for instance in the shade of a tree (preferably near water), or in the shade of a rock face, generally provides the coolest and shadiest protection against heat and the sun.

The surrounding ground that has been shaded will also be relatively cool, whereas if you shelter in the shade of the aircraft wing the ground is likely to be very warm. A cooling breeze of fresh air is also helpful so, if you have a tent, keep the sides or door flaps open during the day.

Avoid sitting or lying on hot ground. Sitting or lying a foot above the warm ground, on cushions or life-jackets or on a bed constructed from branches, may reduce the temperatures that the body is exposed to by some 10–12°C and significantly reduce the loss of fluid through sweating. If moving around is inevitable, then move slowly to conserve energy and avoid sweating.

Consider the risks of setting up camp in a dry river bed – flash floods are possible, with water rushing down from storms miles away.

Be careful of using river rocks to surround a camp fire as they could possibly explode with the heat.

Protect the Eyes and Prevent Sunburn

Wear sunglasses, or make an eye protector from cardboard with small slits to see through, which should prevent the intense sunlight and reflection from the desert surface straining or damaging the eyes.

Being fully covered by clothing and a hat will be some protection against sunburn, but sun-protection cream should also be used to protect exposed parts of the body, such as the face, hands, and neck.

Find Water

In hot, arid areas, the human body requires about 4–5 litres of water a day to remain healthy, and even more if the person is exposed to the sun or is over-energetic in the conditions and perspires a lot.

The need for regular water is much greater than for solid foods – survival may be possible without food for 30 days, but for only a few hours or a day without water in an extreme desert environment. If food is available, only carbohydrates should be eaten as they require little water to be digested, whereas proteins and fats require more water to excrete the wastes formed during their metabolism.

One of the first tasks delegated to one of the survivors should be to retrieve any water or other drinking fluids on board the aircraft. Alcohol should not be consumed, and very sweet drinks are vastly inferior to plain water. Rainwater from any showers can be collected using plastic sheets, or caught in containers as it runs off the aircraft wings. Dew can also be collected at night if it is allowed to form on plastic sheets, canvas, the metal surfaces of the aircraft, plants, stones, etc. – up to a litre per hour can be collected in good conditions for the formation of dew.

Fresh water is vital.

With luck, there might be a running stream in the vicinity, but in desert areas this is unlikely, and a search for underground water might be required. Terrain, vegetation, birds, insects and animal tracks can sometimes provide clues as to where water might be found. Be aware of running towards shimmering mirages in the distance which can give the illusion of an expanse of water, and which have led some survivors to their death.

Fresh water can often be found if a hole is dug in the sand of a dry river bed. Water may be found sometimes just under the surface, but sometimes the hole may have to be a metre or more deep before any dampness is found. Even if the sand in the bottom of the hole is only slightly damp, water may gradually trickle in and accumulate over a period of time. Digging too deep may lead to salty water, which should not be drunk.

Fresh water can also sometimes be found in rock pools, even on stony hills. Ayers Rock in the middle of the Australian desert has rock pools permanent enough to contain fish. Some desert plants and trees also contain water.

Water transpirator bags designed for collecting water in desert environments are commercially available, and these are recommended for desert survival kits.

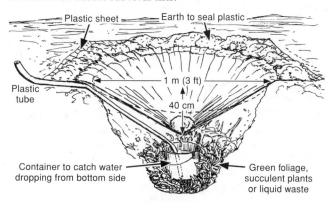

■ *Figure 11-11* **Procuring water**

Conserve Energy and Ration Water

Conserve energy.

Do not consider trying to hike out of the desert area by day unless there is absolute certainty of a water supply. Moving around under a hot sun may reduce survival time by half, compared with resting in a shady area. Travelling in the cool of the night, if travelling is considered necessary, is a much better proposition.

Monitor the condition of the survivors for any signs of dehydration, and ration water accordingly. The colour of urine is a good test of the need for water, with very dark yellow urine indicating some level of dehydration. Extreme thirst, headache, dizziness and disorientation are also indications.

Water is the best fluid to drink. Alcohol should not be consumed, and tea and coffee should be avoided, since they are diuretics, i.e. cause the loss of more fluid than is consumed. Control the activities of the survivors to conserve energy and to minimise the loss of fluids through sweating. If moving is inevitable, then move slowly.

People suffering heat exhaustion may have a flushed face at first, which might then go pale. They may sweat a lot even though their skin might feel cool, eventually becoming delirious or unconscious. They should lie down on their backs in a well-shaded area, and drink some water, possibly with a little salt added. If shivering, keep them warm with a blanket and a hot drink. Heat convulsions may occur in the leg and stomach muscles. A cool drink, possibly with some salt added, plus resting on the back in a cool area is the best remedy.

In an extreme case, a person might suffer heat stroke – indicated by a red face, hot and dry skin with no sweating, the pulse rate increasing and perhaps being very strong, and possible unconsciousness. The person should be laid on the back in the shade, the clothes loosened, and the body cooled with moist cloths and by fanning air.

Survival in a Jungle

Survival in a jungle depends first on making a survivable touchdown, which preferably will be in a clearing, but may have to be in the treetops. If in the unfortunate position of having to land in treetops, you should approach at the lowest possible flying speed.

An aircraft in the centre of a clearing, or suspended in the treetops, should be visible to searching aircraft. An aircraft that has fallen down through the trees, however, may be completely covered by foliage and not be visible from the air.

Gather Survivors and Allot Duties

The leader (normally the pilot-in-command unless incapacitated) should allot duties to fit survivors, such as:

Organise survivors.

- gather other survivors;
- assemble emergency equipment, first-aid kits, rope, etc;
- activate the ELT if so decided, or fire flares if help is nearby;
- have a person stay by the aircraft and use the radio if possible;
- prepare ground-to-air signals;
- collect warm clothing and food and water supplies;
- commence construction of a shelter;
- search for firewood or other combustible material and start a fire;
- prepare hot drinks;
- select a toilet area some distance from the proposed shelter, but itself sheltered if possible;
- have a person maintain watch for possible search aircraft.

If the aeroplane is hidden from the view of searching aircraft, then set up camp in a nearby clearing or on a peak visible from the air. Finding water and food in a jungle may be straight forward – the greatest difficulty will probably be the searchers locating you, so make yourself visible.

Jungle Clothing

Remain fully clothed, with trousers tucked into the socks, as protection against insects, leeches, sharp blades of grass, etc., and always wear shoes. Take the usual protection as described earlier to protect against sunburn if appropriate. Cover all exposed parts including your face, especially during the periods of dusk and dawn, as protection against mosquitoes, which may carry malaria in some parts of the world (e.g. Africa). If no covering is available, smear your face and hands with mud, which will dry and provide some protection.

Try to keep your clothes clean and dry, to avoid skin problems developing. Wring out your clothes after going through water, and dry your body (check for any leeches) and shoes. Try to wash and dry your clothes periodically to keep them clean.

Any wound or infection should be cleaned and disinfected, and then covered, as serious infections can develop very quickly in a warm, moist environment.

Other Inhabitants of the Jungle

Jungles are a great home for all sorts of life, some of which is outright dangerous to humans, and some just of nuisance value.

Meat-eating animals such as tigers or crocodiles, or the piranha fish in some South American rivers, are a consideration, as are venomous or constricting snakes, and poisonous plants. Small animals and insects, such as wasps, bees, mosquitoes, ticks, leeches, spiders, centipedes, ants, and scorpions also need to be protected against. The mosquito can be very dangerous in the long term if it is carrying malaria. Malaria will not develop immediately, but some weeks or months after the victim has been bitten by the mosquitoes, with the effects possibly lasting for many years.

SNAKE BITE. Remember that not all snakes are poisonous. However it is wise to treat all snake bites as potentially dangerous. The modern treatment for snake bites is the *pressure–immobilisation* method:

☐ **Keep the victim lying down and resting;** this will localise the venom as much as possible.

☐ **Immediately apply a broad pressure-bandage** over the two puncture marks made by the fangs; the bandage should be as tight as you would apply to a sprained ankle.

☐ **Then extend the bandaging** by rolling the bandage firmly around as much of the limb as possible.

- Do not remove the clothing, as the movement will help the venom to circulate.
- Leave the bandage in place until medical facilities are reached.
- Apply a splint to the limb to immobilise it (if, as is most likely, the bite is on a limb).
- If possible, transport the patient without panic to the nearest hospital or medical clinic, preferably on a stretcher; otherwise keep the patient still and in shade, and reassure them until medical help arrives.
- Should breathing begin to fail, give artificial respiration.
- Do not attempt to excise the venom from the wound.

LEECHES, which attach themselves to the skin and then grow to a large size as they fill with blood, can best be removed by applying heat from a burning match. It is advisable to check for leeches every 30 minutes or so, as they can work their way through your clothing and on to your legs and arms without you noticing.

Use disinfectant, if available, on any bites or scratches.

Water
Water should be purified before drinking, either by sterilising it by boiling for five minutes or more, by using sterilising tablets, or by filtering it through a cloth. Near a muddy river or pool, clear water can sometimes be obtained by digging a deep hole a few metres away, and allowing water to seep in.

Fresh water is vital.

Coconut milk can also satisfy thirst.

Food
Food may be plentiful in a jungle area, but you need to be careful of disease in meat and poison in plants. Meat should always be well cooked to kill any parasites. Any plant food that irritates the skin or mouth should not be swallowed.

Shelter
Shelter may be needed at night or in rain, as protection against animal and insect life and the elements. Dry and rocky ground in a breezy area is preferable to a swamp. Try to keep above ground level, or separated from the ground by a plastic or rubber sheet, as protection against insects, leeches, and dampness.

Take shelter.

Attracting Attention
Make use of the radio and the ELT if available. If hidden from the view of searching aircraft by foliage, use smoky fires (using damp wood or adding engine oil will assist), or fire some flares when you hear an aircraft overhead.

Alert rescuers.

Now, finally, complete **Exercises 11 – Survival.**

The Air Pilot's **Manual**

Volume 6

Exercises and Answers

About the Exercises

These exercises form a vital part of the course.

We suggest that you take a blank piece of paper and jot your answer down, with the number of the question beside it. This leaves your textbook unmarked and suitable for later revisions. The answers for both sections are to be found at the end of the exercises, just before the index.

Prior to sitting for the examination in Human Performance and Limitations, you should be getting almost total success in the exercises.

Many of the questions which follow are very straightforward; they are intended to serve as reminders of important points in the text, and thereby strengthen your grasp of the material.

We have not included *multi-choice questions* as they are not a good learning aid (continually reading incorrect statements is confusing). In the exam, however, this is the method of examining your knowledge. A good technique for answering multi-choice questions is:

▢ Prior to reading through the selection, think carefully what you feel the answer might be.

▢ Then read the choices – quite often you will find the answer you already have in mind is amongst them.

▢ If not, then proceed to eliminate the incorrect statements.

Human Performance and Limitations Examination

The exam paper consists of 20 multi-choice questions worth 5 marks each. Thirty minutes is allowed to complete the exam, and the pass mark is 70%.

However, for JAR-FCL applicants, or applicants sitting after 30 June 2000, the pass mark is increased to 75%.

Human Factors and Pilot Performance

Exercises 1

Human Physiology and High Altitudes

1 The master controller of the human body is the ....

2 The brain and spinal chord together form the ....

3 The brain (continues/stops) functioning when we sleep.

4 The system that moves blood around the body is known as the .... system. The blood is pumped through the system by the ....

5 Blood carries ...... from the lungs to the body tissues where it is burned to supply energy. This blood is coloured (red/blue).

6 Oxygen molecules passing from the lungs into the blood attach themselves to the h.......... in the red blood cells.

7 After delivering oxygen to the body tissues, the blood then carries ..... products away.

8 The deoxygenated blood, which is somewhat (redder/bluer) in colour, is returned to the heart, which pumps it through the lungs, where the waste .... is removed and then breathed out.

9 The circulation through the lungs is known as the (systemic/pulmonary) circulation.

10 The circulation through the body tissues is known as the (systemic/pulmonary) circulation.

11 The blood vessels carrying blood away from the heart are called ....

12 The blood vessels carrying blood to the heart are called ....

13 The very fine blood vessels are called ....

14 The pump of the circulatory system is the ..... and the rate at which it pumps is called the ..... rate.

15 The process of bringing energy-giving oxygen into the body and removing waste carbon dioxide is called ....

16 External respiration occurs in the (lungs/body tissues), and internal respiration occurs in the (lungs/body tissues).

17 The breathing rate is controlled mainly by the amount of .... in the blood, a high concentration of which causes the breathing rate to (increase/decrease).

18 Lung capacity is about (1/2/5/20) litre(s), but when a person is resting each breath measures about ($\frac{1}{4}$/$\frac{1}{2}$/1/2/5) litre(s).

19 Air pressure (increases/decreases) as altitude is gained.

20 A lack of oxygen in the body is called ....

21 Oxygen deprivation becomes serious above about (1,000/5,000/10,000/20,000/30,000) feet.

22 A sudden depressurisation will cause a sudden (inhalation/exhalation) of breath.

23 What are the symptoms of hypoxia?

24 TUC stands for the t... of .... following sudden deprivation of oxygen.

25 A smoker (will/will not) show symptoms of oxygen deprivation sooner than a non-smoker.

26 The cure for hypoxia is to breathe (more/less) oxygen.

27 Gases trapped in parts of your body will (contract/expand) as the cabin altitude increases. This is called ....

28 Overbreathing may flush (oxygen/carbon dioxide) out of the blood and cause ....

29 The symptoms of hyperventilation are ....

30 The remedy for hyperventilation is to (reduce/increase) the breathing rate.

31 Surfacing too quickly after deep scuba diving can cause .... sickness, also known as the .... Climbing to altitude after scuba diving (will/will not) worsen it.

32 The remedy for the bends is to (increase/decrease) pressure on the body.

33 As a general guide, do not fly at all within .. hours of scuba diving to shallow depths with compressed air, and within .. hours if you dive deeper than 30 feet.

34 What gas associated with the combustion process is colourless, odourless and tasteless, but very poisonous if breathed in?

35 Carbon monoxide (is/is not) found in engine exhaust.

36 Symptoms of carbon monoxide poisoning are ....

37 If carbon monoxide poisoning is suspected, you should (increase/reduce) the supply of fresh air.

38 Equalisation of air pressure on either side of the eardrums is allowed by the .... tubes which connect the ears and the ..... passages.

39 Blocked nasal passages are more likely to cause ear problems during (climb/cruise/descent).

40 If you have a cold, (do/do not) fly.

Exercises 2

Eyesight and Visual Illusions

1 Each eye is connected to the brain by an ..... nerve.

2 To look at a near object, the eyes have to turn slightly (inward/outward).

3 The natural focal point for the eyes when resting is about (1 to 2 metres/20 metres/200 metres/infinity). This is referred to as .... myopia.

4 A person with only one eye (will/will not) have protection from the blind spot.

5 A person with two eyes (does/does not) have blind spots. The second eye (does/does not) provide protection.

6 Focusing both eyes on the one object is called .... vision, and it (helps/does not help) with depth perception.

7 The transparent cap over the lens of each eye is called the ....

8 The cornea can be protected by the ...... closing over it.

9 The coloured membrane between the cornea and the lens is called the .... , and it contains a small, round aperture called the ..... which (can/cannot) change in size.

10 In bright light, the pupil will be (small/wide); in dim conditions, the pupil will be (small/wide).

11 The part of the eye that can change shape and does most of the focusing of the light rays is the ..... . The greater its curvature, the (greater/lesser) the focusing.

12 The ability of an eye to change its focal point is called ....

13 The lens should focus the incoming light rays on the light-sensitive layer at the back of the eye, known as the ....

14 The central section of the retina consists mainly of .... cells which (are/are not) sensitive to colour, (are/are not) sensitive to small details, (are/are not) sensitive to distant objects, and are most effective in (daylight/darkness/both daylight and darkness).

15 The peripheral, outer region of the retina consists mainly of ... cells which (are/are not) sensitive to colour, and (are/are not) sensitive to small details, and (are/are not) sensitive to distant objects and are most effective in (daylight/darkness/both daylight and darkness).

16 The blind spot in each eye is where the ..... nerve leaves the retina.

17 The ability to see clearly and sharply is called visual ....

18 Visual acuity (is/is not) diminished by fatigue or alcohol.

19 In strong sunlight or glary conditions you should wear ....

20 Depth perception when landing is (easier/more difficult) in hazy or foggy conditions.

21 On approach in hazy conditions, the runway may be (closer/further away) than what it appears to be, often causing a pilot to flare too (early, late).

22 Men are (more/less) likely than women to have some form of colour-blindness.

23 The eyes take about .. minutes to adapt to darkness. The most effective retinal cells in darkness are the (rods/cones) which are used for (peripheral/central) vision.

24 Bright light in the cockpit at night can destroy light adaption (immediately/after about 5 minutes), and it then takes about .. minutes to re-establish full light adaption.

25 When scanning for aircraft by day, you should use your (central/peripheral) vision.

26 When scanning for aircraft by night, you should use your (central/peripheral) vision.

27 The resting eye focuses at about ...... metres; this is known as e.... f.... m..... , so we (do/do not) have to concentrate on focusing on distant aircraft.

28 The visual illusion of a single stationary light at night appearing to move is called ....

29 Sloping cloud banks by day or town lights on a hillside at night (can/will not) cause visual illusions of a false horizon.

30 The normal approach path to a runway sloping upwards will appear to be too (steep/shallow), causing a tendency for an inexperienced pilot to fly too (high/low) on slope.

31 The normal approach path to a runway sloping downwards will appear to be too (steep/shallow), causing a tendency for an inexperienced pilot to fly too (high/low) on slope.

32 An especially wide runway will appear to be (closer/further away) than it really is during the late stages of an approach, causing a tendency for an inexperienced pilot to flare too (high/low).

33 An especially narrow runway will appear to be (closer/further away) than it really is during the late stages of an approach, causing a tendency for an inexperienced pilot to flare too (high/low).

34 During a night approach, the apparent gap between the runway edge lights is increasing. The aeroplane is flying to an aiming point (before/at/beyond) the normal aiming point.

35 During a night approach, the apparent gap between the runway edge lights is decreasing. The aeroplane is flying to an aiming point (before/at/beyond) the normal aiming point.

36 It is (good/poor) airmanship to use a v..... a....... s.... i........ at night.

37 An approach at night to a well-lit runway, but with no other lights to be seen, is called a .....-.... approach.

38 The lack of features near a runway, say during a black-hole approach or in white-out snow conditions, make depth and slope perception (more/less) difficult.

39 The term *myopia* refers to (long/short) sightedness.

40 A short-sighted eye focuses the light rays (too much/not enough).

41 A long-sighted eye focuses the light rays (too much/not enough).

42 Short-sightedness is called ......; long-sightedness is called .... or ....

43 Reading becomes more difficult with age because the eyes become more (long-/short-)sighted, known as .... It causes diminished (near/far) vision, and is often corrected by using (full-/half-)glasses.

44 Faulty curvature of the lens is called ....

45 If glasses are required for flying, you should carry (one/two/three) pairs.

Exercises 3

Hearing and Balance

1 The ears are very important for both h...... and b....... .

2 Sound messages are sent from the ear to the brain via the .... nerve.

3 The ear is divided into three areas: the ..... ear, the ...... ear, and the ..... ear.

4 Air pressure either side of each eardrum is equalised by virtue of the E......... t.... .

5 The Eustachian tubes are located in the (outer/middle/inner) ear.

6 Loud and unpleasant noise (can/will not) be fatiguing.

7 A pilot (should/should not) protect the hearing with a good headset or earmuffs while flying.

8 The balance mechanism is in the (outer/middle/inner) ear, and it detects (accelerations/motion).

9 Angular accelerations in all three planes detected by the s...- c....... canals in the inner ear.

10 Linear accelerations are detected by the s..... o.... in the inner ear.

11 The static organ in the ear detects (linear/angular)accelerations. The static organ is composed of the c....., which is g......... material containing small crystals known as o........ . The c..... has small h.... protruding into it which can send signals back to the brain regarding its movement.

12 The static organ detects the *direction* of g-forces, but cannot distinguish their origin, which could be the force of .... or a (linear/angular) acceleration.

13 The more reliable sense is (vision/balance).

14 Once you have settled into a steady banked turn, the balance mechanism will send a message of (level/banked) flight. You should use your .... to verify the true situation.

15 Immediately after rolling level out of a lengthy, banked turn to the left, the balance mechanism will send a message of (level/right-banked/left-banked) flight. This is known as the .... You should ... .

16 Immediately after rolling level out of a lengthy, banked turn to the right, the balance mechanism will send a message of (level/right-banked/left-banked) flight. This is known as the ..... . You should ... .

17 To minimise balance illusions in instrument flight, you (should/need not) hold your head upright relative to your body, and use your ..... .

18 An illusion of rotation when no rotation is occurring, or vice versa, is known as ....

19 Vertigo (can/cannot) be caused by accelerations, strong nose-blowing, and sneezing.

20 An upper respiratory tract infection such as a cold is critical for flying because the infection is likely to have blocked the E........ ....

21 Flying with blocked Eustachian tubes can be painful and, in extreme cases, cause inwards failure of the e....... on descent and lead to p....... v....... .

22 In a steady banked turn, the body experiences (more/less) than 1g, the same feeling as when entering a (climb/descent).

23 After rolling out of a turn, the body experiences (a reduced/an increased) g-force, the same feeling as when entering a (climb/descent). You should ... .

24 A strong forward acceleration can cause an illusion of pitching nose (up/down) and tumbling (forwards/backwards). You should ... .

25 A strong deceleration can cause an illusion of pitching nose (up/down) and tumbling (forwards/backwards). You should ... .

26 Airsickness can often be relieved by (rough/smooth-and-coordinated) flying, lots of (stale/fresh) air, and (no/plenty of) unusual g-forces.

Exercises 4

Am I Fit To Fly?

1 Two factors vital to safe flying are p....... and m..... fitness on the part of the pilot.

2 Smoking promotes the presence of .... in the blood in preference to oxygen, and this reduces the body's ability to produce ....

3 Can a cold cause you discomfort whilst flying?

4 Having consumed a small amount of alcohol, you should not fly for at least ..... hours.

5 The average human body disperses ... unit(s) of alcohol per hour.

6 If you are on medication, the effect of which you are unsure, then you (may/should not) fly.

7 List five common medications considered incompatible with flying.

8 Pilots are advised that in order to prevent the slight risk of post-transfusion faintness they should refrain from donating blood for .... hours before flight.

9 A faulty exhaust system may be dangerous because of the possibility of .... poisoning.

10 Carbon monoxide in an aircraft cabin is:
(a) easily recognisable because of its peculiar odour.
(b) easily recognisable because of its peculiar colour.
(c) difficult to recognise because it is odourless and colourless.

11 The amount of oxygen available (increases/decreases/remains the same) as altitude is gained.

12 Lack of oxygen can affect a pilot dramatically; this is known as ....

Exercises 5

Stress Management, Fatigue and Sleep

1 Excess demands, mental and/or physical, can lead to stress; the cause of the stress being called a ....

2 Stress (can/will not) diminish one's performance and affect the health.

3 When describing stress, 'acute' means (long-/short-) term, and 'chronic' means (long-/short-) term.

4 Stress (is/is not) accumulative in the sense that a number of small stressors (can/will not) result in a larger total stress level.

5 The presence of one form of stress (can/will not) diminish your resistance to other forms of stress.

6 Being fit, healthy, relaxed and well-rested (increases/does not affect/reduces) your ability to resist stress.

7 Being well prepared for a flight (increases/does not affect/reduces) stress during the flight.

8 Your ability to resist stress will be greater if your personal and family life is (happy/disturbed).

9 Too many demands may cause an overload, resulting in ......, and performance (may/will not) drop.

10 (All/not all) pressures are real.

11 Tolerance to pressure is (the same/different) for different people.

12 Tolerance to additional pressure is (greater/the same/less) when stress is already present.

13 A sudden fright causes the release of a........ in the body, which prepares a person for ...... , i.e. to fight or flee.

14 Under-arousal, which can occur if a person is fatigued or not motivated, can lead to (poor/good) performance.

15 Over-arousal to the point of panic can lead to (poor/good) performance.

16 An intermediate level of arousal, optimum arousal, can lead to (poor/good) performance.

17 Sketch a graph of 'output of quality work (i.e. performance)' *versus* 'arousal'.

18 A hot, noisy, vibrating cockpit is likely to be (more/less) stressful than a cool, quiet and non-vibrating cockpit.

19 Stress caused by heat is called h........... ; to minimise heat stress you should (drink/avoid) fluids.

20 Stress caused by low temperatures is called h.......... .

21 A pilot is more likely to be stressed in (calm/turbulent) conditions.

22 Noise stress (can/will not) be reduced by the use of a good headset.

23 Poor eating habits (may/will not) make you more susceptible to stress.

24 Long periods of concentration, such as when flying on instruments, (may/will not) make you more prone to stress.

25 Tiredness (will/will not) make you more prone to stress.

26 Problems at home (may/will not) make a pilot more prone to stress.

27 Extreme worry that results when a person is overloaded is called ....

28 The first step in being prepared to minimise stress and manage whatever demands occur is to be well-prepared both ph........ and ps............. .

29 How could you avoid stress caused by a noisy cockpit?

30 How could you avoid stress caused by turbulence under a cumulus cloud?

31 Sketch a graph of 'pilot capability' and 'demands' *versus* 'time' for the period of a flight, i.e. from start-up to shut-down.

32 Very deep tiredness is called ....

33 The best immediate cure for fatigue is ....

34 A typical person each day requires ..... hours of sleep to prepare for .... hours of activity.

35 In very approximate terms, one hour of sleep gives you credit for ... hour(s) of activity.

36 (Regular/irregular) sleeping times are best.

37 A serious inability to sleep is called ....

38 A pilot should (use/avoid) drugs that induce sleep.

Note: The remaining questions in this group cover the optional material from page 84 of 'Sleep' in the text.

39 The depth of our sleep (varies/remains the same) throughout the night.

40 Very deep sleep normally occurs (early/late) during an eight-hour sleep period.

41 The two basic types of sleep are non-REM sleep and REM sleep, where REM stands for r.... e.. m........ .

42 A person normally wakes naturally during (REM/non-REM) sleep.

43 The body is revitalised during (REM/non-REM) sleep.

44 The brain is revitalised during (REM/non-REM) sleep.

45 Alcohol in the system will (disturb/not affect/improve) the quality of a person's sleep.

46 Sketch a 48-hour period showing the sleep pattern for a person with a good and regular sleep pattern. Also sketch your own.

47 Excessively long sleeping (will/will not) increase your sleep credits and allow longer hours of wakefulness.

48 A shift-worker working different hours each day will have (less/more/the same) difficulty with sleeping compared to a shift-worker with regular hours.

49 The daily body rhythms are called .... rhythms, and the most important one is that of internal b... t.......... .

50 The natural period of the body's circadian rhythm is more likely to be (23/24/25) hours.

51 A natural 25-hour period for body rhythms is pushed back into a 24-hour period by a succession of time-of-day reminders known as z......... .

52 'Zeit' means .... and 'geber' means ....

53 The most powerful zeitgeber is the ... .

54 Alertness and performance capability vary with internal ....

55 The low point in internal body temperature, and in alertness and performance capability, is typically between (9 a.m. and 12 noon/4 a.m. and 6 a.m./midnight and 2 a.m.).

56 The problem caused by moving into a new time zone is called ....

57 When adjusting to a new time zone, different body rhythms all change at (a different/the same) rate.

58 With jet lag, the different body rhythms (remain synchronised/become desynchronised).

59 If you are flying westwards, you are flying (with/against) the sun, and your day will be (longer than/shorter than/exactly) 24 hours.

60 The natural body clock, if not pulled into line by the sun and other zeitgebers, is typically (longer than/shorter than/exactly) 24 hours.

61 Travelling eastwards, you are flying (with/against) the sun, and your day will be (longer than/shorter than/exactly) 24 hours.

62 Travelling (westwards/eastwards) is more in harmony with your natural body clock and will cause less jet lag.

63 Jet lag is likely to be greater when you fly from (Europe to America/America to Europe). Why?

Exercises 6

Information Processing

1 We make our highest level decisions in the ....

2 The brain can be thought of as a c...... d.......-m..... .

3 For high-level decisions, the brain functions as a (multi/single) -channel decision-maker.

4 A number of high-level decisions will be made by the brain (simultaneously/consecutively).

5 Sensory information that we absorb and take note of is said to be p........ stimuli.

6 The common terms for conscious decision making are t....... or c......... .

7 Activities which are so well practised that we can perform them with little or no conscious effort are called s..... , and are run, not by conscious decision-making in the brain, but by m.... p......... .

8 A primitive level of nervous activity not involving the brain, such as the spontaneous withdrawal of a finger from a pin prick, is called a ....

9 A trained 'reflex', where the subject is trained to respond to a second stimulus that is associated with the initial sensory stimulus which causes the response, is called a .... reflex. A good example is P....... dogs.

10 Normal bodily functions such as breathing, heart rate and digestion are not controlled consciously but by the .... nervous system.

11 The aim in the initial hours of flying training is to practise things which initially require a lot of c........ d.......-m..... until they become s..... and can be run by m.... p......... with little conscious thought.

12 Name five senses.

13 Specialised cells which detect sensory information are called .... cells.

14 Continual or repetitive stimulation may cause the receptor cells to ..... to that particular stimulus and not respond to it – for instance, a continual hum or the pressure of clothes we are wearing.

15 Sensory information is stored very briefly in the .... memory before it is replaced by newly sensed information. Visual images last about ... second(s); sounds last about .... second(s).

16 Sensory information (is/is not) more easily perceived and integrated if we recognise it through experience.

17 Sensory information that we expect to receive (is/is not) more easily perceived and integrated when it actually occurs, compared with totally unexpected information.

18 Anticipating receiving sensory information is good, such as a particular radio message, but we must guard against having a m... s.. in case the actual message is different.

19 Sampling stimuli and selecting some of them for further processing is called selective ....

20 Switching our attention between two sets of stimuli is called .... attention or .... sharing.

21 Being under a lot of stress (may/will not) reduce our ability to perceive sensory information.

22 Being fatigued or under-motivated (may/will not) reduce our ability to perceive sensory information.

23 A totally imagined and unreal perception is called a h............ .

24 Misinterpreting stimuli, such as feeling upright when in fact you are in a banked turn, can lead to i.......s .

25 The short-term memory (has/does not have) limited capacity.

26 The short-term memory can hold about ..... items for .... seconds.

27 More information can be retained in the short-term memory by condensing several items into one, for instance '3020' as 'thirty-twenty', a process known as .... information.

28 A *word-play* to assist in remembering a list of items, such as 'PUF' or 'TMP-FISCH', is called a ....

29 In an attempt to commit certain information to our long-term memory we can .... it in our working memory. This is like .... learning.

30 The process of remembering something by understanding it, rather than just rehearsing or repeating it, is called ....

31 Encoding, or understanding, is usually a (better/poorer) way of remembering something over a long period than rehearsal, or rote learning.

32 The part of the memory where information is filed away for later use, perhaps years later, is called the ....

33 The long-term memory appears to have two areas, one where m....... are stored and one where e..... are stored.

34 The meaning part of the long-term memory is also called the .... memory. Giving our full attention to new material so that we really understand it (helps/will not help) in encoding it into our *meaning* memory.

35 Events are stored in a part of our long-term memory which is also known as the .... memory. This part of the memory (is/is not) prone to inaccuracies.

36 The time between perceiving a stimulus and responding to it is called the .... time.

37 Place the expected response times for the following processes in order: action involving a conscious decision-making process; a reflex; action run by a motor programme.

38 Motor programmes, such as turning right, are (often/never) initiated by the central decision-maker.

39 Activities run by a motor programme should (never/periodically) be monitored.

40 Several motor programmes, such as turning right and scratching your head, (can/cannot) run at the same time.

41 You can think about (many things/only one thing) at a time if conscious decision-making is required.

42 Sketch a graph of typical workload demand on a pilot during a complete flight. Also show the pilot capability line.

43 The pilot capability line (can/cannot) be raised by good training, fitness and adequate rest.

Exercises 7

Judgement and Decision-Making

1 For an experienced pilot, judgement of distance above a runway during the landing flare is a p......... judgement.

2 Judgement following a complex thought process and making a conscious decision is called c........ or t....... judgement.

3 Having good knowledge (will/will not) improve the quality of your decision-making and judgement.

4 The quality of your decision-making and judgement (should/will not) improve as you gain experience.

5 When making decisions, you should try to be (emotional/logical).

6 A confident pilot is (more/less) likely to show good judgement and decision-making skills than an under-confident pilot.

7 Outgoing people are (extroverts/introverts).

8 An introvert is (an outgoing/a quiet and possibly shy) person.

9 A good pilot will (exhibit/avoid) 'macho', 'show-off' behaviour.

10 A good pilot will (exhibit/avoid) passive acceptance of whatever occurs.

11 A good pilot will generally (use/avoid) s....... o........ p.......... .

12 A good pilot will be (confident/passive or under-confident).

13 A good pilot will operate in (an orderly/a disorderly) fashion.

14 A good pilot (will/will not) manage the stress level.

15 A good pilot will have a (positive/passive) approach to each task.

16 CRM refers to c...... r....... m.......... .

17 Good CRM begins with being (well/poorly) prepared.

18 Good CRM is more likely in (a tidy/an untidy) cockpit.

19 Good CRM (does/does not) require a good overview of the flight.

20 Being aware of the time (is/is not) a vital aspect of CRM.

21 Being able to set priorities (is/is not) a vital aspect of CRM.

22 Using good judgement (is/is not) a vital aspect of CRM.

23 Managing the level of stress in the cockpit (is/is not) a vital aspect of CRM.

24 Organising and distributing tasks in a multi-crew cockpit is called c... c............ .

25 PF stands for p.... f..... .

26 PNF stands for p.... n.. f...... .

27 A good captain can handle (the task/people/both the task and people).

28 The term PIC stands for p.... i. c....... .

29 Who has final authority over the operation of an aircraft?

Exercises 8

The Flight Deck

1 The pilot–aircraft system is a (closed-loop/open-loop) system because the pilot (can/cannot) continually adjust the flightpath of the aircraft.

2 A pilot using an autopilot (should/need not) monitor its performance.

3 The technical name given to improving the efficiency of people in the workplace, for instance the pilot in the cockpit, is ....

4 For optimum performance, the pilot should adjust the seating position so that the eyes are in the ...... eye position.

5 With the eyes in the design eye position, the pilot should have a good view of (the outside environment/the instrument panel/both the outside environment and the instrument panel).

6 Aeroplane cockpits are designed to accommodate pilots (of all shapes and sizes/within the design population).

7 The cockpit seat should be positioned so that the pilot can achieve (some/moderate/full-and-free) movement of the controls.

8 To be effective, seat-belts (must/need not) be correctly fastened.

9 It is a (good/poor) design technique to standardise controls as much as possible.

10 Name four types of control columns.

11 Each type of control column controls the aeroplane pitch attitude by (fore-and-aft/sideways) movements and the aeroplane bank attitude by (fore-and-aft/sideways) movements.

12 To add power, move the throttle (in/out); to reduce power, move it (in/out).

13 The relative positions of different engine controls, such as the throttle, mixture control and carburettor heat control, is (the same/different) on all aircraft, so a pilot (should/need not) be careful when using them.

14 Fuel tank controls (are/are not) the same on all aircraft. A pilot (need not/must) be careful when switching tanks.

15 Name three functions performed by the rudder pedals.

16 Name several functions that can be controlled from a well-designed yoke.

17 Cockpit displays (should/need not) be easily seen.

18 Cockpit displays (should/need not) be easy to understand.

19 The standard layout for the six main flight instruments is known as the .....-. .

20 Sketch a typical layout of the six main flight instruments, with the basic-T.

21 A pictorial display is known as (a digital/an analog) display.

22 A line of numbers is known as (a digital/an analog) display.

23 Sketch a diagram of the attitude indicator in your aeroplane exactly as it would appear in a descending, 30-degree banked, left turn. Show the artificial horizon, the model aeroplane, the angle-of-bank scale, and the bank pointer.

24 The typical heading indicator is a (gyroscopic/magnetic) instrument. It is also known as a d........ i........ .

25 The HI, or DI, is (easier/harder) to use than a magnetic compass because it (does/does not) experience acceleration and turning errors, and because deciding whether to turn left or right is (more/less) instinctive.

26 The ASI displays (indicated/true) airspeed. In a 'glass' cockpit it may not be the traditional circular dial, but rather a vertically orientated s.... t.... .

27 On the most modern altimeters the QNH (is set automatically/must be set by the pilot).

28 The three-pointer altimeter (can be/is not) a dangerous instrument if not understood properly.

29 The instrument used to show rate of climb or rate of descent is the ...., and is graduated in ....

30 The turn coordinator is calibrated to show a rate-1 turn, which is a heading change of (0/1/3/6/180) degrees per second, to the left or right. With the wings of the model aeroplane aligned with the 'L' marking on the turn coordinator, a complete turn of 360 degrees to the left should take ... .

31 The model aeroplane on the (attitude indicator/turn coordinator/attitude indicator and turn coordinator) shows pitch attitude.

32 A VOR display superimposed upon a heading indicator is called a ...., abbreviated .... .

33 The HSI is (easier/harder) to use than a basic VOR display.

34 Instrument displays shown on cathode ray tubes, or TV-like screens, are known as ..... instruments. They are referred to as an e......... f..... i......... s...... .

35 A pilot can (select and deselect/not alter) information shown on a 'glass' navigation display.

36 A display of flying wings or crossbars superimposed on the AI and programmed by the pilot to give pitch and bank commands needed to achieve a desired flightpath is called a ....

37 Instrument indications projected ahead of the pilot so that he can read them at the same time as looking out of the cockpit window is called a .... or .... .

38 To ensure that vital items are not missed at certain stages of a flight, you should use a ....

39 You (should/need not) be familiar with the manual for your aeroplane.

40 'SOP' stands for s....... o........ p......... .

41 The colour of taxiway lighting is either sideline .... or centreline ..... .

42 What altitudes are indicated on the altimeters in the diagram below?

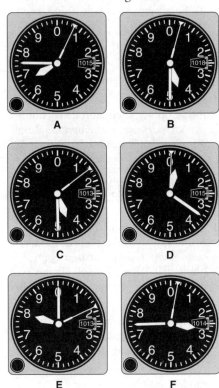

Safety, First Aid and Survival

Exercises 9

Safety and Care of Passengers

1 Passengers (should/should not) be on board while refuelling is in progress.

2 The pilot (should/need not) include a check of appropriate emergency equipment in the preflight inspection.

3 The survival equipment appropriate for a flight over desert areas will be (the same as/different from) the survival equipment appropriate for a flight over an Arctic waste.

4 Cigarette smoking (is/is not) permitted on the apron, especially near an aeroplane that is being refuelled.

5 When stationary, the propeller (should/should not) be regarded as dangerous.

6 Cabin ventilation (is/is not) important for passenger comfort.

7 In a ditching, life-jackets should be inflated (before/after) evacuation.

8 Is it safe to use a BCF (Halon) fire extinguisher in the cockpit and, if so, what precautions should be taken?

9 Does a BCF (Halon) fire extinguisher leave any residue that requires the cockpit, instruments, etc., to be cleaned after its use?

10 Could the use of a dry-chemical fire extinguisher restrict visibility in the cockpit?

11 Is the use of a dry-chemical fire extinguisher more likely to cause breathing difficulties than the use of a BCF (Halon) fire extinguisher?

12 Does a dry-chemical fire extinguisher leave any residue that requires the cockpit, instruments, etc., to be cleaned after its use?

13 Is carbon dioxide suitable for fighting an electrical fire?

14 Is carbon dioxide suitable for fighting an engine fire on start-up, once the engine has been shut down?

15 Is carbon dioxide likely to cause breathing difficulties?

16 What is the reason for not holding the nozzle of a CO_2 fire extinguisher whilst it is discharging extinguishant?

17 Is it recommended to use a carbon dioxide fire extinguisher in a confined space such as an enclosed cockpit?

18 Is a water fire extinguisher suitable for fighting an electrical fire?

19 Is a water fire extinguisher suitable for fighting a fluid fire (e.g. fuel)?

20 Is a water fire extinguisher suitable for fighting a smouldering fabric fire?

21 When combating a fire, the extinguishant (should/should not) be directed at the base of the fire?

Exercises 10

First Aid

1 List five actions to take in the case of a passenger feeling airsick.

2 List four items to take in managing a person who has fainted.

3 In the event of a medical emergency in flight, the safety of the flight (does/does not) take precedence over the individual.

4 An unconscious passenger, evacuated from an aircraft after an accident, should be placed in the .... position to aid blood supply to the brain and any vomit to escape without blocking the ....

5 List the various indications of head injury.

6 Mild head injuries (should/need not) be treated seriously.

7 In the case of a head injury, the pilot may decide to place the patient in the 'coma position' and ensure that .... is unobstructed by the tongue or dentures.

8 Prolonged bleeding can lead to ..... and even ....., consequently it is important to control bleeding as quickly as possible, even before other injuries.

9 Profuse bleeding may be reduced by .... the sides of a wound, applying a .... , or hand pressure to block the blood flow.

10 To manage internal bleeding, the patient should be ...... absolutely, elevating the legs comfortably and .... tight clothing.

11 List the points to follow in managing a fracture.

12 In managing a burn, the clothing in the affected area should be cut away unless it is ..... to the skin.

13 Shock is progressive and may take some hours to become obvious. The pulse may be very .... and ....

14 In considering the safety and care of passengers and crew, it is good airmanship for the operator to provide a .....-.........., although not required by law in non-public transport aircraft.

15 A guide to contents suitable for a first-aid kit can be found in the .... Order, Schedule 4, Scale A.

Exercises 11

Survival

1 When planning to fly across remote or dangerous areas, you (should/should not) submit a flight plan.

2 The level of search and rescue protection is (greater/less) if a flight plan has been submitted.

3 Body core temperature is usually just under ....°C, and any variation above or below this of more than about ....°C will disturb bodily functions, including brain function.

4 Heat production by the body is usually (fairly constant/very variable).

5 Body core temperature is usually maintained just under 37°C by regulating the amount of heat (generated/lost).

6 An emergency radio call is prefaced by the word ...... spoken three times.

7 The emergency squawk code on the transponder is ....

8 Aircraft travelling over remote or dangerous areas should be fitted with an e........ l....... t.......... , abbreviated ... , which, when activated, transmits a very distinctive wailing signal on the emergency frequencies: *civil* ..... MHz and *military* .... MHz.

9 If you hear an ELT signal on 121.5 MHz, you (should/need not) report it.

10 ELT batteries typically last for (1/2/12/24/48/72) hours, and so you (should/need not) consider activating the ELT only when you think its signals may be detected.

11 In bright sunlight, signal mirrors are (very/not) effective in attracting attention.

12 Signal rockets and hand flares should be fired (downwind/into the wind) to protect your body.

13 The morse code for SOS is ... ...

14 The ground signal to indicate that you require assistance is a large (V/X/N).

15 The ground signal to indicate that you require medical help is a large (V/X/N).

16 A forced landing into water is known as a ....

17 When flying for long periods over water in a single-engined aircraft, it is good airmanship to (wear a life-jacket/have a life-jacket handy).

18 In general, it is better to land (along the crest of/into the face of) a large sea swell.

19 A serious reduction in the body core temperature is called ....

20 When immersed in cold water, the body temperature can be conserved by (spreading out/bunching up).

21 For immediate survival, water is (more/less) important than food.

22 Heat loss is minimised by (wet/dry) clothing.

23 In a hot desert area, you should wear (light/no/heavy) clothing.

24 In a very hot environment, you (should/need not) move slowly to conserve energy and minimise sweating.

25 In hot climates, each person needs about (1/2/4/20) litres of water per day.

26 In a jungle, water (should/need not) be purified before drinking.

27 The body (should/need not) be covered in a hot, steamy jungle.

28 If you have to travel by foot in a hot desert area, you should do so by (day/night).

29 Nights in a desert (may be/are never) very cold.

30 It is important in the event of a snake bite to treat the bite as .... , apply a pressure bandage to the affected spot, (immobilise/exercise) the victim, and seek .... as soon as possible.

Human Factors and Pilot Performance

Answers 1

Human Physiology and High Altitudes

1   brain
2   central nervous system
3   continues
4   circulatory (or cardiovascular), heart
5   oxygen, red
6   haemoglobin
7   waste
8   bluer, carbon dioxide
9   pulmonary
10 systemic
11 arteries
12 veins
13 capillaries
14 heart, pulse
15 respiration
16 lungs, body tissues
17 carbon dioxide, increase
18 5, ½
19 decreases
20 hypoxia
21 10,000 feet
22 exhalation
23 *refer to the text*
24 time of useful consciousness
25 will
26 more
27 expand, barotrauma
28 carbon dioxide, hyperventilation
29 *refer to the text*
30 reduce
31 decompression, bends, will
32 increase
33 12, 24
34 carbon monoxide
35 is
36 *refer to the text*
37 increase
38 Eustachian, nasal
39 descent

40 do not

Answers 2

Eyesight and Visual Illusions

1   optic
2   inward
3   1 to 2 metres, empty field
4   will not
5   does, does
6   binocular, helps
7   cornea
8   eyelid
9   iris, pupil, can
10 small, wide
11 lens, greater
12 accommodation
13 retina
14 cone, are, are, are, daylight
15 rod, are not, are not, are not, both daylight and darkness
16 optic
17 acuity
18 is
19 sunglasses
20 more difficult
21 closer, late
22 more
23 30 minutes, rods, peripheral
24 immediately, 30 minutes
25 central
26 peripheral
27 1 to 2 metres, empty field myopia, do
28 autokinesis
29 can
30 steep, low
31 shallow, high
32 closer, high
33 further away, low
34 beyond
35 before
36 good, visual approach slope indicator

37 black-hole
38 more
39 short
40 too much
41 not enough
42 myopia, hyperopia or hypermetropia
43 long-sighted, presbyopia, near, half-glasses
44 astigmatism
45 two

Answers 3

Hearing and Balance

1 hearing, balance
2 auditory
3 outer, middle, inner
4 Eustachian tubes
5 middle
6 can
7 should
8 inner, accelerations
9 semi-circular
10 static organ
11 linear, cupula, gelatinous, otoliths, cupula, hairs
12 gravity, linear
13 vision
14 level, eyes
15 right-banked, leans, use your eyes
16 left-banked, leans, use your eyes
17 should, eyes
18 vertigo
19 can
20 Eustachian tubes
21 eardrums, pressure vertigo
22 more, climb
23 a reduced, descent, use your eyes
24 up, backwards, use your eyes
25 down, forwards, use your eyes
26 smooth-and-coordinated, fresh, no

Answers 4

Am I Fit To Fly?

1 physical and mental fitness
2 carbon monoxide, energy
3 yes

4 eight
5 one unit per hour
6 should not
7 *refer to the text*
8 24 hours
9 carbon monoxide
10 (c)
11 decreases
12 hypoxia

Answers 5

Stress Management, Fatigue and Sleep

1 stressor
2 can
3 short, long
4 is, can
5 can
6 increases
7 reduces
8 happy
9 stress, may
10 not all
11 different
12 less
13 adrenalin, action
14 poor
15 poor
16 good
17 *refer to the text*
18 more
19 hyperthermia, drink
20 hypothermia
21 turbulent
22 can
23 may
24 may
25 will
26 may
27 anxiety
28 physically, psychologically
29 wear a noise-cancelling headset
30 fly away from the cloud and into smoother air
31 *refer to the text*
32 fatigue
33 sleep

use standard operating procedures
confident
an orderly
will
positive
cockpit resource management
well
a tidy
does
is
is
is
is
crew coordination
pilot flying
pilot not flying
both the task and people
pilot-in-command
the pilot-in-command

swers 8

e Flight Deck

closed-loop, can
should
ergonomics
design
both the outside environment and the instrument panel
within the design population
full-and-free
must
good
control wheel (or yoke), control column (or joystick), sidestick, ram's horn
fore-and-aft, sideways
in, out
different, should
are not, must

15 rudder control, nosewheel steering control, differential braking
16 elevator control, aileron control, elevator-trim control, radio transmit button, autopilot disconnect button
17 should
18 should
19 basic-T
20

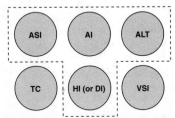

21 an analog
22 a digital
23 *refer to your aircraft*
24 gyroscopic, direction indicator
25 easier, does not, more
26 indicated, speed tape
27 must be set by the pilot
28 can be
29 vertical speed indicator, feet per minute
30 3, 120 seconds, i.e. 2 minutes
31 attitude indicator
32 horizontal situation indicator, HSI
33 easier
34 glass, electronic flight instrument system
35 select and deselect
36 flight director
37 head-up display or HUD
38 checklist
39 should
40 standard operating procedures
41 blue, green
42 A: 6,750 ft B: 4,500 ft C: 14,500 ft (or FL145, as 1013 set) D: 350 ft E: 18,000 ft (or FL180) F: 2,750 ft

34 eight, sixteen
35 two hours
36 regular
37 insomnia
38 avoid
39 varies
40 early
41 rapid eye movement
42 REM
43 non-REM
44 REM
45 disturb
46 *refer to the text*
47 will not
48 more
49 circadian, body temperature
50 25
51 zeitgebers
52 time, giver
53 sun
54 body temperature
55 4 a.m. and 6 a.m.
56 jet lag
57 a different rate
58 become desynchronised
59 with, longer than
60 longer than
61 against, shorter than
62 westwards
63 America to Europe, *refer to the text*

Answers 6

Information Processing

1   brain
2   central decision-maker
3   single-channel
4   consecutively
5   perceived
6   thinking or cognition
7   skills, motor programmes
8   reflex
9   conditioned, Pavlov's
10 autonomic
11 conscious decision-making, skills, motor programmes
12 sight, hearing, smell, taste, touch

13 receptor
14 adapt
15 sensory, one, five
16 is
17 is
18 mind set
19 attention
20 divided, time
21 may
22 may
23 hallucination
24 illusions
25 has
26 seven, fifteen (in very approximat
27 chunking
28 mnemonic
29 rehearse (or repeat), rote
30 encoding
31 better
32 long-term memory
33 meanings, events
34 semantic, helps
35 episodic, is
36 response
37 reflex (shortest response time), mc
    gramme, conscious decision-makii
    est response time)
38 often
39 periodically
40 can
41 only one thing
42 *refer to the text*
43 can

Answers 7

Judgement and Decision-Making

1   perceptual
2   cognitive or thinking
3   will
4   should
5   logical
6   more
7   extroverts
8   a quiet and possibly shy
9   avoid
10 avoid

Safety, First Aid and Survival

Answers 9
Safety and Care of Passengers

1 should not
2 should
3 different from
4 is not
5 should
6 is
7 after
8 yes, ventilate the cabin after its use
9 no
10 yes
11 yes
12 yes
13 yes
14 yes
15 yes
16 the nozzle will become very cold and
    could cause the skin to freeze to it
17 no
18 no
19 no
20 yes
21 should

Answers 10
First Aid

1 *refer to the text*
2 *refer to the text*
3 does
4 coma, breathing passages
5 *refer to the text*
6 should
7 breathing
8 shock, death
9 pressing together, constrictive bandage
10 rested, loosening
11 *refer to the text*

12 stuck
13 weak and rapid
14 first-aid kit
15 Air Navigation Order

Answers 11
Survival

1 should
2 greater
3 37°C, 2°C
4 fairly constant
5 lost
6 Mayday
7 7700
8 emergency locator transmitter, ELT,
    121.5 MHz, 243 MHz
9 should
10 48, should
11 very
12 downwind
13 dit-dit-dit dah-dah-dah dit-dit-dit, or
    ··· – – – ···
14 V
15 X
16 ditching
17 wear a life-jacket
18 along the crest of
19 hypothermia
20 bunching up
21 more
22 dry
23 light
24 should
25 4
26 should
27 should
28 night
29 may be
30 poisonous, immobilise, medical assistance

Index